The Story of Hungary
By
Arminius Vambery

PREFACE.

IN complying with the request of the publishers of the *Nations* Series to write the Story of Hungary, I undertook a task which was out of the range of my previous literary undertakings, which had for the most part been devoted to the geography, history, and philology of Central Asia. The principal reason which induced me to enter upon what is for me a new literary field, was my desire to make American and English readers acquainted with the record of my native country, and to present the various phases of the history of Hungary in the light best suited to attract the attention of the citizens of England and of the Great Republic, to whose opinion we Hungarians are by no means indifferent.

My willingness to prepare the present volume was further due to the fact, that it was not the *History*, but the *Story* of Hungary, I was asked to write; an undertaking in which I had simply to deal with the salient events, the most noteworthy personalities, and the most thrilling episodes in a narrative which covered nearly a thousand years, and was not called upon to consider the philosophical side of the history, or to discuss the deeper-lying motives or the less significant details of national action.

For a task such as that presented to me, I concluded that the knowledge and the ideas of a Hungarian man of letters were not inadequate; I have, nevertheless, had recourse, in certain instances, to the assistance of writers who had given special attention to our national history, with the idea of making as accurate as possible this *the first Story of Hungary written in English*.

The distance between Buda-Pesth and New York rendered it impossible for me to give my personal attention to the proofs while the volume was being put into type. The proof-reading was therefore entrusted to the care of Mr. Louis Heilprin, a gentleman who is evidently thoroughly familiar with the subject, and to whom I desire to express my obligations not only for the care he has taken with the proof-reading, but also for his attention in securing in my English text the most accurate and most effective forms of expression.

I take this opportunity of expressing, also, my thanks for the kind coöperation of my countrymen, Messrs. Sebestyén, Csánki, Acsády, and Vargha.

A. V.

BUDA-PESTH, *August,* 1886.

THE STORY OF HUNGARY.

CHAPTER I.

THE COUNTRY AND THE PEOPLE OF HUNGARY.

ALEXANDER PETÖFI, the great Hungarian poet, in one of his beautiful poems, sings thus of his native land:

"If the earth be God's crown
Our country is its fairest jewel."

And truly were we able to ascend the airy heights and obtain a bird's-eye view of Hungary, we would fain admit that it is one of the fairest and most blessed spots on the face of the earth.

In the Northwest of Hungary, on the banks of the Danube, begins the mountainous region known under the name of the Carpathian range, which for beauty is not surpassed by the Alps, and in extent fairly rivals them. This mountain range, encircling like a gigantic evergreen wreath one half of the country, extends all along its northern boundary and, after enclosing the eastern portion of it, stretches westward to where it is intersected by the waters of the Danube, not terminating there, however, but branching off into the countries lying along the lower course of that river.

The whole range of the Carpathians is characterized throughout its immensely long course by considerable breadth, forming at some places quite a hilly country and high plateaus, as, for instance, in Transylvania which, although properly belonging to Hungary, formerly enjoyed a sort of independence under its own name. This territory is covered almost entirely by the Carpathians, but, of course, designated here by different names.

We shall proceed now in due order.

In the Northwest, there where the Danube enters Hungarian territory near Dévény, the mountain chain begins, under the name of the Northwestern Carpathians; these, describing the shape of a half moon, extend from Presburg (Pozsony) to the Hernád-Tarcza valley. Formerly three groups only were mentioned in connection with this section: namely, the Tátra, Fátra, and Mátra, a representation of which, as well as of the four rivers, the Danube, Theiss, Drave, and Save, is embodied in the arms of the country, whence Hungary is designated as "the country of the three mountains and four rivers." The Northwestern Carpathians are, however, a gigantic mountain mass of immense bulk, subdivided into several distinct ranges. Of these one, the Northwestern border mountain-range, starting near the Danube in Presburg County and extending in the shape of a wide arch in a northeastern direction as far as the sources of the Árva river, divides Hungary from Moravia, Silesia, and Galicia. This ridge is constantly rising, and reaches the highest elevation at its northern edge. Another range is the Little Kreván, which begins in Árva County, and extends through the flatlands between the Vág and Nyitra rivers. East of this are the Gömör mountain-range, famous for its stalactitic caves, including Aggtelek; the Mátra range, extending from Miskolcz to Vácz; and the loftiest of all, the High Tátra, whose highest peaks are those of *Jégvölgy*, Gerlachfalva, and Lomnicz, rising to an altitude of between 8,000 and 9,000 feet. The mountains belonging to this group are snow-covered, and what renders them peculiarly interesting are the so-called *tengerszemek* (eyes of the sea), limpid lakes of unfathomable depth, which, according to popular belief, are connected with the sea, and about which a good many old-time legendary tales are current amongst the people. These lakes are met with at the height of 1,900 metres above the level of the sea.

That range of mountains which extends eastwards from the Hernád-Tarcza valley to the southeastern angle of Mármaros County is called the Northeastern Carpathians. It includes the Wooded Carpathians and the Eperjes-Tokay range, in the southern part of which, the Hegyalja, the king of the wines, the famous Tokay wine, is produced.

The southeastern chain of the Carpathians divides where Mármaros County, Transylvania, and Bukovina converge into an angle, forming several main lines which enclose the territory of Transylvania in an almost quadrangular shape and give it the character of a high plateau.

The name of this group is the Southeastern Carpathians. Parts of it are the Transylvanian northern and eastern border ranges; the Hargita range, with the remarkable Mount Büdös, containing several caves from which issue strong gases, and the beautiful lake of St. Anna at a height of 950 metres; the southern border range, the largest and most massive portion of the Carpathian mountains; the mountain group of the Banate and the mineral mountain range of the Banate, the latter owing its name to the gold, silver, and other ores as well as the coal abounding in it. This group projects as far as the basin of the Danube and forms there the passes known as the Iron Gate, which greatly impede navigation. To the Transylvanian Hungarian range, extending north from the Maros river, belong the mineral mountains of Transylvania, rich in gold and other ore, and the mountain called Királyhágó, which marks the frontier between Hungary and the independent Transylvania of old.

Thirty-eight passes lead from this mountain-system of gigantic dimensions, partly into the countries adjacent to Hungary, partly into the regions divided by them. Of these the most important are: the Jablunka pass, communicating with Silesia and the valley of the Vistula; the Vereczke pass between Munkács and Stry, supposed to be the pass through which the Hungarians entered their present country; the Radna pass, leading into Bukovina; the Ojtóz pass, communicating with Moldavia; the Tömös pass, leading to Bucharest; and the Red Tower pass, leading into Little Wallachia.

Besides the Carpathian mountains Hungary also contains a less considerable portion of the Alps, belonging to the so-called Noric Alps. They lie in trans-Danubian Hungary, the Pannonia of old. They embrace the Austro-Styrian border-range, between the valleys of the Danube and Drave; the Vértes-Bakony ranges, of which the Bakony forest forms a part; and the group of the Buda mountains, producing the celebrated wines of that name.

Croatia and Slavonia, which are parts of the Hungarian realm, are also traversed by mountains belonging to the Alpine system.

We perceive from the preceding account that a large portion of the country is mountainous, but over a third part of it is level land, and so fertile that it may compare to the prairies in North America. The great Hungarian plain, the so-called Alföld (Lowland), boasts of the best soil for the production of wheat, and, stretching down from the offshoots of the Central Carpathians to the frontiers of Servia contains upward of 35,000 square miles.

The extent of the water system of a country and its distribution is always of the first importance. In this respect, too, Hungary has been blessed by nature. Of the sea she has but little; a small portion only of the Adriatic washes her shores, the so-called Hungarian Sea-Coast, where Fiume, the only important Hungarian seaport city, is situated. The country possesses also some interesting lakes; one, Lake Balaton, forty-seven miles long and nine miles wide, has the characteristics of the sea to such an extent that it is called the Hungarian Sea. In this extensive water is to be found the savory *fogas* fish, and on its shores is situated Balaton-Füred, one of the favorite watering-places of Hungary, and near this place is the famous echo of Tihany. Another large lake is the Fertö (Neu-Siedler), eighteen miles long and about five miles wide, which became perfectly dry in 1863, so that even houses were built on its bed, but the waters have returned to it within the last few years.

Several smaller lakes, besides the two mentioned, are scattered throughout the country.

With rivers the country is abundantly supplied. Its mightiest stream is the Danube, after the Volga, the largest river in Europe. The whole of Hungary belongs to its basin. Its length in Hungary is 600 miles, and it leaves the country at Orsova, after having formed several islands in its course. The largest among these is the Great Csalló region, which contains two towns and over a hundred villages; and the most beautiful of them is Margit (Margaret) Island, near Buda-Pesth—quite a miniature paradise, frequented by a great many strangers, who come here to get the benefit of its excellent baths. Of the numerous affluents of the Danube the Theiss is the most important; it has its sources in the country and empties into the Danube on Hungarian soil, near Titel. It is navigable for steamships. The Save and Drave are after the Theiss the largest tributaries of the Danube. All these rivers send their waters, through the medium of the Danube, into the Black Sea.

Thus harmoniously is the soil of Hungary varied by mountains, valleys, plains, and high plateaus, and gratefully watered by rivers and lakes; and if we but add that the country lies between the forty-fourth and fiftieth degrees of northern latitude, that is, in the most favorable part of the temperate zone, we may readily infer the superiority of the climatic conditions prevailing there. There is, of course, great variety of climate. The winter is raw and cold in the Carpathian regions; spring sets in later, winter comes earlier, and the cold sometimes reaches — 22° F. In the hilly and level country the climate is much more genial, the summers hotter, and storms of more frequent occurrence. Wheat, grapes, and maize do not ripen in the regions of the higher Carpathians, whilst the Alföld produces the best and finest wheat, and even rice. The air is most genial on the shores of the Adriatic, and here are grown the fruits of Southern Europe. The climate, as a general thing, is dry, especially in the Alföld, where trees are rare.

Such is the topography and climate of the country which, lying in the central portion of Middle Europe, stretches between Moravia, Silesia, Galicia, Bukovina, Roumania, Servia, Bosnia, the Adriatic Sea, Istria, Carinthia, Styria, and Austria. It covers an area of 125,000 square miles, and has a population of nearly sixteen millions.

Politically the country is divided into three parts, namely: Hungary proper (including the formerly detached Transylvania), the city and territory of Fiume, and Croatia and Slavonia. Dalmatia, too, ought to belong under the old laws to the country, but, for a long time already, it has owned the supremacy of Austria.

Buda-Pesth is the capital of the entire kingdom. Situated on both banks of the majestic Danube, here spanned by three beautiful bridges, amongst them the famous suspension bridge, it is one of the finest cities of Europe. It has nearly 400,000 inhabitants, and is the centre of Hungary's political, cultural, industrial, and commercial life. Fine public and private buildings, some of them beautiful specimens of architectural art, adorn the city, and it boasts wide thoroughfares, among which the delightful Corso along the left bank of the Danube, and the Andrássy Út (Road) leading to the city park, where the national exhibition of 1885 was located, deserve especial mention. The finest and largest cities, besides Buda-Pesth, are: Presburg (Pozsony), on the left bank of the Danube, formerly the seat of the Hungarian Diet; Comorn (Komárom), on the Danube, too, celebrated for its grand fortifications; Stuhlweissenburg (Székesfejérvár), once the capital of Hungary; Raab (Györ); Oedenburg (Soprony); Veszprém, one of the oldest cities; Erlau (Eger), renowned for its excellent wine; Szeged, the metropolis of the Alföld and one of the largest cities, which in 1879 was almost entirely destroyed by the overflowing of the Theiss, but has since been rebuilt, more beautifully than before, after the latest European pattern; Kassa, the finest city in Upper Hungary; Miskolcz; Debreczen, one of the most remarkable cities of the Hungarian Alföld and the seat of a considerable industry; Grosswardein (Nagy-Várad), the scene of many important historical events; Arad, Temesvár, and Carlsburg (Gyulafejérvár), all fortified cities memorable in history; Klausenburg (Kolozsvár), the capital of the former principality of Transylvania; the flourishing Transylvanian towns of Kronstadt (Brassó) and Hermannstadt (Szeben), inhabited for the most part by the descendants of Saxons; Fiume, the seaport on the Adriatic; Agram (Zágráb), the capital of Croatia, a beautiful city, which, however, was greatly damaged in 1880 by a terrible earthquake; and Eszék, the most prominent of the Slavonian towns.

The population of the country is composed of various nationalities. The conquering Hungarians did not oppress the ancient inhabitants of the land but left them undisturbed in the use of their native language, and, even in later days, their tolerance went so far as to actually favor foreign, and, more particularly, German immigrants, and to this exceptional forbearance alone must be traced the survival of so many nationalities, and the lack of assimilation, after so many centuries. Classified as to languages spoken by the inhabitants, the chief nationalities number as follows: 1, Hungarians or Magyars, 6,500,000—the ruling, and, so to say, the political nationality of the country, their language, the Magyar[*] being the language of the state; 2, Germans, 1,900,000; 3, Roumans, 2,400,000; 4, Slovaks, 1,800,000; 5, Croats and Serbs, 2,400,000; 6, Ruthenes, 350,000. Besides these there are other nationalities but in insignificant numbers.

The relative numbers of the various religious denominations are, in round figures, as follows: Roman and Greek (united) Catholics 60%; Eastern-Greek (non-united), 16%; Lutherans, 7%; Calvinists, 13%; Unitarians, 1/3 %; Jews, 4%.

With respect to their cultural condition, the people may be said to be abreast of the nations of Western Europe in every thing but industry, commerce, and some branches of science. In recent years especially a great improvement has taken place in popular education, owing to the large and daily increasing number of schools, and the law which compels children to attend school. There are, for the purpose of advancing learning and cultivating the various branches of science, a variety of conspicuous scientific institutions, literary societies, reading clubs, and public and private libraries. In journalistic literature the country is equal to any country on the European continent.

The constitution of the kingdom is one of the most liberal in Europe. The estates were represented at the Diet up to 1848, but under the present constitution the government is based upon popular representation. The Parliament or National Assembly consists of two Houses, the House of Representatives and the Upper House, or House of Lords, and in these two bodies and the king is vested the legislative power. The national affairs are administered by eight ministerial departments; the affairs in common with Austria are settled by a delegation from the two Houses of Parliament which meets an Austrian Parliamentary delegation once in every year, and administered by three common ministerial departments—for foreign affairs, for the common army, and for the finances, respectively.

In conclusion it may be added that the description given above of the favorable concurrence of soil and climate is fully borne out by the abundance of fine cattle of every description possessed by the country, by a bountiful production of cereals which has earned for Hungary the name of the granary of Europe, by the growth of the greatest variety of fruit and forest trees, and finally by the rich products of the mining regions we have adverted to before.

This chapter, however, would be incomplete were we not to mention the gigantic efforts made by the national government in every direction during the last two decades to raise Hungary from a mere agricultural state to an industrial and commercial state as well, by fostering her domestic industries and providing good highways, a fine net of railways, steam and other navigation, in order to afford an easy and cheap outlet to the abundance of natural products with which nature has blessed her.

These patriotic efforts, considering the short space of time they cover, have been attended with signal success, and have culminated in the National Exhibition of 1885, held at Buda-Pesth, which fitly illustrated to its many visitors, amounting to nearly a million, the extraordinary progress made by the country in the last years.

CHAPTER II.

HUNGARY BEFORE THE OCCUPATION BY THE MAGYARS.

THE historic period of Hungary begins, properly speaking, with the first century before our era, when Pannonia, comprising the regions watered by the Danube and Drave, was conquered by the victorious arms of Rome. Prehistoric traces, however, may be met with in abundance, which, with the aid of archæological inquiry, indicate that the soil of Hungary was already inhabited in the neolithic age and in that of bronze by populations who, judged by the mementoes left behind them, which were unearthed by the present generation, must have stood on the same level of civilization as the rest of Europe at those periods. Certain articles dating from the age of bronze show even such marked national peculiarities as to lead to the supposition that the heterogeneous tribes were all under the influence of one kind of culture. The Pannonians, after a protracted struggle, were subjugated by Tiberius, the stepson of the emperor Augustus. One of the art gems of antiquity, the so-called *Apotheosis of Augustus*, to be seen in the museum of antiquities at Vienna, commemorates the triumph of Tiberius. The conquering general is represented as stepping from his chariot to do homage to Augustus and Livia, who are seated on a throne in godlike forms. Below, Roman soldiers are raising trophies, whilst the conquered leader is sitting on the ground with his arms tied behind his back. The reduction of the Dacians, to whose realm Transylvania belonged, took place under Trajan, a century later. To this day stands in Rome the pillar of Trajan, erected in memory of his successful campaign in Dacia.

In Trajan's time already Pannonia differed in no wise from the other Roman provinces. Under a Roman administration the language of Rome soon gained ground, although the legions placed there were by no means Roman or even Italian, but consisted for the most part of Romanized Spaniards, Belgians, Britons, and inhabitants of the Alpine provinces.The towns became municipalities and colonies, and their inhabitants enjoyed the privilege of self-government conceded to every Roman citizen. Dacia, too, became, under that name, a Roman province, and the Romanizing process was no less rapid there than it had been in Pannonia. The blessings of Roman civilization followed, as usual, in the train of Roman conquests. Cities soon sprang up in the newly organized provinces, and were connected with each other as well as with Rome by fine highways, traces of which may be met with here and there to this day. The cultivation of the vine was introduced under Roman rule, and the regular working of the gold and salt mines of Transylvania began at that period. The life in the provinces was modelled after the Roman pattern, for the Roman brought with him his customs, institutions, language, and mode of life. The newly built cities boasted of public places, of amphitheatres, of public baths, the resort of pleasure-seekers and idlers; nor was the forum with its statues wanting. The border towns had their *castrum*, giving them a peculiar character of their own.

For four centuries these provinces shared the destinies of the Roman empire. The enemies of Rome were their enemies, too, and when, under the emperor Marcus Aurelius, in the latter part of the second century of our era, the German nations combined in an attack on the Romans, the Marcomanni, who were renowned for their savage bravery, made a successful inroad into Pannonia, and crossing the Danube devastated the whole land. Commodus, the son of Marcus Aurelius, was satisfied to maintain only the integrity of the vast possessions he inherited, and was averse to new conquests in the direction of the Carpathians. His policy was to protect and defend the natural boundary line formed by the Danube, a policy which gave the legions located there an undue prominence. From this time forth Rome had to be defended in

Pannonia, for already at that period the mighty revolution, called the migration of nations—the pressing forward of populations from the North and East toward the civilized West and South—began to be felt. It was quite natural that the Pannonian legions should, under the circumstances, become aware of the importance of their position, and undertake to direct the destinies of Rome from that distant province. Roman history records that it was by the proclamation of these legions that Septimius Severus, Maximin, and Aurelian became emperors. The emperors Claudius II., Probus, and Valentinian I. were of Pannonian origin. The infant son of the latter, Valentinian II., was brought by the widowed empress Justina into the camp, and there the legions swore allegiance to him.

The time was now approaching when the waning power of the Roman empire became more and more unequal to the task of defending her provinces. Aurelian already had withdrawn the Roman legions from Dacia and allowed the Goths to settle there, and Probus had introduced the Goths into Lower Pannonia. Roman influence and Roman protection began to be of little value; the great empire, weakened by internal dissensions, by the internecine wars waged against each other by imperial pretenders, torn by religious disputes, and finally divided, hastened to its downfall.

At this period a new people made its appearance in Europe on the shores of the Black Sea and along the banks of the Danube, namely, the Huns, who were pushing before them the Goths towards the West. They differed in race from the Germans, Slavs, and Romans, and they had in Attila a leader capable of uniting under his sway the most discordant ethnical elements. Ostrogoths, Gepidæ, Vandals, Alans, Rugians, mostly Germanic populations, followed the banners of the foreign leader, trusting in his good fortune and awed and magnetized by his great personal qualities. He pushed forward with an immense number of followers, gathering strength as he advanced by the accession of the barbarous nations, bearing down and destroying every thing before him. Theodosius II., Emperor of the East, agreed to pay tribute to the king of the Huns; but in order to disguise to his subjects the disgraceful transaction, he appointed Attila a general of the empire, so that the tribute should have the appearance of official pay. But Attila was not satisfied with this, and broke the peace, overran the Balkan peninsula, pillaged the Byzantine provinces, and destroyed the cities until he obtained his own terms. Priscus Rhetor, who was one of the embassy sent by Theodosius II. to the court of Attila, describes the wooden structure in which the king of the Huns dwelt on the banks of the Theiss, somewhere in the vicinity of Szeged, and the feasting there. Kings sat at the table, lords sang Attila's heroic deeds, and the guests drank each other's health from vessels of gold. Heathen and Christian, Roman citizens and Asiatic barbarians, as well as the representatives of the Germanic tribes, mixed with each other and thronged his court. It was during one of those feasts, in 453, as he was celebrating his nuptials, that the mighty king of the Huns was carried off by a fit of apoplexy. Whilst the sons of Attila were contending with each other for the possession of the empire, the Germanic populations fell upon the divided Huns and drove them back to the Black Sea.

The Gepidæ remained now the masters of the country east of the Danube, whilst the Ostrogoths occupied the ancient Roman province. The latter, however, under the lead of their king Theodoric, migrated in a body to Italy, crossing the Alps, and founded there, on the ruins of the Roman empire, a Gothic kingdom. The Gepidæ remained in consequence the sole ruling people in Hungary; but as they proved dangerous neighbors to the Eastern empire, Justinian invited the Longobards to settle in Pannonia, and gave to the Avars, who now made their first appearance in Europe and had asked him for land to settle on, the left bank of the lower Danube. About this time, too, Slavic populations came into the country, crossing the Carpathian mountains and peopling the deserted land. Gepidæ, Longobards, and Avars could not dwell long in peace together, and the first collision took place between the Longobards and the Gepidæ on the banks of the Danube. This was followed by another hostile outbreak, in which the Longobards obtained the alliance of the Avars against the Gepidæ, resulting in the total overthrow of the latter. Shortly afterwards the Longobards, following an invitation from Italy, emigrated thither. Thus the Avars were left in sole possession of the country, ruling over populations chiefly Slavic. The empire they founded lasted two centuries and a half. The Avars were partly remnants of those Huns who had been the terror of Europe, and their numbers were in part swelled by new recruits coming from Asia.

Baján was the first and most dreaded prince of the Avars. During his reign of thirty-two years the Byzantine emperor was compelled to conciliate the warlike humor of the Avar prince by an annual tribute of splendid presents, which, however, did not prevent the latter from undertaking pillaging expeditions, on more than one occasion, into Thrace, Mœsia, and Macedonia. Although a warlike people the Avars seemed to lack the necessary skill and experience for besieging and capturing fortified places. Their rule was characterized by cruelty, want of faith, and destructive propensities. In course of time they became more inclined to peace; wealth, indulgence in wine, and commerce having rendered them effeminate and less formidable. They were finally conquered, towards the end of the eighth century, by Charlemagne and his Franks, who carried on against them for seven years one of the most cruel and desolating wars known to history. Charlemagne's own historiographer tells us that one might have travelled through the entire land for months, after the termination of the war, without meeting with a single house—so utter and terrible were the ruin and destruction. The downfall of the Avars was irretrievable.

The rule of the Romans had lasted four hundred years in Pannonia; the Huns, Ostrogoths, Gepidæ, and Longobards enjoyed a span of power of a little over a century taking them altogether, whilst the Avars maintained their supremacy for two hundred and fifty years.

A century after their downfall appeared on the scene the Magyars, who founded an empire which still endures, having survived the storms of a thousand years.

CHAPTER III.

THE ORIGIN OF THE HUNGARIANS.

THE story of the origin of the Hungarians is generally derived from two different sources. One, purely mythical or legendary, is said to have come down from the forefathers to the present generation, and, clad in a somewhat fanciful garb, runs as follows:

Nimrod, the man of gigantic stature, a descendant of Japheth, one of the sons of Noah, migrated after the confusion of languages at the building of the tower of Babel to the land of Havila. There his wife, Eneh, bore him two sons, Hunyor and Magyar. One day as the two brothers were out hunting in the forests of the Caucasus, they happened to fall in with a doe. They at once gave chase, but on reaching the moorlands of the Sea of Azov the noble animal suddenly vanished before their very eyes. The brothers, in pursuing the track of their game, had wandered through a wide expanse of country, and perceiving that the rich meadows were admirably suited to the needs of a pastoral people, they immediately returned to their father and asked his consent to their departure. They obtained his consent without difficulty, and settled with their herds of cattle in those regions where grass grew luxuriantly.

The two brothers had lived quietly for five years in their new homes, when the thought occurred to them, more thoroughly to investigate the surrounding country. They accordingly set out on their journey, roaming along the steppes, when their ears were suddenly caught by the sounds of voices singing, which the east wind had wafted in their direction. Led on by the pleasing sounds the wanderers' eyes were met by a lovely sight. Before them the daughters of the dwellers in the woods were disporting themselves beneath their tents, celebrating the Feast of the Hunting-horn, in the absence of their husbands and brothers. Hunyor and Magyar were delighted at this unexpected encounter and quickly carried away the women to their own abode. Amongst the ravished women were two maids of rare beauty, the daughters of Dula, the prince of the Alans. Hunyor took one, and Magyar the other, for his spouse. From them sprang the kindred nations of the Huns and Magyars, or Hungarians, both of which in due course of time, grew to be mighty.

After the lapse of many years the descendants of the two brothers had increased to such an extent that the territory they dwelt in proved too small to support them all. North of their homes lay blessed Scythia, bounded on the east by the Ural mountains, on the southeast by the sandsteppes, rich in salt, and the Caspian Sea, and on the south by the Don river. After having thoroughly reconnoitred this country they drove out the inhabitants, one portion of the people spreading over their newly acquired home and taking possession of it, whilst the remaining portion continued to occupy their former country. The progeny of Hunyor settled in the northeastern part of the country beyond the Volga, whilst the descendants of Magyar, pushing upwards along the Don, pitched their tents on the left bank of the river. The latter were afterwards known by the name of the Don-Magyars, and their country by that of Dontumogeria—that is, the Don Magyarland.

In proportion as the two kindred races increased and came in contact with various other nations, they began to differ from each other more and more widely in their ways and manners. The Huns being more exposed to the attacks of the roving populations than the Magyars, who were protected by the Caspian Sea and endless steppes, became, in consequence, more warlike, and adopted ruder manners. Twenty-two generations had passed away since the death of the two brothers, who had been the founders of their nations, when for reasons unknown the Huns resolved to emigrate from their country. Whilst the Magyars continued to dwell quietly along the Don, the Huns proceeded with an immense army, each tribe contributing ten thousand men, against

Western Europe, conquering and rendering tributary, in the course of their wanderings, numerous nations, and finally settled in the region of the Theiss and Danube. Later on, however, in the middle of the fifth century, when the world-renowned Attila, "the scourge of God," came into power, the Huns carried their victorious arms over a great part of the western world.

The immense empire, however, which had been founded by King Attila, was destined to be but of short duration after the death of its founder. His sons Aladar and Csaba, in their contention for the inheritance, resorted to arms. The war ended with the utter destruction of the nation. All of the followers of Aladar perished; Csaba, however, succeeded in escaping from the destroying arms of the neighboring nations who had fallen on the quarrelling brothers, with but about fifteen thousand men to the territories of the Greek empire. A few thousands, who had deserted Csaba, fled to Transylvania, and settled there in the eastern mountain-regions. The descendants of the latter became subsequently merged with the immigrating Hungarians, and formed with them a homogeneous family under the name of Szeklers, which continues to exist to this day. Csaba, whose mother was an imperial daughter of Greece, met with a friendly reception at the hands of the Greek emperor, Marcianus, and remained in that country for a few years. He returned afterwards with the remainder of his people to the home of his ancestors, on the banks of the Don, where, up to the time of his death, he never tired of inciting the Magyars to emigrate to Pannonia and to revenge themselves on their enemies by reconquering the empire of Attila.

In turning to the second source of the history of the origin of the Hungarians, we are treading upon the firmer ground of scientific inquiry; we can penetrate the hazy light of remote antiquity, and venture the assertion that it is far away in the distant East—namely, in the Altai mountains, that we may look for the cradle of the Magyar race. Here was, as the reader may be aware, the coterminous frontier of the three principal branches of the Uralo-Altaic race—namely, the Mongolians in the east, the Finn-Ugrians in the north, and the Turks in the south. With a population of strictly nomadic habits and of eminently roaming propensities, it needs scarcely to be said that the three branches lived in continual feud and warfare near each other. A great convulsion in the life of these nomads happened, as we presume, in the second or third century after Christ. The Turks, on seeing the more flourishing state of things with their Finn-Ugrian neighbors in the north, fell upon them suddenly, drove them from their homes in the valleys of the Altai mountains, where traces of their industry are still extant, and scattered the various tribes and families, partly to the north—namely, to Siberia; partly to the west—namely, to Southern Russia.

From that extraordinary throng and revolutionary migration emerged the Voguls and Ostyaks, who live at this day on both sides of the great Obi river; the Zyrians, who now live in the governments of Archangel and Vologda; farther the Votyaks and Tcheremisses, a motley crowd of men who are of Finn-Ugrian extraction, but strongly intermixed with Turco-Tartar blood.

Now, of similar origin are the Hungarians, with this difference, that with them the Turco-Tartar origin forms the basis of their ethnical character, and that the Finn-Ugrians who amalgamated with them afterward, being a subjugated population, remained always in a moral inferiority, although they greatly influenced the governing class. We do not know precisely whether the amalgamation took place in the valleys of the Altai, or farther west on the Volga, at some later period, nor can we form an accurate idea as to the part the Hungarians took in the irruption of the Huns, with which event they are associated in national tradition. The Huns were unquestionably Turks by extraction. Their mode of warfare, their religion, and social life present full evidence of this, and admitting that they had in their ranks either pure Finn-Ugrian elements or portions of the above-mentioned amalgamated populations, we may fairly claim that the ancestors of the Hungarians took part in the great devastating campaigns which Attila carried on against Rome and the Christian West as far as France. In this sense, the claim of the Hungarians to descent from the Huns is fully justified. But, as the plan of this work excludes the discussion of questions wrapped in the clouds of scientific speculations we will turn to that portion of the history of the Hungarians which is cleared up by historical evidence, and will begin with the ninth century, when they emerged from the banks of the Volga and began their march toward the West, a march which resulted in their occupation of Hungary.

Before entering into the details of the march of the Magyars towards their present home, we must try to sketch as briefly as possible the geographical and ethnographical conditions of the country between the Volga and the Danube in the ninth century. It must be borne in mind that at that time the Russians were in a considerable minority in those regions. East of the Volga, as far as the Ural River, and even beyond, roamed various tribes of the vast Turkish race, amongst whom the Petchenegs occupied the foremost rank. On the lower course of the Volga and further west, lived the Khazars, a Turkish tribe of advanced culture, who carried on a flourishing trade on the Caspian and Black seas, and had embraced the Jewish religion. These Khazars were the mightiest of the Turkish races of that time, and their wars with Persia and with the rising Mohammedan power became of historic importance. Westward of the Khazars dwelt another fraction of the Petchenegs, the frontiers of whose country extended across Moldavia to the borders of Transylvania, whilst the Magyars or Hungarians, who had occupied a country called Lebedia, were compelled by the Petchenegs to emigrate to Etelkuzu, not remaining there, however, for any great length of time. In fact the whole of Southern Russia of to-day was teeming, during the ninth century, with nomadic populations. These pressed upon each other in the search for pasture grounds for their numerous cattle. There is a great likelihood that the fame of the rich plains of Hungary had remained in the memory of the Magyars from the time when their forefathers fought under the banners of Attila. Suffice it to say that, compelled by circumstances, they made up their minds to go westward, and the seven dukes who stood at that time at the head of the nation, and whose names were Álmos, Elöd, Kund, Huba, Tas, Und, and Tuhutum, united in a solemn league and covenant, and putting Álmos, as the oldest amongst them, at their head, they sealed that union with the old Turkish form of oath, by drinking each of the blood of all, obtained by cutting open the veins of their arms. This form of oath was for a long time a custom in Hungary. The union of the Hungarians was based upon the following five conditions:

1. As long as they and their progeny after them shall live, their duke and ruler shall be always taken from the house of Álmos.

2. Whatever should be acquired by the united strength of all must benefit all those who belonged to them.

3. The chiefs of the people having voluntarily elected Álmos for their ruler, they and their descendants shall always take part in the councils of the prince, and shall have their share in the honors of the empire.

4. Whenever any of their descendants shall be found wanting in the fidelity due to the prince, or shall foment dissensions between him and his kindred, the blood of the guilty one shall be shed even as theirs was flowing when they gave their oaths of fidelity to Álmos.

5. Should a successor of Álmos affend against this oath and covenant of the fathers, then might the curse rest on him.

We have no accurate information concerning the number of Hungarian warriors and of their retinues who entered Hungary towards the end of the ninth century, nor can we point out those localities on the eastern frontier of the country through which the entrance was effected.

As to the numbers, we do not go amiss if we assume that no more than one hundred and fifty thousand fighting men formed the main body of the invaders. Their ranks were swelled partly by Russians who followed in their track, partly by Avars, a kindred Turkish population, whom they found in the country itself, and by Khazars, who, preceding the Hungarians, were leading a nomadic life on the steppe. Regarding the country itself, it must be borne in mind that in those days it was very thinly populated, and the ethnical conditions were somewhat as follows: In the west there were Slovenes and Germans; in the north, namely, in the Carpathian mountains, lived the compact mass of the Slovaks, whose sway extended down to the banks of the Theiss. The country between that river and the Danube belonged to the Bulgarian prince, Zalán, whilst the region on the left bank of the Theiss, as far as the river Szamos, was in the possession of Marót, the prince of the Khazars. The conquest of Hungary was evidently a task of no great difficulty for a warlike nation like the Hungarians, whose strange physiognomy and superior weapons, brought from the Caucasus, struck terror, at the very outset, into the breasts of the inhabitants. The invaders appeared with their small, sturdy, and hardy horses, quick as lightning and strong as iron. Their mode of warfare was strictly Asiatic, similar to that used to this day by the Turcomans, and they were animated precisely by the same spirit which led the Mongolians, under Jenghis Khan, over the whole of Asia and a large portion of Europe. With all this, they could not be called barbarians or savages, when their social and political institutions were compared with those of the inhabitants they subjugated in Hungary. It was the culture of Persia which extended at that time up to the banks of the Volga, penetrating the minds of the motley populations living there, and traces of this culture are clearly to be discovered in the acts of the leading persons amongst the conquering Hungarians. As soon as the Hungarians had taken possession of their present country, under the leadership of Árpád, it became their chief care to give a certain stability to their internal affairs. Scattered over the extensive territory, they more particularly endeavored to bring order into their relations with the former inhabitants. Those only who refused to lay down their arms felt the weight of the conquerors; whilst they reciprocated the friendship and confidence shown to them by others.

Thus it happened that many of the ancient inhabitants were adopted by them for their own countrymen, and that, having entered into a treaty of amity with Marót, a treaty made firmer by the betrothal of Árpád's youngest son, Zoltán, with Marót's daughter, the territory of Bihar was added to Hungary after the death of Marót. According to the fashion of the Scythian populations, they disturbed no one in his faith, nor did they interfere with any one's mode of worship. Nomads as they were, they knew how to appreciate what was still left of the ancient culture in their new country, and they fostered the colonial places still surviving from the Roman period, the cradles of the future city life of Hungary.

There is an account in the history of the Hungarians how the different portions of the invading army spread over the country, what battles they fought, what alliances they entered into with the reigning princes, but the account is based merely upon legendary tradition. We are sadly in want of details about that most interesting epoch, and supported by historical authority we can only state that Leo the Wise, the emperor of Byzantium, asked the military assistance of the Hungarians against the Bulgarians, and that it was the sword of the valiant nomadic warriors which averted a threatening calamity from Constantinople. It is likewise certain that Arnulph, King of Germany, encouraged by the military reputation of the Magyars, asked their assistance against Svatopluk, King of Moravia, and that their first appearance in the country is connected with this occurrence.

The conquest of Hungary occupied the period between 884 and 895.

Within this time falls the utter defeat and tragic end of Svatopluk, the most powerful native prince with whom the Hungarians had to contend. Arnulph had already engaged him in battle when the Hungarians came to the succor of the former. Their timely arrival decided the fate of the battle, which resulted in the complete rout and scattering of the Moravians. Svatopluk, is said to have done wonders of heroism during the battle, but after its fatal termination he could nowhere be found. In vain was the bloody field searched for the body of the unfortunate leader, nor were the messengers sent out to remoter regions to obtain news of him more successful in their quest. Hungarian tradition has it that in his rage and despair at the loss of the battle, he rushed into the Danube, and met there with a watery grave. Slavic tradition, however, represents the matter in a manner more in keeping with the character and reckless disposition of this strange barbarian, who knew but unbridled passions and sudden resolutions formed on the spur of the moment. According to these traditions, Svatopluk, seeing that his fortunes were hopelessly wrecked, mounted a steed and, leaving the battle-field, swiftly rode away into the fastnesses of the interminable forests covering the Zobor mountain, which overlooks in massive grandeur towards the east and south the town and castle of Nyitra, and was then lost to sight. Here in a secluded valley, amidst rocks, and protected by pathless woods, lived three hermits. These holy men passed their lives in offering up prayers to God in a chapel constructed by their own hands, and, entirely absorbed by their pious exercises, they knew no other nourishment but herbs and the fruit growing wild. These men, who did not visit the neighboring cities, had never seen Svatopluk, and this was the very reason that brought the king of the Moravians to their hermitage. As he reached late in the night a place where the forest was densest, he dismounted, killed his horse, and, together with his royal mantle and crown, buried it in a ditch, and covered up the place of burial with earth and leaves. He then tore his garments and soiled them with mud, and in this guise, pretending to be a beggar, he came to the three hermits and told them that, moved by the Holy Spirit, he desired to pass his life with them. He was cordially received by the hermits and lived amongst them a great many years unknown, praying as they did, partaking of the same food they ate, and like them dead to all the memories of the outside world. In his last moments only he told them his real name, and the hermits, in their childlike astonishment at this incredulous adventure, placed the following inscription on his tombstone: "Here rests Svatopluk, the king of Moravia, buried in the centre of his kingdom."

CHAPTER IV.

THE REIGN OF THE DUKES.

ÁRPÁD, called by the Greek writers Arpadis, was the first ruler of Hungary, who laid the foundations of the present kingdom, and whose statesmanlike sagacity may well excite admiration, considering that under his lead a strictly Asiatic nation succeeded in penetrating into the very interior of Christian Europe and moulding a state out of the heterogeneous elements of old Pannonia. For this reason we find it improper to call him a rude barbarian, as contemporary Christian writers are in the habit of doing. He evidently was penetrated with the Persian culture and his Oriental statesmanship not only equalled but even surpassed the political ideas of the ruling men at that time at the head of affairs in Pannonia and Eastern Germany. Arriving, as he did, with a restless and adventurous nomadic people; he could not mitigate at once the martial rudeness of the latter. Like other Turkish and Mongolian masses the Hungarians, very soon after the occupation of the country, rushed out into the neighboring lands to gratify their lust of adventure and booty. They penetrated into Germany, spreading terror and devastation everywhere. On a larger scale was their inroad into Italy in 899, where King Berengar was defeated on the banks of the Brenta. Twenty thousand Italians were slain, the wealthy cities of Milan, Pavia, and Brescia were plundered, and the invaders crossed even the Po. It was only by the payment of a large ransom that the Italians could free themselves from the scourge of these Asiatic conquerors. Encouraged by this success the Hungarians, in the following year, entered Germany, trying their arms with varying fortune, until a common decision of the chieftains arrested these incursions. In 907 the nation was saddened by a mournful event. The ruler who had founded the new empire, who for nearly twenty years had directed the destinies of the nation with so much wisdom and energy, and in whom the glory of great statesmanship and generalship was united, had ceased to be amongst the living. His body was, according to ancient custom, burned and his ashes buried near a brook flowing at that time in a pebbly bed towards Etzelburg, the Old-Buda of to-day. His grateful descendants, after the introduction of Christianity, erected on that spot a church, called the White Church of the Virgin, in commemoration of the immortal prince. He was succeeded by his son Zoltán, who had to seize the reins at a comparatively tender age, and who was therefore assisted by three governors. This circumstance encouraged the neighboring princes to fall upon Hungary in order to drive the new conquerors out of the country. Luitpold, Duke of Bavaria, and Ditmar, Archbishop of Salzburg, together with others, led the united army in three different columns, flattering themselves with the hope that, imitating the tactics of Charlemagne against the Avars, they would be as successful as that famous ruler of the Franks.

The Hungarians, menaced by such an imminent danger, concentrated all their forces to resist the onslaught. Always quick to resolve and as quick in their movements, they anticipated the attack, and the two hostile armies met in 907 in the environs of Presburg. The struggle on both sides was a bitter one. The zeal of the Germans, on the one hand, was excited by the prospect of ridding themselves and the whole Occident of the disagreeable neighborhood of these dangerous intruders, whilst with the Hungarians, on the other hand, it was a question of self-preservation, for in case of a defeat they had every thing at stake. The latter, therefore, fought with the utmost vehemence, not in regular battle array, after the German fashion, but with their storming divisions, furious attacks, feigned retreats, and renewed onslaughts, their arrows and javelins descending every time like a hailstorm, they broke through the serried ranks of the Germans and rode down every thing that was in their way. The sun rose and set three times over the heads of the fighting armies before the great battle was decided. The Germans were hopelessly defeated. Duke Luitpold lost his life fighting, and with him the Archbishop of Salzburg, as well as most of the bishops, abbots, and counts, laid down their lives during those three fatal days.

It was but natural that, encouraged by this successful battle, the Hungarians should eagerly continue their marauding expeditions in every direction into Germany and even France. Dividing into small bands, just as the Turcomans used to do up to quite recent times in Persia, the Hungarians infested the whole of Saxony and Thuringia, and penetrated as far as Bremen. They crossed the Rhine, flooded a part of France, and quick as were their inroads, no less promptly did they return, always laden with rich booty and driving before them a long file of slaves of both sexes. The entire Occident was continually harassed by them, and this gave rise to those dire misrepresentations of the Hungarians and to the execrations against them which could be heard all over the western world during the tenth century, and which were faithfully copied into the chronicles of that time. In these chronicles they were charged with devouring the hearts of their enemies in order to render themselves irresistible in battle. Signs in the heavens were said to herald their approach. Virgins devoted to the service of God foretold the irruptions of the Hungarians and their own martyrdom. Mere human power seemed hopeless against them; the litanies of that time, therefore, abound in special prayers asking for the protection of the Lord. Impartial history easily recognizes in all this partly exaggerations, partly outbreaks of dismay, and the effects of fright, but these utterances, overdrawn as they are, contribute much to our knowledge of the violence of the struggle between the western Christians and the Asiatic Hungarians. Quite differently and by no means so dreadfully are the Hungarians described by the Byzantine historians. Their reputation for ferocity, and the knowledge of the terror they inspired, enhanced their valor and audacity. Neglecting all precautionary measures, and undervaluing their enemies, they began to meet here and there with small disasters, and, as the Germans on the other hand, becoming familiar with their mode of warfare, and more accustomed to the strange appearance of Asiatic warriors, grew bolder and bolder, we may easily account for the turn which gradually took place in the war fortunes of the Magyars. It was Henry the Fowler, King of Germany, who, after making preparations for nine years, inflicted the first heavy loss upon the Hungarian adventurers near Merseburg in 933. The Germans rushed into the battle with the cry of "Kyrie eleyson," whilst the Hungarians were wildly shouting "Hooy, Hooy." The Saxon horsemen caught up the Hungarian arrows with their shields, and in solid ranks threw themselves in fierce onset upon the Hungarians. The latter perceived with surprise and dismay that they were opposed by a well-organized enemy. During the hand-in-hand fight which now ensued the Germans achieved victory by their determined bravery. A great many Hungarians fell in the fight, and many more were killed during their retreat. The number of killed is assumed to have been thirty-six thousand. The Hungarian camp with all the baggage fell into the hands of the victors. Henry commanded that a universal thanksgiving feast should be observed throughout the whole of Germany, and ordered that the tribute hitherto paid to the Hungarians should be divided between the churches and the poor.

The Hungarians now refrained from entering Germany in a northern direction, but the more frequent and more vehement grew their irruptions into Bavaria and also into the northern portion of the Byzantine empire. It was the old lust of conquest and adventure, and greediness for booty which spurred their activity. Duke Taksony, who succeeded his father Zoltán in 946, and reigned until 972, was animated by the same lawless spirit, and the Hungarians would have continued to be the scourge of the neighboring countries if the defensive measures taken by the Germans about this time had not acted as a dam against their devastating flood. In the year 955, on the river Lech, near Augsburg, King Otto the Great inflicted a terrible defeat upon the Hungarians—a defeat by which nearly the whole of the Hungarian army, numbering forty thousand men was annihilated. Their generals, Bulcsee and Lehel were captured; the chains of gold they wore around their necks, as well as other trinkets of gold and silver, were taken from them, and at last they were carried to Ratisbon, and were made to suffer a disgraceful death by being hanged. A part of their fellow captives were buried alive, whilst the others were tortured to death in the most cruel manner. The remainder of the army was destroyed in its retreat by the people who had everywhere risen, and, according to tradition, but seven were left to reach their homes. The Magyars, a proud nation even in their misfortune, were so incensed against these fugitives for having preferred a cowardly flight to a heroic death, that they were scornfully nicknamed the *Melancholy Magyars*, and condemned to servitude. Even their descendants wandered about through the land as despised beggars.

A tradition has survived amongst the people to this day, about the death of Lehel and his reputed ivory bugle-horn, upon which there are carved representations of battles. It is true that archæological inquiry has proved its sculpture to be of Roman workmanship and that it was a drinking-cup rather than a bugle. The legend, however, as still current amongst the Hungarians, deserves to be told for the sake of its romantic character.

Amidst the confusion and wild disorder incident upon the disastrous battle of Augsburg, Duke Lehel found no time to give thought to his battle-horn. His horse had been killed under him, and whilst he lay buried beneath it the trusty sword was wrenched from the hand of the hero before he could pierce his own heart with it. Taken prisoner he was led captive into the presence of the victorious Otto.

Princely judges sat in judgment on the princely captive and condemned him to death. This sentence caused Lehel no pain; he felt he had deserved it, not, indeed, for having given battle but for losing it. Yet it hurt him to the soul to see the rebel Conrad seated amongst his judges, the traitor who had invited the Hungarians to enter Germany, and who, by his defection, had caused their defeat. The success of his dastardly desertion had, however, conciliated the victors and restored him to their confidence.

Lehel begged but for one favor, and that was to be allowed to wind the horn, his faithful and inseparable friend, once more, and to sound on it his funeral dirge. The horn was handed to him. He sounded it for the last time; and, as he drew from it the sad strains which sounded far and wide and were mournfully re-echoed by the distant hills, the dying warrior on the field of Lech lifted up his head, eagerly listening to the familiar bugle, and the soul which had come back to him, for one instant, took wings again as soon as the sad strains died away. The dying music, plaintively quivering, told the tale of an inglorious death terminating an heroic life. The very henchmen were listening with rapture.

At that moment Lehel broke away from his place, and, seeing Conrad before him, felled him to the ground, killing him with a single blow from the heavy horn. "Thou shalt go before me and be my servant in the other world," said Lehel. Thereupon he went to the place of execution. There is discernible on Lehel's horn, in our days, a large indentation which posterity attributes to the event just narrated.

Not only in Germany but also in the southeast of Europe the marauding Hungarians experienced more than one disaster, and it may be properly said that in 970, when they attacked the Byzantine empire and were defeated near Arcadiopolis, their long series of irruptions into the adjoining countries was brought to a conclusion. They became convinced that while they themselves were steadily decreasing in numbers and wasting their strength in continuous wars, the neighboring nations were becoming every day more formidable by dint of their unanimity, organization, courage, and skill in warfare, and that, in consequence, the Hungarian name inspired no more the terror which the first successes had earned for it. They saw that if they went on with their inroads, as hitherto, they would thereby but bring about the dissolution of the empire from within, or that they might provoke on the part of foreign nations a united attack which they would be unable to withstand. For this reason they renounced those adventurous campaigns which began already seriously to menace their existence and their future in Europe.

They were strengthened in the wisdom of this course by Duke Geyza, who succeeded his father in 972, and reigned until 997. Baptized during the life of his father at Constantinople, and having married Sarolta, the mild-tempered daughter of Duke Gyula, of Transylvania, he became very early awake to the necessity of refining the rude manners of his people. His disposition became much more apparent when, after the death of his first wife, he married the sister of Miecislas, the prince of Poland, a lady famous for her beauty, and also conspicuous for her energy and masculine qualities, for she vied in riding, drinking, and the chase with her chivalrous husband, upon whom she really exercised an extraordinary influence. Extremely severe in his rule, it was Geyza who began to transform the manners and habits of the Magyars. They began to show greater toleration towards foreign religions, and were really on the eve of changing their Asiatic manners and habits into those of Europe. More than a hundred years had passed since their migration from the ancestral steppes. Historical events, difference of climate, and, above all, the separation from their Asiatic brethren had carried into oblivion very many features of that political and social life which, originating in Asia, could not be well continued in the immediate neighborhood of, and in the continual contact with, the western world.

The great crisis in the national career appears to have arrived at its culmination during the reign of Duke Geyza, and to have found its ultimate solution in the conversion of the Magyars to Christianity, a most important act in the national life of the people, which deserves consideration in a separate chapter.

CHAPTER V.

THE CONVERSION TO CHRISTIANITY.

THE Hungarians, when entering their present homes, were heathens, and professed what is called *Shamanism*, the faith common to all the branches of the vast Uralo-Altaic race, and which has survived to this day amongst the populations of Southern Siberia and Western Mongolia. The doctrines and principles of Shamanism being generally but little known, it is proper to sketch here its outlines, in order to make clear the character of the Hungarian religious rites and customs.

The believers in Shamanism adored one Supreme Being called *Isten*, a word borrowed from the Persians, who attach to it to this day the meaning of God. Besides the supreme being, they adored sundry spirits or protecting deities, such as the gods of the mountains, woods, springs, rivers, fire, thunder, etc. These divinities were adored either by prayers or through sacrifices offered to them in the recesses of woods, or near springs. What these prayers of the Hungarians were we do not know; we can form, however, some idea of their character on reading the prayers of the present Shaman worshippers, a specimen of which is here subjoined:

> "O, thou God living above, Abiash!
> Who hast clad the earth with grass,
> Who hast given leaves to the tree,
> Who hast provided the calves with flesh,
> Who didst bring forth hair on the head,
> Who didst create all the creatures,
> Who prepares every thing present!
> Thou hast created the stars, O God!
> O, Alton Pi, who hast exalted the father,
> O, Ulgen Pi, who hast exalted the mother,
> Thou creator of all created things,
> Thou preparer of all that is prepared,

O God, thou creator of the stars,
O give us cattle, O God!
Give food, O God!
Give us a chief, O God!
Thou preparer of all things prepared,
Thou creator of all things created!
I prayed to my Father
To bestow on me his blessing,
To give me help,
To me, in my house,
And to my cattle, in the herd!
Before thee I bow down.
Give thy blessing, O Kudai,
Thou Creator of all things created,
Thou preparer of all things prepared!"

The sacrifices consisted in the offering up of cattle and particularly, on solemn occasions, of white horses. Their priests, called *Táltos*, occupied a pre-eminent place, not only in the political but also in the social life of the Magyars. They were a kind of augurs and soothsayers, whose prophecies were based either upon certain natural phenomena, or upon the inspection of certain portions of slaughtered animals, such as the intestines, the heart, and shoulder-blade, which latter was put into the fire, good and bad auspices being prognosticated from the different positions of the cracks produced.

Religious faith being always open to outside or foreign influence, it was but natural that the Hungarians, in that long march from the interior of Asia into Europe, should have borrowed many novel features from the religious life of the countries through which they passed. Thus, in the earlier faith of the Magyars, we meet with many distinctive traits of the Parsee religion, of that of the Khazars, and of the religions of many Ugrian races, for, like other families of the Uralo-Altaic race, the

Magyars were conspicuous for their spirit of toleration towards other believers.

The numerous Christian prisoners they had brought with them from various parts of Europe were not only left in the undisturbed practice of their creeds, but were even permitted to influence to a very considerable degree the faith of their conquerors and masters. Under these circumstances it was by no means a hazardous undertaking, on the part of Duke Geyza, to give permission to missionaries and priests to come into the country and preach the gospel. A Suabian monk named Wolfgang was the first who tried to spread Christianity in Hungary in 917. A greater success was achieved by Pilgrin, the bishop of Passau, who, taking the matter of conversion into his hands, was able to report to the Pope in 974 that nearly five thousand Hungarians had been baptized, and that "under the benign influence of the miraculous grace of God those heathens even who have remained in their erring ways forbid no one the baptism, nor do they interfere with the priests, allowing them to go where they please. Christians and heathens dwell together in such harmony that here the prophecy of Isaiah seems to be fulfilled: 'The wolf and the lamb shall feed together, and the lion shall eat straw like the ox.'"

Considering the difficulty of turning inveterate Asiatics to western views of life, and, particularly to the totally different doctrines of the Christian religion, we may easily realize that the total conversion of the Magyars was a work attended with many struggles and difficulties. After Pilgrin we find Bruno engaged in the pious undertaking; but by far the most successful of all of the missionaries was St. Adalbert, the bishop of Prague, who came to the country in 993, and, remaining there for a considerable period of time, had the good fortune to baptize several members of the reigning family, amongst whom was the son of Duke Geyza, called Vayik, to whom was given the Christian name of Stephen. This conversion being regarded as one of the most momentous events in the history of the Hungarians, it will be worth while explaining the accompanying illustration, representing this act. In the baptistry, we perceive, as the principal personage, Stephen, in his baptismal robes. Next to him is seen St. Adalbert, robed and adorned in keeping with his episcopal dignity and the apostolic office of conversion. To the left in the foreground, as witnesses to the baptism, are standing the Emperor of Germany, Otto III., who was brought there by his friendship for Geyza and his interest in the baptism of Stephen, and Count Teodato, of San Severino, a knight who had emigrated from Apulia, and to whom Geyza had entrusted the education of his son. Behind the latter stands Duke Henry of Bavaria, who, attending the emperor, is present as a guest. Farther in the background we perceive Duke Geyza and his consort, sunk in pious revery. We see Stephen after the act of confessing his faith and knowledge of Christianity. Already he had turned his face toward the west, had renounced Satan and devoted himself to the eternal war of the children of God, and then, turning to the east, had vowed, with exalted enthusiasm, obedience and devotion to the Law of God as revealed through Christ. Now we see him, according to the custom of the Church at that time, in the act of descending into the baptismal font in order to receive from the hands of the holy bishop the sign of the Cross, the sacrament of spiritual regeneration.

Pious emotion is reflected in the countenances of the attendant Magyars, although there may be discernible here and there the expression of a hidden spirit of antagonism. And the supposition of such an expression can, in no way, be called a groundless one. The worship of God on the banks of rivers, in woods and groves, the offering of sacrifices, and sundry superstitions connected with the soothsaying of the Shaman priests, certainly impressed more forcibly the minds of the free and independent dwellers of the steppes than the mass pronounced in Latin, and the rites of the Catholic Church, introduced by the monks and priests of the West. Conversion to Christianity had to be unconditionally followed up not only by the relinquishment of the old national religion, but also by the renunciation of the ancient habits and manners, to which the Hungarians clung in spite of the generations that had passed since their coming to the banks of the Danube and Theiss. The reluctance, shown here and there, must be also ascribed to the overbearing attitude assumed by the foreign missionaries towards the ruling race of the Magyars, upon whom these Bavarians, Suabians, Czechs, Italians, etc., looked down as contemptible barbarians, a title they by no means deserved, for it was only the difference in culture and not the want of culture which separated the two elements. Suffice it to say that traces of this discontent became visible very early, and that the slumbering spark broke out in open rebellion in 997, in the very year when Stephen ascended the throne, made vacant through the death of his father, Geyza. History records three different risings, which took place with the intention of doing away with the newly introduced Christian religion, together with all the changed modes of life borrowed from western civilization. In the first instance the movement was headed by Kopán, a nobleman in the county of Sümeg. His object was to drive out the foreign Christian missionaries and priests, to dethrone Stephen, and to re-establish the old pagan faith. A vast multitude of discontented Hungarians gathered under his banners, but Stephen was not at all afraid. Collecting his army and the foreign Christian knights about him, he left his regal seat Gran (Esztergom), and marched on straight against the rebels. The engagement took place in the vicinity of Veszprém. It was a hard contested struggle, and only after a bitter fight and the death of Kopán himself, did his adherents lay down their arms. The happy issue of the battle decided the victory of Christianity in Hungary, and all that was still needed, was to strengthen the new faith. The effects of this victory were, nevertheless, of short duration, for in the year 1002, another anti-Christian movement broke out in Transylvania, whose ruler, Duke Gyula, uniting with the partly pagan, partly Mohammedan Petchenegs, made an inroad into Hungary, carrying devastation and bloodshed everywhere. Stephen now had to march against this dangerous enemy, and not only vanquished the Hungarian duke Gyula, but continued his march into the country of the Petchenegs, defeated their prince, Kaan, and looting his camp got possession of all the rich treasures these Petchenegs had carried away from the Greek empire.

The third and decidedly the most dangerous rising took place in 1046, when a certain Vatha, a zealous adherent of the former pagan religion, and an offspring of Duke Gyula, availing himself of the disturbances arising from the contest for the succession to the throne, incited the people against the Christian religion and its institutions. They urged Andrew, the pretender to the throne of the country, "to abolish the Christian religion and its institutions; to re-establish the ancient religion and the laws brought from Asia, and demanded that they should be permitted to pull down the churches, and to drive out the priests and the foreign immigrants." Unaware of the number and strength of the rebels the prince did not venture to refuse their request. This the rebels took for a tacit compliance, and, emboldened by it, they fell, with wild rage, upon the Christians. The Germans and Italians that were found in the country, especially the bishops and priests, were persecuted with most inhuman cruelty. The churches and other places devoted to Christian piety were destroyed, the ancient pagan religion was restored, and everywhere the people resumed the former mode of life according to their ancient customs and heathen faith, offering up sacrifices, as before, in woods and groves and near springs. During these disorders St. Gerhard, the former tutor of St. Emeric, and at that time bishop of Csanád, lost his life. He was on his way to Pesth, to meet Andrew, when he fell into the hands of the enraged populace, was killed by them on the mountain opposite Pesth, called Gellérthegy (Mount Gerhard) to this day, and his body was thrown into the Danube. Utterly dangerous as the symptoms of these risings were, we see, however, how deeply even at that time Christianity had taken root in Hungary. It very soon became apparent that the revolution was not only of a religious but of a political and social character. King Andrew issued rigorous laws, menacing every one who did not return to the Christian religion and renounce the practice of heathenish customs, with loss of life and property. The destroyed churches were to be rebuilt, and the order of things introduced by Stephen be respected again. These laws and the punishments inflicted upon some of the stubborn adherents of paganism did not fail to produce their effect, and, in a short time, the rebellion was crushed and order and quiet gradually restored throughout the country.

And, strange to say, just as the Mohammedan Turks of our day ascribe the decline and downfall of their power to the many innovations introduced into their religious and social life, and discover the main source of their ruin in the assimilation to the West, precisely so spoke and argued the Hungarians of that day. They laid particular stress upon the fact that the nation, whilst adhering to the religion and customs of its ancestors, had been independent, strong, and mighty, and had even made the whole of Europe tremble; but that now, since it had adopted the religion and customs of the West, the nation was weakened by internal dissensions, strangers had become her masters, foreign armies had penetrated into the very heart of the country—nay, Hungary had lost her independence and had become the vassal of a foreign power. Such representations could not fail to produce their effect. It was easy to convince the uncultivated Hungarians, who were not yet confirmed in the Christian religion and but ill brooked its severe discipline, that all those troubles and misfortunes which had visited the country were the consequences of the introduction of Christianity, and that to achieve a splendid future for the nation, in harmony with its glorious past, this must be done upon the ruins of Christianity and of the institutions introduced by Stephen.

This great change, however repugnant it may have seemed to the Hungarians, was, nevertheless, unavoidable. As previously stated, the foreign elements which flooded the country, owing to the very large number of captives the Hungarians brought with them from every part of Europe, had wrought that change in the manners and habits of life in spite of all the reluctance of the former Asiatic nomads. These captives greatly outnumbering their masters, were mostly used for agricultural purposes, but their close contact with the ruling class unavoidably produced a mitigation of the rude military habits of the latter. The Hungarians eagerly listened to the Christian chants and prayers of their subjects. They imitated them in their food and dress, and, although nearly two centuries had to pass before the former wanderers on the Central-Asian steppes could get accustomed to permanent habitations, and, despite the aversion the proud warrior felt to the plow, the ice, nevertheless, began to break. The Asiatic mode of thinking had to be given up, and with the tenets of Christian tradition habits of Christian life were gradually introduced.

This process of transformation was greatly quickened by the personal intercourse and family connections of Duke Geyza and his chieftains with the court and nobility of the neighboring countries. Besides the involuntary immigration caused by the forays, we meet with a remarkable influx of foreign noblemen who, on the invitation of Duke Geyza, settled in the country, towards the end of the tenth century. The brothers Hunt and Pázmán came from Suabia, Count Buzád from Meissen, Count Hermann from Nuremberg; the Czech knights Radovan, Bogát, and Lodán came with large retinues; many others immigrated from Italy and Greece, so that the high nobility of Hungary, already at the beginning of the conversion of the Magyars, had a large infusion of foreign blood. It may be added that the entire clergy of that day was composed of Czechs, Germans, and Italians. The ground was, therefore, duly prepared, and it wanted only the iron hand of a resolute and wise ruler to achieve the work of conversion, and to accomplish the great task of transforming a formerly warlike and nomadic nation into a Christian and peaceful community. This ruler was King Stephen I.

CHAPTER VI.

ST. STEPHEN, THE FIRST KING OF HUNGARY. 997-1038.

KING STEPHEN led the Hungarian nation from the darkness of paganism into the light of Christianity, and from the disorders of barbarism into the safer path of western civilization. He induced his people to abandon the fierce independence of nomadic life, and assigned to them a place in the disciplined ranks of European society and of organized states. Under him, and through his exertions, the Hungarian people became a western nation. Never was a change of such magnitude, and we may add such a providential change, accomplished in so short a time, with so little bloodshed, and with such signal success as this remarkable transformation of the Hungarian people. The contemporaries of this great and noble man, those who assisted him in guiding the destinies of the Hungarian nation, gave him already full credit for the wise and patriotic course pursued by him, and the Hungarian nation of the present day still piously and gratefully cherishes his memory. To the Hungarians of to-day, although eight and a half centuries removed from St. Stephen, his form continues to be a living one, and they still fondly refer to his exalted example, his acts, his opinions, and admonitions, as worthy to inspire and admonish the young generations in their country.

This need be no matter for surprise, for at no period of Hungary's history has her political continuity been interrupted in such a way as to make her lose sight of the noble source from which its greatness sprang. No doubt a complete change has taken place in the political and social order, in the course of so many centuries, but the state structure, however modified, still rests upon the deep and sure foundations laid by the wisdom of her first king. One day in the year, the 20th of August—

called St. Stephen's day—is still hallowed to his memory. On that day his embalmed right hand is carried about with great pomp and solemnity, in a brilliant procession, accompanied by religious ceremonies, through ancient Buda, and shown to her populace. The kingdom of Hungary is called the realm of St. Stephen to this day, the Hungarian kings are still crowned with the crown of St. Stephen, and the nation acknowledges only him to be its king whose temples have been touched by the sacred crown. The Catholic Church in Hungary although it no more occupies its former pre-eminent position in the state, still retains enough of power, wealth, and splendor to bear ample testimony to the lavish liberality of St. Stephen. Thus the historian meets everywhere with traces of his benignant activity, and whilst the fame and saintliness of the great king have surrounded his name with a luminous halo in the annals of his nation, that very brilliancy has prevented from coming down to posterity such mere terrestrial and every-day details as would assist in drawing his portrait. The grand outlines of his form detach themselves vividly and sharply from the dark background of his age—but there is a lack of contemporary accounts which would help to fill up these outlines, and the legends of the succeeding generations, which make mention of him, can but ill supply this want, for they regard in him the saint only, and not the man. His deeds alone remain to guide us in the task of furnishing a truthful picture of the founder of his country, and well may we apply to him the words of Scripture, that the tree shall be known by its fruit.

Stephen was born in Gran (Esztergom), the first and most ancient capital of Hungary, about 969, at a time when his father had not yet succeeded to the exalted position of ruler over Hungary, and a magnificent memorial chapel in the Roman style of the tenth century, erected there, marks the event of his birth in that place. His mother Sarolta, Geyza's first wife, was the daughter of that Gyula, Duke of Transylvania, who, whilst upon a mission to Constantinople, in 943, had embraced the Christian faith and subsequently endeavored to spread it at home. Thus a Christian mother watched prayerfully at the cradle of young Stephen, and in early childhood, already, the tender mind of the boy was guided by the pious Count of San Severino. Adalbert, the Archbishop of Prague, who sought a martyr's death and subsequently won the martyr's crown, introduced him to the community of professing Christians. With his wife Gisella, a Bavarian princess, at his side, he took his place among the Western rulers as their kinsman. While his long reign proved him to be true to his country and his nation, yet the paganism of the ancient Hungarians was quite foreign to his soul.

After the first half of the tenth century religious ideas began to exercise a more powerful influence in Europe than before. The great movement which originated in the monastery of Cluny, in France, held out to the world the promise of a new salvation. Men of extraordinary endowments began again to proclaim with evangelical enthusiasm the mortification of the flesh, in order to exalt the soul, and the suppression of earthly desires for the purpose of restoring the true faith to its pristine glory. They insisted that the shepherd of the faithful souls, the Church, should be freed from all earthly fetters and interests, for, just as the soul was above the body, so was the Church superior to the worldly communities. The Church therefore, they taught, must be raised from her humiliating position, her former dependence changed into a state of the most complete freedom. As a consequence, the visible head of the Church, the Pope, could not be allowed to remain the servant of the head of the worldly power, the emperor, for it was the former that Providence had entrusted with the care of the destinies and happiness of humanity. These ideas spread triumphantly and with incredible rapidity throughout all Europe. They were heralded by a sort of prophetic frenzy; and soul-stirring fanaticism followed in their train. The age of asceticism, long past and become an object almost of contempt, was rescued from oblivion and revived. The despised body was again subjected to tortures and vexations, and the purified soul longed for the destruction of its own earthly existence in order to soar on high freed from mundane trammels. It was the miraculous age of hermits, saints, and martyrs who made it resound with their wailing and weeping, changing this home of dust into a valley of tears, so that the soul transported to the regions of bliss might appear in greater splendor to the dazzled eyes of the earthly beholder. The popes, moreover, riding high on the unchained waves, guided the Church through the tempest of the newly awakened religious passions, with a watchful eye and steady persistence toward one end—the exaltation of the papal power over that of the emperors. At the end of the tenth century Pope Sylvester II. was the representative of the spirit of the age clamoring for the aggrandizement of the papal power, and Otto III. represented in opposition to him the imperial power, undermined by the new ideas. Since the overthrow of the Western Roman empire the world had not been called upon to witness a contest of greater import than the impending struggle between these two rival powers. The great upheaval, indeed, which was to shake Europe to its very centre, did not take place until half a century later, but the seeds, from which the war of ecclesiastical investiture, the stir of the crusades, and the universality of the papal power were to spring, were already scattered throughout the soil which had lain barren through many centuries.

This was the age which gave birth to Stephen and in which he was educated, but his exalted mind rejected the exaggerations, eccentricities, and errors of his time and accepted only its noble sentiments and ideas. His sober-mindedness was equal to his religious enthusiasm, and as his innate energy exceeded both, he left it to religious visionaries to indulge in ascetic dreams. He desired to be the apostle of the promises of his faith, but not their martyr. He made the maintenance, defence, and extension of Christianity the task of his life, because he saw in its establishment the only sure means for the safety and happiness of his people. He pursued no schemes looking to adventures in foreign lands, but devoted all his thoughts, feelings, and energies to his own nation, subordinating to her interests everybody and every thing else. He defended these alike against imperial attacks and papal encroachments. His eyes were fixed on the Cross, but his strong right arm rested on the hilt of his sword, and his apostolic zeal never made him forget for a single moment his duty to a people which had gone through many trials, whose position amongst the European nations was a very difficult one, whose destinies rested in his hands, and who were yet to be called upon to play a great part in the history of the world.

Stephen was about twenty-eight years old when he succeeded his father in 997. He at once embarked with the enthusiasm of youth, coupled with the deliberation and constancy of manhood, on his mission to bring to a happy conclusion the task begun by his mother. In this work he was sedulously assisted by Astrik and his monastic brethren, and the gaze of the foreign Christian lords, who had immigrated with his Bavarian wife, as well as of the great number of lay and ecclesiastical persons who came, flocking to the country, was centred upon the young royal leader, who surpassed them all in zeal and enthusiasm. He spared no pains, nor was he deterred by dangers; he visited in person the remotest parts of the realm, bringing light to places where darkness prevailed, and imparting truth where error stalked defiantly. He sought out the men of distinction and the mighty of the land, and the hearts which were closed to the message of the foreign monks freely opened to his wise and friendly exhortations. Where he could not prevail by the charms of his apostolic persuasion he unhesitatingly threw the weight of his royal sword into the scale. Whilst battling with the arms of truth he did not recoil from using violence, if necessary, in its service. Fate did not spare him the cruel necessity of having to proceed even against his own blood.

The more rapidly and successfully the work of conversion went on, the greater became the apprehension and exasperation of those who looked upon the destruction of the ancient pagan faith as dangerous and ruinous to their nation. Nor did these recoil from any hazard to maintain their faith and to prevent the national ruin anticipated by them. They took up arms on more than one occasion, as has been previously mentioned, but Stephen succeeded in quelling the dangerous rebellions. Assisted by the foreign knights, he broke the power of paganism, and he showed no regard for any pretence of national aspirations. Those who still harbored the ancient faith in their hearts kept it secretly locked up there, and for the time being at least did homage to the new faith and the power of the king. The possessions of the rebels were devoted to ecclesiastical uses, and the king, at the same time, bestirred himself in the organization of the triumphant Church. He divided the converted territory into ecclesiastical districts, providing each with a spiritual chief, and placing the ecclesiastical chief of Gran at the head of all and of the Church government instituted by him. He caused fortified places to be erected throughout the newly organized Church territory for the defence of Christianity, as well as for the maintenance of his own worldly power, which began nearly to rival that of the other Christian kings.

But in order successfully to carry into effect these measures, Stephen had to obtain their confirmation by at least one of the leading powers which then shared in the mastery over Europe—namely, imperialism and papacy. The emperors, on the one hand, claimed supreme authority over all the pagan populations converted to Christianity, while the papal see, on the other hand, was inclined to protect against the empire the smaller nations, which were jealous of their independence, in order to gain allies for the impending struggle of the Church against the empire. Stephen was quick to choose between these two. The German Church—except in the abortive attempt made by Bishop Pilgrin—had contributed but little to the conversion of the Hungarian people, and it could therefore lay no claim to exercise any authority over the Church of Hungary. Nor had the German kings done any thing to assist Geyza and Stephen in their attempts at conversion. Stephen had before him the example of his brother-in-law, Boleslas of Poland, who had but recently applied to the papal see for the bestowal of the royal crown, in order to secure the independence of his position as a ruler and that of the Church in his realm. The religious bent of Stephen's mind, combined with his acute perception of the true interests of his country, induced him, at last, in the spring of 1000, to send a brilliant embassy to Rome, under the lead of the faithful, experienced, and indefatigable Astrik.

Pope Sylvester II., than whom no one exerted himself more strenuously to increase the papal power, received the Hungarian envoys cordially, and upon learning from Astrik their mission, he exclaimed: "I am but apostolic, but thy master who sent thee here is, in truth, the apostle of Christ himself!" He readily complied with Stephen's every request, adding even more signal favors. He confirmed the bishoprics already established, and empowered him to establish additional ones, conferring upon Stephen, at the same time, such rights in the administration of the affairs of the Church of Hungary as hitherto had been allowed only to the most illustrious princes in Christendom, the sovereigns of France and Germany. He granted to Stephen and his successors the right of styling themselves "apostolic kings," and to have carried before them, on solemn occasions, the double cross, as an emblem of their independent ecclesiastical authority. As a further mark of his favor, the Pope presented Stephen with the crown which had been destined for Boleslas of Poland, in order to symbolize for all times to come the blessing bestowed upon the Hungarian kingdom by God's representative upon earth. The crown of to-day, weighing altogether 136 ounces, is not quite identical with the crown that adorned St. Stephen's head. It now consists of two parts. The upper and more ancient part is the crown sent by Pope Sylvester, the lower one has been added at a later date. The former is formed by two intersecting hoops and connected at the four lower ends by a border. On its top is a small globe capped by a cross, which is now in an inclined position, and beneath it is seen a picture of the Saviour in sitting posture, surrounded by the sun, the moon, and two trees. The entire surface of the two hoops is adorned with the figures of the twelve apostles, each having an appropriate Latin inscription, but four of these figures are covered by the lower crown. The lower or newer crown is an open diadem from which project, in front, representations of ruins, which terminate in a crest alternating with semicircular bands. The seams of the latter are covered with smaller-sized pearls, and larger oval pearls adorn the crests. Nine small drooping chains, laid out with precious stones, are attached to the lower rim. A large sapphire occupies the centre of the front of the diadem, and above it, on a semicircular shield, is a representation of the Saviour. To the left and right of the sapphire are representations of the archangels, Michael and Gabriel, and of the four saints, Damianus, Dominic, Cosmus, and George, and, finally, of the Greek emperors, Constantine Porphyrogenitus and Michael Ducas, and of the Hungarian king Geyza, with inscriptions. With regard to the upper crown no doubt whatever is entertained as to its being the one sent by Pope Sylvester, and concerning the lower crown Hungarian historians state that it was sent, about 1073, by the Greek emperor, Michael Ducas, to the Hungarian duke, Geyza, as a mark of gratitude for the good services rendered to him by the latter. The exact date when the two crowns united cannot be ascertained. This minute description of the crown of Hungary may be well pardoned, considering the antiquity and the high veneration in which this relic of the past is held by the Hungarian people.

The legend of St. Stephen speaks thus of Astrik's mission to the Eternal City: "Father Astrik having accomplished his errand in Rome, and obtained even more than he had asked for, returned joyfully home. As he was nearing Gran the king came out to meet him with great pomp, and Father Astrik showed him the presents he had brought with him from Rome, the royal crown and the cross. Stephen offered up thanks to God, and subsequently expressed his gratitude to the Pope for the presents received. The great prelates, the clergy, the lords, and the people having listened to the contents of the letter conveying the apostolic benediction, with one heart and soul and with shouts of joy acclaimed Stephen their king, and having been anointed with the sacred oil, he was crowned on the day of Mary's ascension (15th of August) at Gran."

That highly important letter brought by Astrik from Rome, which established the independent authority of the Hungarian kings over the national church, has been preserved to this day. The following lines of the papal bull may in some measure characterize the age in which they were written, and illustrate, at the same time, the importance which was ascribed to these missives during many centuries:

"My glorious son," the letter proceeds to say, after having in the introduction exalted Stephen's apostolic zeal, "all that which thou hast desired of the apostolic see, the crown, the royal title, the metropolitan see at Gran, and the other bishoprics, we joyfully allow and grant thee by the authority derived from Almighty God and Saints Peter and Paul, together with the apostolic and our own benediction. The country which thou hast offered, together with thy own self, to St. Peter, and the people of Hungary, present and future, being henceforth received under the protection of the Holy Roman Church, we return them to thy wisdom, thy heirs, and rightful successors, to possess, rule, and govern the same. Thy heirs and successors, too, having been lawfully elected by the magnates of the land, shall be likewise bound to testify to ourselves and our successors their obedience and respect, to prove themselves subjects of the Holy Roman Church, to steadfastly adhere to, and support the religion of Christ our Lord and Saviour. And as thy Highness did not object to undertake the apostolic office of proclaiming and spreading the faith of Christ, we feel moved to confer, besides, upon thy Excellency and out of regard for thy merits, upon thy heirs and lawful successors, this especial privilege: we permit, desire, and request that, as thou and thy successors will be crowned with the crown we sent thee, the wearing of the double cross may serve thee and them as an apostolic token, even so that, according to the teachings of God's mercy, thou and they may direct and order, in our and our successors' place and stead, the present and future churches of thy realm. * * * We also beseech Almighty God that thou mayest rule and wear the crown, and that He shall cause the fruits of His truth to grow and increase; that He may abundantly water with the dew of His blessing the new plants of thy realm; that He may preserve unimpaired thy country for thee, and thee for thy country; that He may protect thee against thy open and secret foes, and adorn thee, after the vexations of thy earthly rule, with the eternal crown in His heavenly kingdom."

The brilliant successes so rapidly achieved by Stephen during the first years of his reign secured the triumph of Christianity and of the royal authority in the western half of the country only. The adherents of the ancient faith and liberty still remained in a majority in the eastern, more-thinly peopled regions beyond the Theiss and in Transylvania. Gyula, the duke of Transylvania, and the uncle of Stephen, was not slow in protesting against the new kingdom and the innovations coupled with it. The rebellion failed, as we have already seen. Gyula and his whole family were made captives by the victors, and neither he nor his posterity ever regained their lost power. Transylvania was more closely united with the mother country, and from that time, during a period extending over more than five centuries, was ruled by *vayvodes* appointed by the kings. Soon after Stephen opposed victoriously the Petchenegs, the allies of the defeated Gyula, who were settled beyond the Transylvanian mountains in the country known at present as Roumania, and having also defeated Akhtum, who, trusting in the protection of the Greek emperor, was disposed to act the master in the region enclosed by the Danube, Theiss, and Maros, there was no one in the whole land who—openly, at least—dared to refuse homage to the crown pressing the temples of Stephen and to the double cross. During the twenty years succeeding the events just narrated, history is entirely silent as to any great martial enterprise of Stephen. It is true that hostilities were frequent along the northern and western borders against the Poles and Czechs, but they were never of a character to endanger the territorial integrity of the country. During those years of comparative peace Stephen firmly established the Hungarian Christian kingdom.

The Christian Church was the corner-stone of all social and political order in the days of Stephen. The Church pointed out the principal objects of human endeavor, marked out the ways leading to the accomplishment of those aims, drew the bounds of the liberty of action, and prescribed to mankind its duties. It educated, instructed, and disciplined the people in the name and in the place of the state, and in doing this the Church acted for the benefit of the state. Hence it was that Stephen, in organizing the Hungarian Christian Church and placing it on a firmer basis, consulted quite as much the interests of his royal power as the promptings of his apostolic zeal. Where the Christian faith gained ground, there the respect for royalty also took root, and the first care of royalty, when its authority had become powerful, was to preserve the authority of the Church.

Immediately on his accession to the throne, Stephen addressed himself to the great and arduous task, and in all places where the promises of the holy faith, scattered by his proselyting zeal, met with a grateful soil, he established the earliest religious communities. Later, as the number of parishes rapidly increased, he appointed chief prelates to superintend and maintain the flocks and to keep them together. The ecclesiastical dignities and offices were conferred, in the beginning, without exception, upon members of the religious orders, they being at that time the most faithful warriors of Christianity against paganism, and the most devoted servants of the triumphant church. Stephen took good care of them, and rewarded them according to their merits. He founded four abbeys for these pious monks, who all of them belonged to the religious order of St. Benedict. The abbey of Pannonhalom was the wealthiest and most distinguished among these; and to this day, it maintains the chief rank among the greatly increased number of kindred societies. The first schools were connected with the cathedrals and monasteries, and although their mission consisted mainly in propagating the new church and faith, they yet cultivated the scanty learning of the age.

Stephen endowed the bishoprics and monasteries with a generosity truly royal. He granted them large possessions in land, together with numerous bondsmen inhabiting the estates. The Hungarian Catholic Church has preserved the larger part of these grants to this day. His munificence was displayed in the cathedral at Stuhlweissenburg (Székesfejérvár), built in honor of the Virgin Mary, of whose marvels of enchantment the old chronicles speak with reverential awe. The chronicler calls it "the magnificent church famous for its wondrous workmanship, the walls of which are adorned with beautiful carvings, and whose floor is inlaid with marble slabs," and then he proceeds in this strain: "Those can bear witness to the truth of my words who have beheld there with their own eyes the numerous chasubles, sacred utensils, and other ornaments, the many exquisite tablets wrought of pure gold and inlaid with the most precious jewels about the altars, the chalice of admirable workmanship standing on Christ's table, and the various vessels of crystal, onyx, gold, and silver with which the sacristy was crowded."

Stephen's munificence was not confined to his own realm, and numerous memorials of his beneficence and generosity are still preserved in foreign lands. As soon as Christianity had gained a firm foothold in the land, and the Hungarian people felt no more as strangers in the family of Christian nations, the natives, either singly or in larger numbers, began to journey to the revered cities of Rome, Constantinople, and Jerusalem. Stephen took care that these pilgrims should feel at home in the strange places they visited. Thus, amongst other things, he had a church and dwelling-house built in Rome for the accommodation of twelve canons, providing it also with a *hospitium* (inn). In Constantinople and Jerusalem also he caused a convent and church to be erected, within whose hospitable walls the Hungarian pilgrim might find rest for his weary body, after the fatigues of the long journey, and spiritual comfort for his thirsting soul. He was ever mindful of the interests of Christianity both at home and abroad. He not only founded the Hungarian Christian Church, but knew how to make it universally respected, and, in his own time already, the popes were in the habit of referring to Hungary as the "archiregnum"—that is, a country superior to the others.

In establishing the Hungarian kingdom Stephen necessarily shaped its institutions after the pattern of the Western States, but fortunately for the nation he possessed a rare discrimination which made him imitate his neighbors in those things only which were beneficial or unavoidable, whilst he rejected their errors and refused to introduce them into his own land. At that period feudalism, although it had sadly degenerated, prevailed, England alone excepted, throughout the whole

West. It was a system which did not permit the strengthening of the central power of the state, and the countries subjected to it were divided up into parts but loosely connected, each of which acknowledged an almost independent master, who, although he held his county or duchy from his king, and owned and governed it by virtue of that tenure, was yet powerful enough to defy with impunity the sovereign himself. Without adverting to the pitiful dismemberment of Italy, we need only mention that France was divided into about fifty, and Germany into five small principalities of this character. The kings themselves might make use of their kingly title, they might bask in the splendor of their own royalty, but of the plenitude of their royal power they could but rarely and then only temporarily boast.

Stephen's chief aim was to enhance the royal power by rendering it as independent as he possibly could of restrictions on the part of the nation, and to introduce such institutions as would prove most efficacious in the defence of the integrity and unity of nation and country. He left the nobility—the descendants of those who had taken possession of the soil at the conquest of Hungary—in the undisturbed enjoyment of their ancient privileges; he did not restrict their rights, but in turn did not allow himself to be hampered by them. He only introduced an innovation with reference to the tenure of their property, which he changed from tribal to individual possession, using his royal authority to protect each man in the possession of the estates thus allotted to him. The nobles governed themselves, administered justice amongst themselves, through men of their own selection, and the king interfered only if he was especially requested to judge between them. The nobles had always free access to the king's person, not only during Stephen's reign, but for many centuries afterwards. The nobility was exempted from the payment of any kind of taxes into the royal treasury, and they joined the king's army only if the country was menaced by a foreign foe, or if they chose to offer their services of their own free will.

Inasmuch as the great power of the nobility had its foundations on freehold possessions in land, Stephen was careful to support the dignity of the royal power by the control of large domains. The royal family were already the owners of private estates of large extent, and to these the king now added those vast tracts of land which, scattered throughout the whole realm, and more particularly extending along the frontiers, were without masters, and could not well pass into private hands, as the scant Hungarian population was inadequate for their occupation. These domains, which, for the most part, were thinly inhabited by the indigenous conquered populations, speaking their own languages, and the colonization of which by foreigners became a special object with the kings, were now declared state property, and as such taken possession of and administered by Stephen. He divided these possessions into small domains, called in Latin *comitatus*, county, and in Hungarian *megye*, eyre or circuit, and placed at the head of the administration of each county a royal official styled *comes*, count. These districts subsequently gave rise to the county system, which was destined to play such an important part in the history of the country, but originally they were designed to answer a twofold purpose, one financial and one military. One portion of the people living on these royal lands had to hand over to the royal treasury a certain part of their produce, whilst another portion was bound to military service for life. In this way the royal counties furnished a sort of standing army, always at the disposal of the king, and supplied, at the same time, the revenues necessary to support that army. Stephen found also other means to replenish his treasury and to add to his military strength. The revenues derived from the mineral and salt mines, and from the coining of money, flowed into the royal coffers; he levied, besides, a thirtieth on all merchandise, market-tolls at fairs, and collected tolls on the roads, and at bridges and ferries. The towns and the privileged territories had to pay taxes, and, on a given day, to send presents to the king. Stephen added, besides, to his military strength by granting to individuals—mostly to native or foreign noblemen of reduced circumstances—extensive estates in fee, subject to the obligation, in case of need, of joining the royal army with a fixed number of armed men. The Petchenegs, Szeklers, and Ruthenes settled as border guards along the frontiers were also obliged to render military service, and even the royal cities sent their contingents of troops equipped by them. This brief enumeration of the means employed by Stephen to strengthen his throne, will make it evident that he provided abundant resources for maintaining the royal power, such as none of his neighbors, or even the rulers of the countries further west, had, then, at their disposal.

The royal court was the centre and faithful mirror of that kingly power, and, in its ordering and conduct, Stephen was careful to imitate foreign courts, not only in their main features, but at times even in their most minute details. The court of his imperial brother-in-law, Henry II. of Germany, especially, served him as a model. Thus it was held that the person of the king was sacred, and that to offend against him who was the embodiment of the majesty of the state, was looked upon as a crime to be punished with loss of life and fortune. The king stood above all the living, and above the law itself. Stephen surrounded himself with the distinguished men, lay and ecclesiastical, of the realm, and, aided by their counsel, administered the affairs of the country, but his word and will was a law to everybody. Amongst the officers of his court were a lord-palatine, a court-judge, a lord of the treasury, and many others, who, in part, assisted him in the government of the state and, in part, ministered to the comforts of the court. At a much later period only, after the lapse of centuries, did the offices of palatine, judge, and treasurer, become dignities of the realm.

The government of the country in time of peace involved no great care or trouble, for only the royal domains or counties and the royal cities possessing privileges fell within the sphere of the direct power of the king and court. The Church and nobility governed themselves and applied to the king in cases of appeal only, the royal towns conducted their affairs through the agency of judges and chief magistrates elected by themselves, whilst the bulk of the people, composed of the various classes of bondmen and servants, were completely subjected to the authority and jurisdiction of the lords of the land. The bondman might move about freely, but he could never emancipate himself from the tutelage of the landlords. The Hungarian nation was composed of the same social strata which were to be met with everywhere in the West, and the growth of these pursued the same direction, differing, however, in one particular—the relation of the large landed proprietors, the nobility, to their king. To these exceptional relations must be attributed the fact that the political changes in the country did not run in parallel grooves with those of the other western states. Stephen granted no constitution, all complete, to his people; its growth was the work of centuries, but the country was indebted to him for having organized the state in such a manner that, whilst there was nothing in the way of a free and healthy development of its political institutions, its inherent strength was such that it could successfully resist the many and severe shocks to which in the course of nearly a thousand years it was subjected.

The country prospered during the long reign of King Stephen, thanks to his untiring labors and to the rare moderation with which he tempered his passionate zeal. The nation became gradually familiar with the changes wrought, and began to accept the new order of things, although it could not quite forget the old ways. Old memories revived again and again, and those especially who bowed down before the crown and cross from compulsion and not from conviction, were filled with anxiety as to the uncertain future. Stephen thoroughly understood the feelings and prejudices of his people, and he carefully avoided every act, and steered clear of every complication which might tend to rouse their passions. He well knew that time alone could give permanence and stability to the institutions created by him, and that years of peace and continued exertions were necessary to consolidate his work. Two great objects, therefore, occupied his mind continually, even in his old age; in the first place, to defend the realm against external dangers, and in the second place, to raise a successor to himself to whom he might safely entrust the continuation of the work commenced by him.

But fate denied him the accomplishment of either of his objects. As long as Henry II., his brother-in-law, reigned there was peace between Hungary and the German empire, but the death of the latter in 1024 severed the bond of amity between the two countries. The feelings entertained by Conrad II. toward the kingdom of Hungary were very different from those manifested by his predecessor, and this change of sentiment was soon shown by Conrad's laying claim, by virtue of his imperial prerogative, to the sovereignty over Stephen's realm. Conrad, with his ally, the Duke of Bohemia, and the united forces of his vast empire, began war in 1030, and overran with his armies the country on both banks of the Danube, as far as the Gran and the Raab. Stephen was undismayed, his courage rather rose with the perils environing him. He bade the people throughout the land to fast and pray, for not alone his kingdom was at stake, but the independence of the Hungarian Church was menaced by the imperial forces. Those who looked with indifference at the cause of the Hungarian crown and the cross, had their enthusiasm excited by the proud satisfaction of fighting in defence of the national dignity and liberty. Amongst those western nations who had been for so long a time harassed by the military expeditions of the Hungarians, the German people, feeling its strength, was the first to turn its arms against the former assailants. But Conrad's attack proved unsuccessful against the united strength of the king and the nation, between whom the peril from without had restored full harmony, and he was compelled to leave the country in the autumn of the very year in which he entered upon the war, dejectedly returning to Germany after a campaign of utter failure instead of the expected triumphs. Peace was concluded in the following year, and the emperor acknowledged the independence of the young but powerful kingdom. Conrad's son, who subsequently succeeded to the imperial throne as Henry III., visited Stephen at his court, in order to draw closer the ties of amity between the two countries. The danger had passed for the time being, but the apprehensions of Stephen were far from being allayed as he pondered on the future. The peace just concluded did not satisfy him; there were no guaranties for its preservation, nor had he any faith in its being a permanent peace, for he well knew that the German kings, as long as they wore the imperial crown, would not fail to repeat their attacks on the independence of the young kingdom. Reflections of this sombre nature often filled his soul with despondency, and then came occasions when he entertained fears that the nation might not be strong enough to withstand the dangers threatening her, or that if she triumphed she would, in the intoxication of her victory, turn with exasperation against those innovations which had brought the foreign foes upon her.

All his hopes centred in Duke Emeric, his only son, who, under the care of the pious Bishop Gerhard, grew up to be a fine youth, full of promise, in whom his fond father discovered all those qualities which he wished him to possess for the good of his nation. The young prince was, indeed, very zealous in his faith; his piety amounted almost to frenzy, and he turned away from the world, despising its joys and harassing struggles, and seeking the salvation of his soul in self-denial and the mortification of his flesh. He was, in truth, the holy child of a holy parent, but not born to rule as the fit son of a great king. He preferred the cloister to the royal throne, and, far from inheriting the apostolic virtues of his august father, he was rather inclined to indulge in the errors of the age he lived in. But the aged king, dazzled by the lustre of his son's holiness, was blind to his shortcomings. He had faith in him, for in him he saw his only hope. In order fitly to prepare him for his future royal mission, he set down for him in writing the experiences of his long and beneficent rule, and the wisdom and goodness treasured up in his heart and mind. These admonitions addressed to his son have been spared by all-devouring time, and to this day they are apt to delight and instruct us as one of the most precious relics of that age. The reader will surely be pleased with a few specimens of these exhortations:

"I cannot refrain, my beloved son," Stephen wrote, "from giving thee advice, instruction, and commands whereby to guide thyself and thy subjects. * * * Strive to obey sedulously the injunctions of thy father, for if thou despisest these thou lovest neither God nor man. Be therefore dutiful, my son; thou hast been brought up amidst delights and treasures, and knowest nothing of the arduous labors of war and the perils of hostile invasions by foreign nations, in the midst of which nearly my whole life has been passed. The time has arrived to leave behind thee those pillows of luxuriousness which are apt to render thee weak and frivolous, to make thee waste thy virtues, and to nourish in thee thy sins. Harden thy soul in order that thy mind may attentively listen to my counsels."

After enlarging in ten paragraphs upon the topic of his counsels, he proceeds as follows: "I command, counsel, and advise thee, above all, to preserve carefully the apostolic and Catholic faith if thou wishest thy kingly crown to be held in respect, and to set such an example to thy subjects that the clergy may justly call thee a Christian man, * * * for he who does not adorn his faith with good deeds—the one being a dead thing without the others—cannot rule in honor."

Stephen then lays down rules of conduct towards the magnates of the realm, the lay lords, the high dignitaries, and the warriors, as follows: "They are, my dear son, thy fathers and thy brothers, neither call them nor make them thy servents. Let them combat for thee, but not serve thee. Rule over them peaceably, humbly, and gently, without anger, pride, and envy, bearing in mind that all men are equal, that nothing exalts more than humility, nor is there any thing more degrading than pride and envy. If thou wilt be peaceable, every one will love thee and call thee a brave king, but if thou wilt be irritable, overbearing, and envious, and look down upon the lords, the might of the warriors will weaken thy kingly state, and thou wilt lose thy realm. Govern them with thy virtues, so that, inspired by love for thee, they may adhere to thy royal dignity."

He then recommends, above all, patience and careful inquiry in the administration of justice in these words: "Whenever a capital cause or other cause of great importance be brought before thee for judgment, be not impatient, nor indulge in oaths beforehand that the accused shall be brought to punishment. Do not hasten to pronounce judgment thyself, lest thy royal dignity be impaired thereby, but leave the cause rather in the hands of the regular judges. Fear the functions of a judge, and even the name of a judge, and rather rejoice in being and having the name of a righteous king. Patient kings rule, impatient ones oppress. If, however, there be a cause which it is fit for thee to decide, judge mercifully and patiently to the enhancement of the praise and glory of thy crown."

Speaking of the foreigners settled in the country, he says: "The Roman empire owed its growth, and its rulers their glory and power, chiefly to the numerous wise and noble men who gathered within its boundaries from every quarter of the world. * * * Foreigners coming from different countries and places to settle here bring with them a variety of languages, customs, instructive matters, and arms, which all contribute to adorn and glorify the royal court, holding in check, at the same time, foreign powers. A country speaking but one language, and where uniform customs prevail, is weak and frail. Therefore I enjoin on thee, my son, to treat and behave towards them decorously, so that they shall more cheerfully abide with thee than elsewhere. For if thou shouldst spoil what I have built up, and scatter what I have gathered, thy realm would surely suffer great detriment from it."

The preference of Stephen for the immigrants from abroad did not degenerate into contempt for ancient customs, for he thus concludes: "It is both glorious and royal to respect the laws of the forefathers and to imitate ancestors worthy of reverence. He who holds in contempt the decisions of his predecessors will not keep the laws of God. Conform, therefore, my dear son, to my institutions, and follow without hesitation my customs, which befit the royal dignity. It would be difficult for thee to govern a realm of this character without following the precedents laid down by those who governed before thee. Adhere, therefore, to my customs, so that thou shalt be deemed the first amongst thine, and merit the praise of the stranger. * * * The evil-minded ruler who stains himself with cruelty vainly calls himself king; he but deserves the name of a tyrant. I therefore beseech and enjoin upon thee, my beloved son, thou delight of my heart and hope of the coming generation, be, above all, gracious, not only to thy kinsmen, to princes, and to dukes, but also to thy neighbors and subjects; be merciful and forbearing not only to the powerful but to the weak; and, finally, be strong, lest good fortune elate thee, and bad fortune depress thee. Be humble, moderate, and gentle, be honorable and modest, for these virtues are the chief ornaments of the kingly crown."

But the young duke was not fated to realize the hopes of his fond father. In the very year (1031), and on the very day, say the chronicles, on which Stephen intended to have his son annointed before the nation as his successor, the mysterious edict of divine Providence suddenly took him away. In place of the crown of terrestrial power, his unstained life, nipped in the bud, was to be rewarded by the glory of everlasting salvation.

This sad blow prostrated the aged king, who had already been ailing, throwing him on his bed, and from that moment up to the day of his death he was unable to recover either his bodily or mental strength. Bereft of all hope and left to himself with his great sorrow and harassing doubts, he looked about him irresolutely for one on whose shoulders the cares of royalty should rest after his departure. The descendants of his uncle Michael were still living, and his choice fell upon them, they being rightfully entitled to succeed to the throne. But he was foiled in his intention by the opposition of the court, where the foreigners rallying round Queen Gisella had obtained the mastery, and where they now resorted to every evil scheme to compel the decrepit king to designate as his successor Duke Peter, who resided at the court, and was the son of one of the king's sisters, and Ottone Urseolo, the Doge of Venice. He finally yielded, and by this act the vessel of State which he had piloted for nearly half a century with a strong arm and great circumspection, was drawn into a most dangerous current. Stephen was the founder of the kingdom of Hungary; to others was left the inheritance of defending and strengthening it. He died in 1038 on Mary's Ascension Day, the anniversary of the same day on which, thirty-eight years before, he had placed the crown on his head. On the day of his death Stephen gathered about him his courtiers and the magnates of the land, and commended the realm to their care, but, as if distrustful of them, he, in his last prayer, placed both the church and the kingdom founded by him under the patronage of the Holy Virgin Mary. Five centuries later Stephen was canonized and placed upon the calendar of saints by the Church of Rome, and the event of the exaltation of their first king and apostle was celebrated as a great national holiday by the people. Time has preserved St. Stephen's right hand and the crown which his piety earned for him, but the brightest and noblest monument he erected to himself is the creation of a commonwealth whose free institutions, unimpaired strength and independence have survived the storms of nearly nine centuries.

CHAPTER VII.

THE KINGS OF THE HOUSE OF ÁRPÁD.

THE crown of St. Stephen remained in the dynastic family of Árpád for three centuries. The kings of this dynasty erected, upon the foundations laid by the first great king of that house, the proud and enduring structure of the Hungarian Church and State. The liberty of the nation and the independence of the country were maintained by these rulers against the ever-recurring attacks of both the Eastern and Western empires, and the paternal meddling of the popes, as well as against the barbarians invading Europe from the East, whose devastations menaced the complete destruction of every thing that lay in their path.

But while they repulsed with an ever-ready and strong arm all hostile attacks—from whatever quarter they might come—they willingly extended the right hand of friendship and hospitality to those who came to settle in the country with peaceful intentions, and brought with them the valued seeds of Western culture. The Hungarians themselves could be but with difficulty weaned from their ancient customs, and they still continued to be the martial element of the country, inured to war and laying down their lives on fields of battle; but the populations which had emigrated from the West, protected by royal immunities, were the fathers of a busy and prosperous city-life, and laid the foundations of civilization in Hungary. A few monumental memorials, spared by the hand of time, proclaim to this day the artistic taste and wealth of those remote centuries, and the scant words to be found in ancient and decayed parchments speak loudly, and with no uncertain sound, of the cities of that time as busy marts of industrial activity and thriving commerce. From the list of the annual revenues of one of the Árpáds, Béla III., and those of the country in the twelfth century, which was submitted by him when asking for the hand of the daughter of the French king, the civilized West learned with amazement of the enormous wealth of the king ruling near the eastern confines of the Western world. The king's wealth was but a reflex of the prosperity of the people. During the era of the Árpáds Hungary surpassed many a Western country in power and wealth, and in the work of civilization either kept pace with them or faithfully followed in their footsteps. These three hundred years produced great kings, who, distinguished by their abilities, character, and achievements, made the country strong and flourishing; but this era produced also weak and frivolous rulers, whose faults will forever darken their memory. Posterity, however, cherishes the memory of all with equal piety, and is accustomed to look at the entire period in the light of the lustre of the great kings only. No wonder, therefore, if the ancient chroniclers, in describing the events of that era, are led by their piety to weave into the text gorgeous tales and legends for the purpose of enhancing the glory of the great kings, and of palliating the shortcomings of those kings who were weak and frail.

The history of those three centuries may be divided into three periods. The first, comprising the first two centuries, may be called the heroic period of the young kingdom, in the course of which both the foreign and domestic foes were triumphantly resisted, the attacks of the neighboring nations repulsed, and the risings of paganism quelled. The second comprises the early part of the thirteenth century. During this period the royal power entered upon a state of decay, and was no longer able either to secure respect for the law or the execution of its behests. At this time too the nobility extorted from royalty a charter called the Golden Bull, confirming their immunities. During the third period an oligarchy, recruited from the ranks of the nobility, rose to power, and became the scourge of the nation, defying the royal authority and trampling upon all law. The licentiousness of this class ruined the country, which was then very near becoming a prey of the Mongols, who made an unexpected invasion. The realm, however, was saved from utter destruction by the devotion of one of her great kings and a happy conjuncture of circumstances.

The misgivings which filled Stephen's soul when he closed his eyes in eternal sleep soon proved to have been well founded. Four years had hardly elapsed after his death when the armies of the German emperor were already marching on Hungary, and in another four years paganism arose in a formidable rebellion, with the avowed purpose of destroying the new church and kingdom.

Peter (1038-1046), Stephen's successor, who was of foreign descent and of a proud and frivolous nature, despised the rude and uncivilized Hungarians. He surrounded himself with foreigners, German and Italian immigrants, who divided amongst themselves the chief dignities of the State, preyed upon the prosperity of the country, and ruined the morals of the people. The nation did not tolerate his misrule very long. The fierce hatred and exasperation with which they looked at every thing foreign found its vent against Peter, whom they drove from the country and then elected in his place one of their own nation, Samuel Aba (1041-1044), the late king's brother-in-law. Peter did not renounce his lost power, but asked the help of the German emperor, which he readily obtained. The Emperor Henry III. opened with his German troops the way to the forfeited throne, and Samuel Aba, who marched against him, having fallen on the battle-field, Peter for the second time had the crown of St. Stephen placed on his brow, but this time he took the oath of fealty to the German emperor. Thus did Hungary for the moment become a vassal state of the German empire. But the vassalage was short, for hardly had the emperor withdrawn from the country when the passionate wrath of the nation rose higher than ever against Peter.

This time, however, the wrath was not alone against his person, but menaced destruction to every thing opposed to the ancient order of things, and produced a bitter contest against both Christianity and the royal dignity. Peter would have fain escaped now from his persecutors, but he was captured, thrown into prison, and deprived of his sight, and then, from the depth of his misery, he vainly bewailed the giddiness which had conjured up the storm of passions that had deprived him of his throne, his eyesight, and liberty.

The leader of the pagan rebellion was Vatha. At his command firebrands were thrown into the churches and monasteries, the crosses were demolished, and every thing proclaiming the new faith was reduced to ruins; and by his advice ambassadors were sent to the dukes of the house of Árpád, who, after Stephen's death, had sought refuge in foreign countries, to summon them to return to the country and restore there the old order. King Andrew I. (1046-1061), to whom the supreme power had been offered, and who, during his exile in Russia, had married the daughter of the Prince of Kiev, immediately obeyed the summons, not, however to submit to the behests of paganism, but to rule in accordance with the principles and in the spirit of his illustrious kinsman, King Stephen. For a while, indeed, he was compelled to bear with the outbreaks, massacres, and devastations of paganism, but as soon as he felt secure in his new power, and especially after having taken up his residence in Stuhlweissenburg, then the capital of the country, where he was able to collect around him the Christian inhabitants of the West, who lived there in large numbers, he at once turned his arms against the pagan rebels. He dispersed their armies, captured their leaders, and crushed the rebellion with merciless severity.

The double cross shone out again triumphantly, but the crown was still menaced by danger. After the defeat of paganism the Emperor Henry III. sent envoys to Andrew, asking satisfaction for the cruelties inflicted upon Peter and calling upon the king to renew the oath of fealty to the emperor of Germany. Andrew felt that unless he maintained the independence of the country, and the dignity of the crown, he incurred the risk of losing the throne itself. He therefore rejected Henry's claims and prepared for the defence of the country. At the same time he summoned home his brother Béla (Adalbert) who, during his exile in Poland, had won high distinction as a soldier, and had obtained, as a reward for his military services, the hand of a daughter of Miecislas. Andrew himself was in ill-health, and he did not care to face the brewing storm single-handed. He wanted to have at his side the powerful arm of his brave and mighty brother, whose very appearance was sufficient to inspire the distressed nation with confidence and hope. He gave Béla one third of the realm, and, being childless, promised him the crown after his decease. Neither Andrew nor the nation were disappointed in Duke Béla, who was believed by the people to be irresistible. It was in vain that Henry III. collected the entire armed force of the empire, and three times in succession (1049-1052) threw this force upon Hungary. In each campaign Duke Béla succeeded in dealing deadly blows upon the invaders. His triumph was so complete that the emperor was compelled to solemnly proclaim peace, again acknowledging the independence of the kingdom.

The nation was not permitted long to enjoy the peace following her almost miraculous escape. Domestic dissensions took the place of the dangers threatening from abroad, and this time the feuds did not originate with the people, but with the royal family itself. All the glory of the important results of the German wars, of the driving the enemy from the country, and of her happy escape from the besetting dangers, centred in the person of Duke Béla. The nation looked with love and admiration upon the knightly form of their favorite, and his popularity was so great that it quite overshadowed that of Andrew, notwithstanding all his kingly power. Andrew's feelings were deeply hurt by the popularity of his brother, nor could he help being terrified by it. But it was not his brother's popularity alone which troubled him.

During the war a son had been born to Andrew, who was christened Solomon. Andrew now repented of his promise to Béla. He wished his infant son to succeed to the throne, and in order to insure it to him, he caused Solomon to be crowned in spite of his tender age. Not satisfied with this, but fearing that Béla, aggrieved by these proceedings, might rise against Solomon at some future time, he betrothed his little son to the daughter of the recently humbled emperor, in order to secure for Solomon the powerful aid of the German empire against Béla's attacks. Every movement of Andrew was dictated by fear, and he saw cause for trembling in every thing. What troubled him most was that Béla had never breathed a word about his griefs or wrongs. Andrew would often ask himself whether Béla was candid in his apparent indifference, or whether, under the cover of this calm repose, he was not concocting dangerous schemes against him and young Solomon. He determined to put Béla's candor to the proof. He had been ailing, and made his feeble condition a pretext for inviting his brother to the court. He received Béla with kindly words, confided to him his misgivings, appealed to his generosity, and repeatedly assured him that he did not intend to defraud him of his rights by the acts done in favor of his son Solomon. Andrew concluded by saying that he left it to Béla to decide whether he would rather succeed to the throne after his own death, or be satisfied to remain at the side of young Solomon as the military chief of the nation and the protector of the realm. The old chronicles relate that Andrew, having finished his sweet speech, caused to be placed before Béla the royal crown and a sword, calling upon him to choose between the two. "I take the sword," exclaimed Béla, unable to conceal his indignation, "for if I coveted the crown, I could always obtain it with the sword."

The feud between the two brothers became henceforth irreconcilable. The nation sided with Béla. The emperor spoken of before was dead, and a boy occupied the German throne. Andrew had sent his queen and young son some time before to the German court, and now he marched against Béla, who was prepared to meet him. The two brothers confronted each other near the Theiss, and Andrew lost both the battle and his life, whilst Béla was on the field of battle proclaimed king of the realm.

Béla and his family occupy a conspicuous place in the history of the first century of the Hungarian kingdom. He himself, two of his sons, and one of his grandsons were destined to successfully defend the country, to pacify the nation, and, pursuing the work of Stephen, to complete the creations of that great king. They were all endowed with eminent qualities befitting the great task allotted to them. The heroism, devotion, and wisdom of the father descended to the children, in whose character the inherited virtues shone out with even a brighter and purer light. They were zealous guardians of their kingdom and devout Christians, and they were wedded, heart and soul, to their nation, which beheld in its kings with feelings of delight the embodiment of its own best qualities. The imagination of the people soars towards them after the lapse of so many centuries, and loves to make their lofty forms the heroes of fabulous legends. Hence it is that the events recorded of them in the pages of the chronicles are nearly choked up by the ever-gorgeous poetical creations of the imagination of the people.

The reign of Béla I. was short (1061-1063), but even during this brief period he succeeded in rendering important services to his country. While he was king paganism once more reared its crest under the lead of James, son of the Vatha who had been put to death during Andrew's reign. James stirred up the multitude against Christianity and royalty, but Béla nipped the rising in the bud. This last attempt of paganism having failed, its power was completely broken, and it finally lost entirely its hold upon the imagination and passions of the people. Some there were yet who continued to resort secretly to the sacred places in the groves, but their persecutors traced them even to these hallowed spots, until, at last, the sacred fire burning on the secretly elevated and visited altars was completely extinguished by the laws enacted under Kings Ladislaus and Coloman. The imperial court of Germany made strenuous efforts to place Solomon, whom it had received under its protection, upon the throne of St. Stephen. Armies were collected and marched against Hungary in the hope of being able at last to assert the imperial supremacy over the kingdom which had been hitherto so unsuccessfully proclaimed. The nation shrank from young Solomon, who was badly brought up and frivolous, and in whom they saw only the tool of the German power. The voice of the people designated amongst Béla's chivalrous sons either the righteous Geyza or the brave and pure Ladislaus, as the princes best fitted for the crown.

These generous princes, however, desiring to save their country from the calamities of an attack by the Germans, abdicated their power in favor of young Solomon, and gave him a friendly reception on his ascending the throne, stipulating only this, that their cousin should leave them undisturbed in the possession of their paternal inheritance, which comprised about one third of the realm. Solomon (1063-1074) promised every thing and kept nothing. He was distrustful of his cousins, perceiving that the nation idolized them, and bowed down before him only from compulsion. It was in vain that his royal kinsmen supported him with an unselfishness almost touching, and strove hard to lend him the lustre of their own popularity in order to obtain favor for him in the eyes of the nation. Solomon persisted in seeing in them his rivals, from whose grasp his crown was not safe, and not his brothers, the upholders and guardians of his royal power. The foreign advisers poisoned the mind of the wavering and fickle king against his young kinsmen, not because they doubted the unselfishness of their devotion, but because his civil counsellors well knew that the two brothers were sworn enemies of German expansion and supremacy. The chronicles of the country abound in praise of the heroic deeds performed by Solomon in conjunction with his cousins while he lived in harmony with them, and in accounts of the intrigues which disturbed that harmony, and finally led to their utter estrangement from each other. The foreign counsellors of Solomon succeeded in working upon his fears and jealousy to such an extent that they finally prevailed upon the king to hire assassins to do away with Duke Geyza. The trap was laid but the victim for whom it was destined succeeded in making his escape. The feud of the fathers revived in their sons, and King Solomon and the dukes Geyza and Ladislaus confronted each other in the same hostile spirit in which their fathers, Andrew and Béla, had once stood face to face. The question which the sword was to decide was not merely whose should be the crown, but as to whether the German power should become the master of the Hungarian kingdom, or not. Fate decided against Solomon. He lost the battle of Mogyoród, and with it his throne, and with his defeat vanished all hopes of establishing German supremacy over Hungary.

The vacant throne was filled first by Geyza (1074-1077), and, after his short reign, by his brother Ladislaus. Solomon escaped, and turned now to his imperial brother-in-law, Henry IV., now again to the adversary of the latter, Pope Gregory VII., for help, moving heaven and earth to regain his lost throne. It was all in vain, the mischief was done and could be remedied no more. The chroniclers delight in adorning the story of the erratic life and repentance of the unfortunate youth. They relate of him that, perceiving the utter failure of all his attempts, he was filled with loathing against himself and the blind passions which had made him the enemy and scourge of his country, retired from the world, and became a hermit in order to atone for the faults of his brief youth by doing penance during the remaining years of his life. A cave on the shores of the Adriatic, near Pola, is pointed out to this day, in which Solomon is supposed to have led the life of a hermit. The chronicle adds that he lived to a high old age, became the benefactor of the inhabitants of the vicinity, prayed for his nation, and that the last wish of his departing soul was the happiness of his country.

Ladislaus (1077-1095), who succeeded his older brother Geyza, was one of the noblest, most noteworthy of the kings of the royal line of the Árpáds. He was great not only in the light of the important achievements of his reign, but by his eminent personal qualities. His character was a happy combination of strength without violence, of wisdom without vacillation, of piety without fanaticism, and of lofty majesty without pride. He was the hero, the model, and the idol of his nation, which had never clung to any of its kings with more boundless affection, greater devotion, and more respect. He identified himself with the nation, drew strength from her affection for him, and rendered her powerful in return. He gave the kingdom, founded by his illustrious ancestor, a permanent peace, restored the faith in its strength, and insured its development. He put an end to the era of attacks from the West, and even intervened in the troubles of Germany by siding with the papal party against Henry IV. An ancient chronicler informs us that he had been offered the crown of Germany but refused to accept it, because "he wished to be nothing but a Hungarian." Although he aided the popes in their contest with Germany, he yet defended the interests of the kingdom against papal pretensions. Pope Gregory VII. having reminded him that the Hungarian kings had obtained their crown from one of his predecessors, Sylvester II., and that it was fitting therefore that they should submit to the supremacy of the Pope, Ladislaus replied, in a letter sent to the Pope, that "he was ready to obey with filial submission and with his whole heart the holy see, as an ecclesiastical power, and his holiness the Pope, as his spiritual father, but that he would not subordinate the independence of his realm to anybody or any thing." Nor did the king in his acts deviate from his professions, and the popes prized his alliance too highly to find it advisable to turn his friendship into enmity by forcing upon him their supremacy.

Ladislaus was not satisfied to merely defend his people and country against hostile attacks; he exerted himself to increase the population and to add to the territory. Under him Croatia was added to the kingdom (1089), and, having founded a bishopric at Agram, he spread the Christian faith amongst the Croatians and organized their church. About the same time, the Kuns (Cumans), having invaded the country from the East, Ladislaus routed them, and, making a great number of captives amongst them, he colonized with these prisoners the lowlands of the Theiss. Croatia is still a member of the realm of St. Stephen, and the Kuns have been entirely absorbed by the Hungarian element, sharing the weal and woe of the latter. History has preserved in the fragments of the laws enacted by him clear proofs of the greatness of Ladislaus in the affairs of peace; a severe judge and wise leader, he defended with his sword the blessed seeds planted by him in time of peace. He compelled the people to settle down permanently, and taught them by severe penalties to respect the persons and property of others. He visited with severe punishment the followers of ancient paganism, and overwhelmed the Christian church with benefits. It was at his request that Stephen, his son Emeric, and the martyred bishop Gerhard, Duke Emeric's tutor, were canonized and placed upon the list of saints by the Church of Rome. We need not wonder, therefore, if, confronted with such grandeur and majesty, posterity abstained from applying to him human standards, and loved to see in his acts the manifestations of a higher and a divine power. Thus the chronicler speaking of him says with deep emotion: "He was rich in love, abounding in patience, cheerful in his graciousness, overflowing in the gifts of grace, the promoter of justice, the patron of modesty, the guardian of the deserted, and the helper of the poor and distressed. Divine mercy raised him in the gifts of nature above the common worth of man, for he was brave, strong of arm, and pleasant to the sight; his whole appearance was marked by leonine strength and majesty; he was so tall of stature that his shoulders were visible above those about him, and, blessed with the fulness of divine gifts, his aspect proclaimed him to have been created to be a king." His mortal remains lie enshrined in the cathedral of Grosswardein (Nagyvárad), which was built by his munificence, and the piety of the nation has made of the place of his burial a miracle-working resort for devout pilgrims. A pious tradition has lived for centuries amongst the people, that whenever danger menaces the country the king leaves his bed of stone and, followed by the invisible hosts of his departed braves, combats against the assailants of his country.

Ladislaus was still living when the religious movement which took the form of a holy warfare began to agitate the west of Europe—a movement which was destined to maintain its hold upon the minds of the inhabitants of the western world for two hundred years. According to a tradition of the nation, Ladislaus was offered, as the most chivalrous king, the chief command over the western Knights and crusading armies, but was prevented by death from assuming the leadership. Most of the crusaders went eastward by the valley of the Danube, passing through Hungary, and the waves of the first expedition reached the country during the reign of Coloman (1095-1114), the successor of Ladislaus. It was fortunate for the country that a king like Coloman kept guard at this time over her frontiers; a king who, although he may have lacked the ideal qualities of his predecessor, possessed both the strength and the courage to protect and defend the realm. Although he was well aware that his attitude would provoke the anger of the popes and place him in opposition to the public opinion of the whole Christian world, he was not deterred from mercilessly driving away from the borders of the country the first motley host of unruly and lawless crusaders that approached them. The only crusaders to whom he gave a friendly reception, permitting them to pass through the country, were the troops of Godfrey of Bouillon, but even as to these, he exacted the most rigorous security for their good behaviour. Coloman's firmness alone saved the country from being engulfed by the movement, and prevented its domestic peace, which was not as yet firmly established, from being disturbed.

But while he was thus guarding the interests of the country with a watchful eye, an unmoved heart, and a strong arm, he still found time and opportunity for increasing the territory of the realm. He completed in Croatia the conquests begun by Ladislaus, and added to the new acquisition Dalmatia, which he wrested from the grasp of the Venetian republic. Coloman was the first Hungarian king who styled himself King of Croatia and Dalmatia.

Coloman won the admiration of his contemporaries and posterity, not merely as a leader of armies, but as a ruler whose great erudition and wise laws served to perpetuate his memory. These qualities obtained for him the epithet *"Könyves"* (bookish) or learned King Coloman. The chronicles extol him for putting a stop by process of law to the prosecution of witches, and for declaring in one of his laws: "Of witches who do not exist at all no mention shall be made." He bestowed great care upon the administration of justice, and among his laws occurs the following admirable direction given to the judges: "Every thing must be so cautiously and anxiously weighed on the scale of justice, that innocence, on the one hand, shall not be condemned from hatred, and, on the other, sin shall not be protected through friendship."

The last years of Coloman's reign were embittered by the ambition of his brother Álmos, who coveted the throne. The energetic and erudite king, who had spent his whole life in consolidating the glorious work begun by Stephen, saw with a sorrowing heart how the restless ambition of single individuals was uprooting the plants he had so carefully nursed. Duke Álmos rose three times in rebellion against his royal brother, nor did he reject, on these occasions, foreign aid. Coloman defeated him each time, and pardoned him each time. But seeing that the incorrigible duke could not be restrained by either his power or his magnanimity, and that he was again collecting an army against him, Coloman caused Álmos and his young son Béla to be thrown into prison, where both were deprived of their sight. This dark and cruel deed, the ferocity of which can be palliated only by the rudeness of the age, was Coloman's last act, and, in thinking of the retribution of the life to come, it could not fail to disturb his peaceful descent into the grave.

The risings of Álmos initiated that period of civil strife which continued for two hundred years, until the house of the Árpáds became extinct, and which, on the one hand, afforded the Greek emperors an opportunity to meddle with the affairs of the country, and to attempt the extension of their supremacy over the kingdom; and, on the other hand, undermined the authority of royalty, lifted the oligarchs into power, and sapped the foundations of the institutions established by Stephen.

Álmos, the blinded duke, planned again a rising against Coloman's son and successor, Stephen II. (1114-1131), but the plot having been discovered he fled to the Greek court for protection and aid. The Hungarian and Greek armies were already confronting each other on the banks of the lower Danube, but the shedding of blood was prevented on this occasion by the sudden death of Duke Álmos.

His son Béla II. (1131-1141), who had also been made blind, ascended the throne after the death of Stephen II., but he gave no thought to pacifying the restlessness of the people or to restoring peace to the country. One feeling alone held the mastery over his soul, shrouded in darkness—that of vindictiveness against those who had robbed him and his father of the light of day. His revengeful feelings were still more fanned by his masculine queen, Ilona, the daughter of the prince of Servia, by whose advice he summoned the diet to meet in

Arad, on the southern confines of the country, for the sole purpose of avenging himself on this occasion. The lords, anticipating no evil, assembled in large numbers, although there were many among them who might have had good reasons for dreading the king's wrath. They came, however, confiding in the forgiveness of Béla, which had been publicly proclaimed by him. According to the information gleaned from the chronicles, the diet was opened by Queen Ilona herself, who, after describing in a passionate strain the sad fate of her blinded husband, and inveighing against the crime of those who were the causers of his affliction, herself gave the signal for the awful work of vengeance. A dreadful struggle ensued between the adherents of the king and those who had been singled out by the court as victims. Many remained dead in the hall of the diet which had thus been changed into a battle-field, but many others, who succeeded in escaping, took away with their wounds feelings of undying hatred against their king. These bloody proceedings gave the disaffected a fresh cause for placing their hopes in the Greek court, and expecting from that quarter relief from the tyranny which oppressed them.

But when open hostilities finally broke out between the two nations, Béla II. was no more among the living. When the war commenced, Geyza II. (1141-1161), the son of Béla, sat on the Hungarian throne, which the Emperor Manuel, the most powerful of the Comneni, ruled in Constantinople. The war was a protracted one, and its scene was chiefly on the southern frontier, along the course of the Danube and the country near the Save, but Manuel, with all his power and wariness, was unable to obtain an advantage over the younger and more energetic neighbor. After the death of Geyza, his son Stephen III. succeeded to the throne. The Greek emperor refused to recognize him as the king of Hungary, and attempted to place upon the throne as his vassals, successively, the two brothers of Geyza who had found a refuge at his court, but he did not succeed with either of the pretenders. One of his protégés died young, while the other was driven from the country by the lawfully elected king, Stephen III.

Manuel, seeing all his schemes overthrown, and perceiving that, as an enemy, he had utterly failed, pretended now to feelings of friendship, and offered peace to the Hungarians. As a further pledge of peace he requested King Stephen III. to permit his brother Béla to reside with him at Constantinople, promising that he would adopt him as his son and heir. Manuel, having no sons to whom he might leave the imperial throne, in all probability secretly cherished the hope that his adopted son would at some future day succeed to the Greek throne, and would also inherit the crown of St. Stephen, and that by this means the two neighboring countries, which he did not succeed in uniting by force of arms, would, in the course of time, become one. Fate, however, seemed to have conspired to frustrate the best laid plans of the Greek emperor. He carried Duke Béla with him to Constantinople, adopted him as his son, declared him his heir, and every thing appeared to point to a happy realization of his ambitious dreams, when unexpectedly a son was born to him, an event which completely upset his calculations. It became now impossible for Manuel to continue to keep the young Hungarian duke at his court, unless, indeed, he wanted to raise a rival to his own son; he, therefore, deprived him of all the distinctions he had heaped upon him, and sent him hurriedly back to his native country, where the throne had just become vacant by the death of Stephen III. Manuel, however, made the young duke take a solemn oath before he allowed him to depart that he would never attack the Greek empire, and this empty formality was all that he was able to achieve in furtherance of his scheme to impose his supremacy upon Hungary. The same duke, however, who had been nurtured in the culture of Greece, and became King of Hungary as Béla III., completely banished Greek influence from the country, and secured its independence for a long time to come.

Béla III. (1173-1196) was one of the most powerful and respected rulers of Hungary. He possessed great kingly qualities, and his character commanded universal respect. He had a great deal to contend with, after his return from Constantinople, before he succeeded in being firmly seated on his throne. He was received with feelings of suspicion by the powerful nobility, the chief dignitaries of the church, and by the queen-mother herself, who all looked upon him as a partisan of the eastern despotism, and as an enemy to the Roman Catholic Church, and who were anxious to place his brother Geyza upon the throne. Béla triumphed before long over all his enemies. He had his brother thrown into prison, sent his mother into exile, restrained and humiliated the powerful oligarchs, and conciliated the friendship of the high prelacy by his munificence and liberality towards the church of the country. Having restored order at home, he devoted himself to the task of obtaining again possession of the territory Manuel had seized. The reconquering of the Dalmatian seashore involved him in a war with Venice, the envious rival of the Hungarian kingdom, in the course of which Béla had occasion to give proof of his military power on a new scene of action, where the valor of his ancestors had never had an opportunity of shining, by achieving over the proud republic a great triumph on the sea. Béla had learned a great deal at the Greek court, but all his valuable acquirements he employed for the advantage of his country. He did not exactly open new avenues for the development of the nation; his chief merit consisted rather in leading her back to the road marked out by Stephen, and successfully pursued by King Ladislaus and King Coloman. His every effort tended to bring the nation closer to that western civilization which had fostered her tender beginnings, and the rejection of which all this time would have amounted to a stultification of her past, and a certain risk of her future. Two things, however, were of paramount necessity to enable the people to prosper by the king's judicious exertions in this direction: to restore to the country the needful rest she had not now enjoyed for half a century, and to reëstablish order within the kingdom, torn by the partisanship of the last fifty years. Béla resolutely set to the task of establishing peace and order. He relentlessly pursued the thieves and robbers who rendered life and property insecure and had increased to a frightful extent since Coloman's time, and, in order to do it more effectually, he appointed special officers in every county for that purpose, establishing, at the same time, a royal chancery at the court with a view to giving greater effect to the government of the country and the administration of justice. The proceedings in important affairs of state or private law-suits taken before the king—which hitherto had been oral—now had to be carried on in writing. The country, under Béla's well-ordered government, became more prosperous, and the nation more polished. Béla's first wife was a Greek princess, and his second a French princess. Both the queens, with the retinues following them to the court, introduced there the good taste, culture, and manners of the Greeks and French, so that a German chronicler happening to visit the court at that time, could not find adequate words to extol its magnificent splendors. Culture was not confined to the court; it spread to the nation itself, for we find that the university, recently established in Paris, was attended by a number of Hungarian youths.

All the acts of Béla indicate that he had selected for his model in government one of his most distinguished ancestors, Ladislaus, for whom, as an expression of his own and the nation's piety, he had also, in 1192, secured a place on the list of saints recognized by the Church of Rome.

Béla, while thus advancing the interests of the kingdom and the nation, did not lose sight of the claims of the age upon kings and rulers to support the holy wars waged by Christendom against the infidels. He followed with sympathy the movements of the crusaders, and upon Jerusalem's falling into the hands of the infidels in 1187, he planned himself to lead an army for the purpose of reconquering the holy city. The third crusade was begun in 1189, and the German forces, under the lead of the emperor, Frederic Barbarossa, passed on their way to the Holy Land through Hungary. Béla received his distinguished guest with royal pomp, abundantly provided the German troops with every thing necessary, but he himself did not join the crusaders. What the circumstances were that prevented the king from taking part in the crusades it would be difficult now to determine, but that they must have been weighty ones is amply proved by the fact that he had been long preparing for a crusading campaign, and had for that purpose collected a great deal of treasure. The idea was present before his mind at the time of his death, for he directed that his elder son, Emeric, should succeed him on the throne, and the younger, Duke Andrew, should inherit the treasure collected for the pious object, and employ it in the carrying out of the paternal intentions. Béla's fate had that in common with the fate of the most conspicuous kings of Hungary—that posterity praised his grand achievements, while his own children failed to respect and preserve the inheritance left to them by a distinguished sire.

The feud between the two brothers broke out immediately after the death of Béla III. Andrew collected troops for the pretended purpose of executing the last will of his father, but in reality to employ them against his own brother. He succeeded in defeating the army of King Emeric, who was taken unawares, and was, besides, vacillating and incapable, and, after occupying Croatia and Dalmatia, to which he added fresh territory, he proclaimed himself, in 1198, Duke of Croatia, Dalmatia, Rama, and Chulmia (Bosnia and Herzegovina). Emeric vainly urged Innocent III., the most powerful pope since Gregory VII., to compel the rebellious duke to carry out the pious vows of his father. Andrew did not stir one step towards the Holy Land, but, persevering in his sinful perverseness, continued to repeat his attacks against the lawful king. At last, during one of his outbreaks, he was overtaken by an avenging Nemesis.

The armies of the two brothers confronted each other on the banks of the Drave. The camp of Andrew was stirring with a strong and numerous army which, in anticipation of a certain victory, was loudly revelling and making merry. King Emeric's eyes sadly surveyed his own scant following, whose devotion and determination, great as they were, did not seem sufficient to make up for the deficiency in numbers. The collision between the opposing armies was inevitable, and the king felt that his utter discomfiture would be the result of the battle. His desperate condition inspired him with a sudden resolution, and, without communicating his intention to any one, he went into the enemy's camp, dressed in kingly state, and, sceptre in hand, made straight for his brother's tent. The revelling warriors, in surprise, were struck with awe at the marvellous spectacle suddenly bursting in upon their dazed eyes. "I wish to see the man who will dare to raise a sinful arm against his king and master," were the magic words which opened him the way through the gaping multitude. Upon arriving in his brother's tent he seized the rebellious duke's hands and led him captive to his own camp. The above narrative of the event, as gleaned from the chronicles, may not agree in every particular with the actual occurrence, but Duke Andrew became the king's prisoner, and remained captive until the latter called him to his deathbed, generously confiding to his care his infant son, Ladislaus, who had already been crowned king.

Andrew proved as faithless a guardian as he had been a false brother. He could not restrain his ambition, but deprived Ladislaus of his crown, and drove him and his mother from the court. Shortly afterwards, the unhappy youth died, and Andrew could, at last, in 1205, ascend the throne he had so long coveted, and whose possession he had attempted to achieve by means in the choice of which he never consulted his conscience.

The reign of Andrew II. (1205-1235) deserves a conspicuous place in the history of Hungary, not for its beneficence, but for its weakness and shortcomings. The never-ending civil wars of the last century, especially the internecine struggle between the two brothers, had the effect of weakening the kingdom, lowering the royal power and authority, and, as a consequence of the decay of the latter, of increasing the overbearing spirit of the oligarchs. Andrew II. could not escape the condign punishment brought upon himself by his own acts. His whole reign was a series of feeble attempts to free himself from the entangling web caused by his own faults and the licentiousness of the oligarchy. He presented the spectacle of a man whose ambition was greater than his abilities, and whose levity equalled his ambition. In the beginning of his reign he was completely under the influence of his wife, Gertrude, who was of Tyrolese descent, and who suffered the country to become a prey to her foreign relations and favorites. Yet when the great and powerful lords rose against the plundering foreigners, the licentious court, and the tyrannical and wicked queen, killing the latter in her own palace, Andrew had neither the courage nor the power to exert his royal authority against the rebels, but was rather glad that the storm had passed over his head and had not singled him out for its victim. Instead of resenting the injury done to him, he conciliated his enemies by presents and gifts, and indulged in schemes of a new matrimonial alliance. He was fond of pomp, splendor, generous expenditure, and the ostentatious display of the court, but the royal revenues soon proved inadequate to pay the sums thus squandered, reduced as the royal domains had been by grants of entire counties. The king, in order to raise the revenues, mortgaged the imposts and tolls, and, by debasing the coinage, dishonestly added to his resources. The din of the revels of the court prevented the loud complaints of the people, who were oppressed and worried in a thousand ways by the oligarchs and the tax- and toll-gatherers, from reaching the ears of the king. At times his restlessness and ambition still involved him in adventurous enterprises. Thus he wished to elevate his son, Duke Béla, to the throne of Galicia, but lacked the strength to accomplish his scheme. The campaign against Galicia only added to the expenditures of the country, and, indeed, it happened that the king with his son and the whole army were in the most imminent danger of destruction. His mind was also disturbed by his failure to carry out the wishes of his father, and, at last, he determined, in 1217, to march an army to the Holy Land. In order to raise the money necessary for the campaign he plundered the churches and monasteries, and sold to Venice the city of Zara, the bulwark of the Dalmatian seashore. He finally left the country with the army thus collected, but while he was roaming about in the Holy Land without aim or purpose, the orphaned country was reduced to the brink of misery. "When we returned home from our expedition," complained the king himself, in a letter addressed to the holy see, "we found that both the clergy and the laymen had been guilty of wickedness such as surpasses all imagination. All the treasure of the country we found squandered, and fifteen years will not suffice to restore our land to her former better condition." The condition of the country must have been sad, indeed, if the state the king had left her in might be called good in comparison with it, and however heavily the responsibility of the fresh calamities rested upon the king, his truthfulness in this instance cannot be doubted.

The gloomy rule of Andrew II. was relieved by one cheering event which contained the germ of a better future. The gentry, comprising in its ranks the largest part of the freeholders of the country, unable to bear longer the weak government of the king, the violence of the oligarchy, and the scourge of the army of extortionate gatherers of taxes and tolls, at last lifted their heads and asked the throne to listen to their complaints and to remedy their wrongs. Béla himself, the king's son, whom Andrew II. had caused to be crowned before going to the

Holy Land, was the leader and spokesman of the nobility, who had stood up in defence of the sacredness of the constitution, and who now urged the return to the rule of law in the land.

Their wrongs, and the remedies exacted by the gentry were set forth in the following strain: The king should not, at the expense of the patriots, bestow favors upon foreigners, nor elevate them to dignities, and distribute among them the domains of the country; entire counties or dignities of state should not, as a practice, be granted in perpetuity, and he should not suffer avaricious nobles to grasp a greater number of offices than they could efficiently administer. He should guard the ancient immunities of the nobles, so that they might freely dispose of their property, and not be molested in their persons without lawful judgment, and should not be burdened with taxes or extortionate exactions of any kind. He should take care that the tax-and toll-gatherers and other officials be taken from the ranks of the gentry, and should remove from his service the Ishmaelites and the Jews. Every thing opposed to these requirements he should at once bring to an end. The county estates, granted away to the injury of the land or dishonestly obtained, should be taken back by the king, and he should, in pursuance of the ancient custom of the country, every year, on St. Stephen's day, convoke the diet, whose duty it was to act upon the complaints of the nation and to defend her liberty when attacked.

The king, however, moved neither by the voice of truth, nor by the misery of his people, refused to accede to these requests. In the breast of Andrew II., who, during his whole reign, had utterly neglected the duties coupled with his exalted station, awoke on the present occasion a feeling of injured royal dignity. But the gentry were determined to enforce their demands, and, gathering around the heir to the throne, they took up arms in order to obtain by force the concessions they deemed necessary for the good of the country. Father and son with their armies were already confronting each other, when the chief prelates interfered, and prevailed upon Andrew to listen to the wishes of the gentry. The concessions were drawn up in form of a royal letter and the king bound himself and his successors by oath to observe the stipulations contained in it. Posterity has given this royal letter the name of the *Golden Bull*, owing to the fact that the seal appended to it by a silk string rests in a box made of gold.

This remarkable document, which terminated the internal strife extending over a period of a hundred years, and to which for six centuries the past generations of Hungary were in the habit of proudly referring as the foundation of the constitution of the Hungarian nobility, reads, omitting passages of minor importance, as follows:

King Andrew, who had to be compelled by force to issue the Golden Bull, could, however, not be coerced by any power to observe the promises he had made therein. The exertions of the heir presumptive and the nobility as well as the wrath of the pope were of no avail. Nine years later he confirmed its contents by a fresh oath, but hardly two years elapsed when he incurred the curse of Rome for again disregarding his oath. Struggles, extending over many centuries, were necessary to realize the words of the Golden Bull. Time had then already effaced the memory of Andrew's follies and frailties, and posterity saw him only in the reflected light of the great concessions made by his royal missive. The estates of the diet which met at Rákos in 1505 spoke of him in terms of extravagant praise as the king "who had made the Hungarians great and glorious, and had raised their fame to the very stars."

The struggles which resulted in the issuing of the Golden Bull were by no means over. The nobility had obtained from royalty the concession of their rights, but were lacking the power to maintain them, and to secure their permanency. The very charter of their liberties furnished matter for fresh disputes and dissensions. In these contests, however, the nobility now seldom attacked royalty, the weakening of which would have proved injurious to their own interests, but they usually allied themselves with the kings against the oligarchs, who treated with contempt both law and right, having no need of the protection of either, and who indulged in tyrannical violence against the throne as well as the nation. The licentiousness and increasing power of the oligarchs were the sore spot in the body politic during the period of the last Árpáds, and in a greater and lesser degree, now apparently healed, now more envenomed than ever, it continued to be for centuries a disturbing element in the public life of the country.

The struggle between royalty, supported by the nation, and the unruly great lords had just commenced, when the storm of the Mongol invasion broke loose upon the country, shaking it to its very foundations. When the storm subsided only the weak ones were found to have suffered, the strong ones came out of the nation's calamity more powerful than ever. The national misfortunes only served to advance the interests of the oligarchs, who, about this time, began more frequently to surround the crests of the mountains with stone walls, and, dwelling in their rocky nests, defied royalty with increasing boldness, and oppressed the people with greater impunity than ever. The chroniclers in recalling this period mourn with bitter wailing the gloom which had settled upon the country, the incapacity of the kings, the pride and violence of the lords, and the miserable condition of the people. That the power of the nation was not entirely gone, however, was shown by the cheering fact, casting a ray of light into the gloom of those days, that at the very time when the authority of royalty had sunk to the lowest ebb, the Hungarian arms were able to cope with the powerful Slavic empire ruled by Ottokar, king of Bohemia, and to assist in establishing the power of the Hapsburgs. Unfortunately the national strength was for the most part divided against itself, and the very triumph of the Hungarian arms against Ottokar proved injurious to the nation at large, for it redounded only to the glory of the oligarchy, and tended to confirm their power.

After the death of Andrew II., his son, Béla IV. (1235-1270), devoted himself with youthful energy to the task of restoring the ascendancy of the royal power and authority, of insuring respect to the laws, and of humbling the pride of the oligarchy. He removed the evil counsellors of his father, sent the principal ringleaders to prison, surrounded himself with good patriots, and where gentle words proved inefficacious he resorted to arms in order to obtain possession of the royal domains and county lands which single oligarchs had contrived to acquire by grant during his father's life or from his ancestors, or which had been lawlessly appropriated by them. The efforts made by the youthful king were, however, of no avail. The very successes which attended here and there his policy served only to excite to a higher pitch the anger and resentment of the great lords, and deepened the estrangement between them and the throne. The disaffected oligarchs, whose selfishness was not tempered by patriotism, and whose passions did not know the bridle of the law, were so base as to elevate a foreign prince, Duke Frederic of Austria, to the throne, in opposition to their lawful king. The watchfulness of Béla alone prevented the royal inheritance from passing, at that time already, from the Árpáds into foreign hands. Béla succeeded in driving back Frederic, and in defeating the treasonable schemes of the oligarchy, but he became, at the same time, convinced that until he was able to present to the opposing lords a more formidable front he would have to renounce the realization of the fond hopes of his youth.

Béla looked about him for fresh resources to strengthen his authority and to add to his power. Pious Dominican monks, just then returning to the country from the regions of the Volga, told the tale that in the far east, along the banks of that river, they met with that fraction of the Hungarians who, during the period preceding the occupation of

Hungary, had parted from their brethren near the Black Sea, where the latter continued their march westward. These accounts suggested to Béla the scheme of inviting the distant Eastern brothers to settle in his realm, hoping to augment the royal power by the aid of the new settlers, and to be thus enabled to resume successfully his contest with the proud lords. This scheme, however, failed, but the same circumstances which frustrated his plans as to his countrymen near the Volga, assisted him in obtaining aid from another quarter. The Mongol hordes, which came rushing from Central Asia toward the western world, swept in their impetuous onward march the Hungarians near the Volga out of existence; but the same wild current drove also the Kuns (Cumans) out of their habitations near the Black Sea, and the latter, after having roamed about homeless for a time, and then reached the frontiers of Hungary, begged of King Béla to allow them to come into the country and to settle there. Forty thousand families were in search of a new country, and forty thousand fierce warriors offered their services to King Béla. The people of Hungary were averse to receiving immigration on so large a scale, and the great lords loudly protested against the reception of the new comers, being convinced that the latter would only enhance the king's power, and become instrumental in humbling their order. The king, however, considering the good of the country only, braved the opposition, and admitting Kuthen, king of the Kuns, with his people, into the land, assigned to them as their future abode the plain of the Theiss. Nor did he forget to make their conversion to Christianity a condition of their admission. The good effects Béla had anticipated from his new colony were slow in showing themselves, but the evil consequences of the recent settlement became manifest at once. The great numbers of this rude and barbarous element, who were as little disposed to live in fixed habitations as to embrace Christianity, soon disgusted the people by their lawlessness, violence, unruliness, and the devastations committed by them amongst the Hungarian population. The complaints of all classes, without distinction, which reached the king's ear, became daily louder. Béla was unable to come to the relief of the people, for to have turned against the Kuns, as he was asked to do, would have shaken them in their fidelity to him. But by showing a preference for the new comers he also forfeited the affection of his old adherents, the good patriots who had firmly stood by him, hitherto, in all his troubles. Dissensions arose between the king, who was animated by the purest intentions, and his people, who were unable to fathom the patriotic motives of his actions; and they were at their highest when the hurricane which had swept away the Hungarians on the banks of the Volga, and driven the Kuns to the plains of the Theiss, reached at last the crests of the Carpathian mountains.

The successors of Jenghis Khan, wishing to extend the frontiers of their vast Asiatic empire toward the west, crossed the Volga, overran the Russian steppes, and reduced Moscow to ashes in 1238. Proud and beautiful Kiev was soon after, in 1240, humbled by their victorious arms. The Hungarians were aware of the approach of the formidable foe, but their internal dissensions, and their troubles with the Kuns and with their king, made them forget the imminence of the danger that menaced them. They indulged, besides, in the hope that the mighty Carpathian mountains would arrest the fierce current in its onward course. But the nation was soon roused from its fancied security and awoke to a dread sense of the true situation. The mournful fate of Kiev, the sufferings of the Polish people, and the threatening language of the embassy sent by Batu Khan, the general of Oktai, the Great Khan, who had been the terror of the Russians, dispelled the illusions, of the most sanguine.

The mind of King Béla was beset with anxious thoughts, but his courage did not fail him. Although it was rather late for efficient military preparations, he labored day and night to put the country into a state of defence against the coming peril. He demolished the forests, and barricaded with the timber thus obtained the Carpathian passes. He invited his adherents to take counsel with him, and called to arms the ecclesiastical and lay lords, the soldiery of the counties, and every man in the country capable of bearing arms. According to ancient custom he caused the bloody sword to be carried about throughout the land. His active zeal was not confined to his realm alone, but, sending his ambassadors to the western courts, he instructed them to beg, admonish, and urge the rulers of the West, in the name of Christianity, to come to his aid. It was all in vain. The foreign courts did not stir, and the Hungarian lords, in their surprise and dismay, instead of devising means to meet the danger, were wildly looking about them for some one to be made responsible for the coming peril, and to serve as a victim of their anger. They turned with passionate hatred upon the king and the Kuns, saying that he with his Kuns should defend the country, and that the king need not count upon them in this emergency. The spring of 1241 was already nearing, and still the royal banner, floating over Pesth, proclaimed to the world the absence of troops and the defencelessness of the country. The Mongolian armies had, meanwhile, already begun to press forward. Their right wing marched on Poland and Silesia, in order to effect an entrance into the country from the north-west; the left wing, passing through Moldavia, approached the snowy mountains of Transylvania; whilst the army of the centre was led by Batu Khan himself across the northwestern Carpathians to the pass of Bereczke. Thus the two arms of the Mongol armies were preparing to crush, in a deadly embrace, the doomed country.

Batu Khan crossed the Carpathians on the 12th of March, 1241, and, having dispersed the troops of Palatine Hérdeváry, at the foot of the mountains, the active Mongol cavalry troops overran with such suddenness the plain watered by the Theiss, that four days later the smoke of the burning villages, set on fire by the ruthless enemy, could be discerned from the walls of Pesth. The Hungarian lords, even at this critical moment, failed to arrive with their contingents, and those who were under arms near Pesth nursed their wrath, not against the enemy, but against the hated Kun immigrants whom they denounced as the spies and allies of the Mongols, and as traitors to Hungary. They rushed upon the unsuspecting Kuns with savage rage, massacring their king, Kuthen, together with his household, at his quarters in Pesth. The Kuns, incensed at this treachery, were not slow to retaliate. One portion of them left the country, killing, burning, and devastating every thing before them, whilst the other joined the Mongols in order to avenge more thoroughly their unjust persecution.

Towards the latter end of March, Béla, inspired by despair rather than by any hope of success, led the royal army which had gathered around Pesth, and numbered altogether from 50,000 to 60,000 warriors, against the Mongols. This scanty force was all that the Hungarian nation, shorn of its valor and sadly wanting in public spirit, opposed to the invading enemy. The Mongol army retreated before Béla as far as the Theiss, and there Batu Khan, falling back with both wings of his army, pitched his camp in the angle formed by the Sajó and the Theiss. King Béla was intent upon reaching the same point, and placed his forces on the plain extending along the right bank of the Sajó, opposite the Mongol camp. Here on the plain of Muhi took place the dreadful conflict between the two armies. From the dawn of day to late in the night lasted the bloody engagement which ended with the complete annihilation of the Hungarian army. On the fated battle-field perished the chief prelates of the church, the highest dignitaries of the state taken from the ranks of the best patriots, thousands of the gentry, and the hope and last prop of the nation, her only army. Only few amongst those who did not fall amidst the shock of battle could escape with their lives. The pursuing enemy was everywhere close upon the track of the fugitives. "During a march of two days," says Rogerius, a contemporary writer, who had been an eye-witness of these horrors, "thou couldst see nothing along the roads but fallen warriors. Their dead bodies were lying about like stones in a quarry."

Yet, amidst all these misfortunes, there was one gleam of comfort in store for the nation. Every thing, indeed, was lost, but her king was saved, and whilst he lived the nation still kept up her hopes and faith in a better future. A few devoted followers had rescued Béla from the perils of the bloody engagement near the banks of the Sajó, and the fugitive king, wandering for a while amidst the mountains of Upper Hungary, finally arrived at the court of Frederic, Duke of Austria, to whom he had previously sent his family and royal treasures. Here, however, instead of meeting with hospitality, he was made prisoner, and succeeded in regaining his freedom only by abandoning to his avaricious neighbor, who turned Béla's misfortunes to his profit, his treasures, his crown, and the possession of three counties. Béla then sent his family to the Dalmatian seashore, whilst he himself hurried back to his unfortunate land, to the region near the Drave, in order to save what could yet be saved. The Danube alone interfered with the further advance of the Mongols. Two thirds of the realm had already fallen a prey to the fierce rage, greed, and brutal passions of the enemy. Whilst the Mongol Khan was dividing one half of the country, as conquered territory, into hundredths and tenths, and the people, lured from their hiding-places, lowered their necks, terror-stricken under the new yoke, Béla collected anew an army in the western part of the realm, and despatched ambassadors to the rulers of the western states. But before he could yet see the results of his renewed exertions, the severity of the winter, by covering the Danube with ice, afforded the Mongols an opportunity to penetrate into the western half of the country. The places which guarded the most sacred memorials of Hungarian royalty and Christianity, became a mass of smouldering ruins. The waves of the Mongolian inundation closed now upon the entire land. Béla was again compelled to seek safety in flight, and, mistrusting the continent, he sought a refuge near the sea. He retired, together with his family, first to Spalato, and subsequently to his fortified castle Trau, which was defended on almost every side by the sea. But his pursuers, who seemed to look upon their victories as incomplete as long as the king was not in their power, were on his track even there, and, devastating the seashore, as far as Ragusa, they, at last, desperate with rage, laid siege to Trau.

The last hopes of the nation had centred upon the sea-fortress, and now these hopes, too, seemed to vanish, when suddenly, as by a miracle, the besiegers ceased their hostilities, folded up their tents, and departed for the East. At the command of Batu Khan the whole Mongolian army, with all their followers, left the razed country, the flood of the invaders receding to the banks of the Volga, whence it had come. Oktai, the Great Khan, was dead, and Batu Khan hurried back to be present at the funeral feast, and to make his powerful voice, emphasized by the arms of his entire army, felt in the election of the new ruler.

After the Mongols had withdrawn, King Béla returned, in company of a few of his trusty followers, to his desolated land. He tottered under the weight of the misfortunes and woes of his people. To use the words of a contemporary writer and eye-witness describing the scene of desolation which met Béla's eyes: "Here and there a tower, half burnt and blackened by smoke, and rearing its head towards the sky, like a mourning flag over a funereal monument, indicated the direction in which they were to advance. The highways were overgrown with grass, the fields white with bleaching bones, and not a living soul came out to meet them. And the deeper they penetrated into the land, the more terrible became the sights they saw. When at last those who survived crept forth from their hiding-places, half of them fell victims to wild animals, starvation, and pestilence. The stores laid up by the tillers of the soil, the year before, had been carried away by the Mongols, and the little grain they could sow after the departure of the enemy had hardly sprung up when it was devoured by locusts. The famine assumed such frightful proportions that starving people, in their frenzy, killed each other, and it happened that men would bring to market human flesh for sale. Since the birth of Christ no country has ever been overwhelmed by such misery."

Great deeds spring up in noble souls harrowed by misfortune. Béla showed himself greatest in the extreme misery of his nation. In order to relieve the wants of the people and to enable them to till the soil, he caused to be imported seed for sowing and draught cattle from the neighboring countries. He colonized with new inhabitants the depopulated regions, held out inducements to German artisans, miners, and traders to settle in towns, and invited again the Kuns, who were roaming in the regions of the Lower Danube, to return to their former habitations on the rich lands of the Theiss. He bestowed especial care upon the cities, founded new ones, and granted additional privileges to the old ones. He was also the founder of Buda, which stands to this day. He ordered the larger cities to be surrounded by walls, caused forts, built of stone, to be erected in the neighborhood of more important roads, and encouraged the great lords to build similar forts. He was careful to guard the eastern frontiers, but remembering that the durability of the internal order was as powerful a support of the security of the land as well defended frontiers, he was bent upon making the laws respected. Hardly five years had passed since Béla engaged in his arduous task, and already the country recuperated to such an extent that the nation could receive with composure the news that the Mongols were making fresh preparations for a second attack, and was even, for years, able to turn the weight of her whole power against the Western states.

The nation which stood in such great need of peace, was unfortunately doomed never to enjoy its blessings. Béla himself, as soon as he had gained sufficient strength, deemed it his first duty to punish Frederic, the faithless Austrian duke, and to recover the treasures retained by the latter's treachery. The war between the two neighbors began in 1246. The contest in itself was of no great significance but its consequences were highly important. Béla achieved, with the help of his Kun warriors, a complete triumph over Frederic, who lost his life on the battle-field. Frederic was the last of the Babenberg line, and the inheritance of the Babenbergs, the Austrian principalities, were, through his death, left without a master. Béla coveted for himself the masterless countries, but was opposed in his schemes in that direction by Ottokar, the powerful king of Bohemia, who then already labored for the realization of his ambitious dream, the founding of a great Slavic empire. The Hungarian king could not expose his country to the dangers involved in the erection of such a Slavic empire along the western borders, and was therefore opposed, from the beginning, to Ottokar's aspirations. The contest between Hungary and Bohemia was at first waged for the Babenberg possessions, but its original cause was lost sight of, and the war continued for many years, to terminate only with the overthrow of Ottokar and the ruin of his empire. Béla was engaged in these wars during the last years of his reign, and they were continued by his son Stephen V., and his grandson Ladislaus IV.

These wars brought into a community of interests the kings of the house of Árpád and the Hapsburgs, whose first great ancestor, Rudolph, ascended in 1273, the German imperial throne, the stability of which was endangered by Ottokar. The latter had seceded from the German empire, and was now building up at its expense his own great Slavic kingdom. It was quite natural, therefore, that Ladislaus IV., King of Hungary, and Rudolph of Hapsburg, should enter into an armed alliance for the purpose of combating the common enemy, who, confident in his power, threatened both his eastern and his western neighbor.

Twice they led their joint armies against Ottokar, and, at last, in the course of the second campaign in 1278, they completely routed the Czech armies near Stillfried and Diernkrut in the plain of the Morava, or March. Side by side with Rudolph's ten thousand men fought forty thousand Kun warriors against Ottokar, the preponderance of the Hungarian arms securing at last the triumph of the allies. Ottokar's power was overthrown and he himself fell, buried beneath the ruins of his kingdom. Rudolph strengthened the German throne, whose fate the events of subsequent centuries closely identified with that of his family, and the Austrian principalities became the hereditary provinces of the Hapsburgs. Hungary derived but an unequal benefit from this triumph. To be sure the gratitude of the ally, freed from a formidable enemy, was fervent, and his vows of friendship (not always respected by his successors) most earnest. Thus Rudolph writes to Ladislaus IV.: "Tongue cannot tell, nor pen describe, the immense joy we feel at your having risen with so powerful a force to avenge our common injuries. Wherefore, glorifying God, we express the greatest gratitude of which we are capable to your Majesty, and loudly promise that no vicissitude shall shake us in the indissoluble alliance which we have vowed to you." The booty, gratifying the avarice of a few and the vanity of the nation, could also hardly be reckoned a solid advantage. One important result accrued, undoubtedly by the triumph of the allies, also to Hungary, in the destruction of Ottokar's Slavic kingdom. In other respects the victory proved rather a disadvantage, for, instead of strengthening the power of the state, it relieved the minds of the powerful lords in the land, who now, freed from anxiety, once more indulged their self-seeking propensities, and labored to ruin the country.

Ladislaus IV. (1272-1290) not only did not possess the qualities which might have enabled him to oppose the corruption of his age, but, by his levity, undermined even the last remnant of the royal authority which had become more and more feeble in the course of the last century. The king, unmindful of his crown, and indifferent to the interests of the nation, deserted his ancestral court, and, pitching his residence amongst the tents of the Kuns, passed there his life in the society of his boon companions in riotous living and revels, destructive alike of his dignity as a man and king, and detrimental to the hopes of the nation. The great of the land imitated the example set by their king. They were led exclusively by their insatiate self-indulgence, and neither the law of the land nor the commands of the Church, the voice of faith or morality, could prevail upon them to respect themselves, and to have regard for the rights of others. The weak became the victims of the strong, and the most powerful were making preparations to divide amongst themselves the masterless and defenceless country. The Brebiris along the sea-shore, the Németujváris beyond the Danube, the Csák family in the regions of the Vág, and the Apors in Transylvania, were in reality the little kings of the country. They broke off a piece from the domain of St. Stephen whenever it suited them, and of the size they wanted. They let their troops loose upon the people, and carried on wars in their own way with one another, and with the neighbors. And if any thing escaped the greed of the oligarchs, it fell into the hands of the Kuns, who, trusting in the protection and favor of the king, plundered and devastated the land like marauding armies. "Then descended," says the chronicler, "Hungary from the grandeur of her glory. Owing to the domestic wars the cities became deserted and the villages reduced to ashes, peace and harmony were trampled upon, the wealthy became impoverished, and the nobles, in their misery, turned peasants. It was at this period that the two-wheeled cart got the name of St. Ladislaus' wagon, for owing to the universal plundering of the draught-cattle, the number of the latter had decreased to such an extent that people were compelled to draw these carts themselves."

The country before long, however, was free from the misrule of Ladislaus, but his death did not extricate it from the misery into which he had plunged it. A number of Kun youths, apparently from motives of private vengeance, assassinated him in his tent. The death of Ladislaus became a new source of trouble to the country, for there was now but one male descendant of the house of Árpád to ascend the throne, Duke Andrew, the grandson of Andrew II., the king who had given the Golden Bull to the Hungarians. Stephen, the father of Duke Andrew, had left Hungary early in life, and, settling in Venice, married there Tomasina Morozzoni, a lady descended from a distinguished patrician family.

Andrew III. (1290-1301), the last king of Hungary of the Árpád line, was born in Venice, where he received his education and remained until he attained the age of manhood. Hitherto he had lived entirely a stranger to the events which had plunged the country with rapid strides into the uttermost misery. There were many within the land, and among the neighbors abroad, who did not look upon him as a genuine Hungarian and who refused to acknowledge his right to the inheritance of the Árpáds. During his brief reign he gave, nevertheless, ample proofs of possessing abilities befitting an eminent ruler, and no blame can attach to him for having been unable with his inadequate strength and power to contend against the difficulties of that period. To put down the little kings in the country, and to keep away from the borders those foreign powers who, under the pretence of kinship and led by unblushing avariciousness, announced their claims to the inheritance at this early date, was a task to which Andrew III. was not equal. But he struggled bravely and manfully against the difficulties that beset his royal path. He opposed to the oligarchs the gentry, whose ancient immunities he confirmed, and whom he attached to his person by granting them new ones. Duke Albert of Austria, the son of Rudolph of Hapsburg, who was the first to claim the throne, was driven from the country, but the diplomacy of Andrew turned him subsequently from an enemy into a friend and ally. He entered upon the contest with the Neapolitan Anjous, who, being the descendants in the female line of the

Árpáds, were the most pressing and determined claimants to the throne. But at the very outset of the struggle, when the shock of the collision of hostile interests is generally most severe, and just as Andrew was preparing to enter upon the campaign against Charles Robert of Naples, death suddenly took him in 1301. The chronicles contain traces of a suspicion that he died by poison administered by his Italian cook, who had been hired for that foul purpose by the Neapolitan party, and that thus, the doom of the house of Árpád was sealed by the wiles of an assassin. The sun of the Árpáds set amidst dark and storm-portending clouds, and the new dynasty of Anjou inherited the great task of reconciling the oligarchs with the gentry, and both classes with the crown, and thus of restoring the ancient power and splendor of the Hungarian kingdom.

CHAPTER VIII.

THE ANJOUS IN HUNGARY.

THE male line of the house of Árpád became extinct by the death of Andrew III. His only daughter, Elizabeth, retired to a convent, and the nation was once more called upon to exercise its ancient right of electing a king, and three candidates, a Czech, a German, and an Italian, at once came into the field. Each of these claimants had a party in the country, and not until the strength of the nation had been wasted by internal strife and warfare during a period of eight years did the Italian party succeed in placing on the throne Charles Robert, who became the founder of the Hungarian Anjous. It will be our task now to relate how the newly elected ruler, taking the reins of government into his own hands, introduced into the country the glorious era of chivalry. Under the reign of the Anjous we shall see the culture and customs of Western Europe gradually taking root in Hungarian soil, the name of Hungary becoming the object of respect and admiration abroad, the boundaries of the kingdom extended by a powerful hand, the crown of a brave and chivalrous neighbor, the Polish nation, placed upon the brows of the Hungarian king, until, at last, as the Hungarian poet Bajza sings, "the shores of three seas formed the frontier walls of the kingdom."

At first the Czech party was victorious. Wenceslaus, the aged king of the Czechs, who, through the female line, was related to the house of Árpád, not feeling equal to the task of governing Hungary himself, offered to his party, in his place, his son and namesake, who was but thirteen years old. On the 27th of August, 1301, at Stuhlweissenburg the sacred crown of St. Stephen was placed on the head of young Wenceslaus; but his reign was of short duration. The curse of the Church of Rome was pronounced against his partisans, but the citizens of Buda were little affected by this interdict, and caused the curse to be hurled back on the anathematizers by their own prelates. Yet the party of the boy-king grew so weak that his father deemed it advisable to recall him home. Wenceslaus the elder entered Hungary, pillaged the wealthier cathedrals, and expressed but one wish concerning his son— to see him for once attired in the royal Hungarian robes. His adherents complied with the wish of the old king, and, dressed in the royal robes and bearing the crown on his head, young Wenceslaus proceeded homeward, surrounded by his soldiers and under the protection of armed body-guards.

The Italian party, intent upon avenging this affront, invaded the territory of the Czechs, and by frightful massacres made the people atone for the abduction of the king. The fierce Kuns, or Cumans, throwing Czech children, strung together by means of holes bored through the palms of their hands, across their saddlebows, wildly tore through the land, devastating every thing. Very soon Albert, emperor of Germany, with Otto the Bavarian, came to the rescue of Wenceslaus, who, grateful for their assistance, delivered the crown to Otto.

The German party, in their turn, were now victorious, and obtained possession of the crown of St. Stephen, the most sacred relic of the nation. Otto marched into the country, but under the auspices of a bad omen. The crown was, through some accident, lost on the road, although his attendants discovered it afterwards, buried in the mire. Otto, whose vanity prompted him to display, marched in a procession through the capital, Buda, adorned with all the paraphernalia of royalty, and from that day on, every king succeeding him has, after the coronation, repeated this special pageant. Otto was as much the shadow of a king as Wenceslaus had been before him. In order to consolidate his power he asked in marriage the daughter of the most powerful Hungarian lord, Ladislaus Apor, the vayvode of Transylvania. Receiving a favorable reply, he hastened, full of hope, to Transylvania, but on his arrival was thrown into prison by the wily vayvode. After his liberation, which took place soon afterward, he turned his back for ever upon

Hungary, and was satisfied with the empty title of King of Hungary. The crown, however, remained in the possession of the vayvode.

The Italian party were now left masters of the field. The most obstinate and uncontrollable oligarchs were by this time tired of the disorders prevailing in the country, and all combined with a hearty good-will to place Charles Robert, of Anjou, upon the throne of Árpád. On the 27th of August, 1310, Charles Robert was crowned for the fourth time, but in this instance with the sacred crown, which had been at length obtained from Apor. Charles was now the lawful king (1309-1342), and could, without interference, set about the task of restoring order in the country, a work to which he proved fully equal.

The king had many difficulties in his way. The ruler *de facto* and *de jure* could call but a small portion of the kingdom really his own. The endless dividing up of the territory, which was characteristic of Germany at the close of the last century, was to be found in miniature also in Hungary. The disorders prevailing under the rule of the last Árpád, and of the two kings succeeding him, had encouraged the lawlessness of the marauding nobles. Every one appropriated as much territory as he could, and exercised royal or princely authority in the domains thus acquired by him. While so many had become the possessors of large estates, the king was without any personal patrimony. These little kings had to be reduced, one by one, to submission, and deprived of the usurped lands. The most powerful of them was Matthias Csák of Trencsén, and his subjection gave the greatest trouble, and consumed the most time.

The power and territory of Matthias Csák extended from the Northwestern Carpathians to the Theiss and Danube. The castle of Trencsén was the seat of this petty king. From this fortified castle on the Vág, built on a rocky eminence near the commercial road leading from Silesia to Hungary, he was in the habit of sending his marauders to devastate the neighboring country. He pounced like a bird of prey from his rocky nest upon the unwary merchants who were passing with their ships below, and the poor traders esteemed themselves fortunate if they got safely off by leaving a portion of their wares in the freebooter's hands. The plunder thus got together enabled him to display royal pomp, and such was the dazzling sumptuousness and luxury exhibited at his castle that, compared to it, the king's palace seemed to be but a poor hut. Csák had his own palatine treasurer and other officers of high rank, and when he went about he was attended by an escort of several thousand armed men. It was only after a good deal of solicitation that Csák consented to receive the Pope's legate, Cardinal Gentilis, and even then the legate had to meet Csák at the place specified by the latter, who wished this church dignitary to understand that he should feel highly honored by being permitted to shake his hand.

In the beginning, Csák seemed to submit to Charles, and, swearing fealty to the king, he consented to be represented at the third coronation. In order to win Csák's friendship and support, Charles made him the Guardian of the Land. But this new honor did not prevent him from very soon becoming weary of his subordinate position, and when a law had been passed ordering the restitution of the royal castles and domains which had come into the possession of subjects or strangers, his wish to be independent became even greater than before. An armed contest soon ensued between the king and his powerful subject. It was preceded, however, by a papal excommunication of Csák and his adherents, extending even to the dead, but the impious rebel retorted by laying waste the lands of the neighboring high prelates. Csák's power stood at that time at its height. He was the master of a domain containing over thirty fortified castles, which, to this day, is called by the people, after him, Matthias Land, and it was quite natural that the king was reluctant to beard the lion in his own den. The king's troops first entered the territory of Szepes, hoping to find there the weak point of the antagonist, but they were compelled to retreat before the captains of Csák. The decisive battle took place in 1312, north of the town of Kassa. The engagement was sharp and bloody, and terminated in the defeat of Csák's men. The ancestors of the Báthorys, Tökölyis, Drugets, and Széchenyis, who were amongst the most powerful families in Hungary, fought on this occasion by the side of the king. Although humbled, Csák's power was not greatly impaired, for we find him, a few years later, strong and bold enough to attack John, king of Bohemia, and take from him the fortified castle of Holics.

Charles Robert then turned his attention to his other rebellious subjects, reducing them to submission, one by one, leaving Csák to be dealt with by Providence. He had not, however, to wait very long, for in 1321 this great lord died. The manner of his death is described to have been frightful. Worms generated by his own body consumed him slowly. There was no one after his death to inherit his vast estates and with them his great power. Matthias Land was divided up in smaller sections, and distributed amongst the king's favorites. The subjects of Csák, amongst them his palatine Felician Zách, submitted at once to the king.

The king's attention was too much engaged by this domestic warfare to allow him, while it lasted, to display the energy which marked the subsequent years of his reign, an energy which was destined to make Hungary an influential power in Central Europe. During these days of civil strife he had his seat in Temesvár, and his household was so little befitting royalty that its poverty frequently elicited the complaints of the higher clergy. But matters quietly changed when Charles transferred his residence to Visegrád, the royal palace to which cling so many fond and sad national memories, and which in our days still, though in ruins, looms up on the right bank of the Danube as a monument of Hungary's ancient power and glory. Charles was full of ambitious schemes to raise his family to the greatest possible power, and the extension of the power of Hungary was deemed by him to be the readiest means of accomplishing this aim. First of all he stood in need of money and soldiers, but his genius enabled him to procure both. He exploited the rich mines of the country, and raised the commerce and industry of the realm to a flourishing condition, and the wealth of the people increased to such an extent that he felt warranted in levying direct taxes, a mode of taxation which had before been entirely unknown in Hungary. The manner in which he created an army bears witness to his ingenuity. The county system had become so loose and disorganized that no soldiers could be expected from that source. He had to look for them in another quarter. Charles knew, very well, the chivalrous disposition of the nation, which, in the matter of display, had still preserved its Oriental character; he knew, too, from history, that those who appealed to the vanity of the Hungarian were never disappointed, and he laid his plans accordingly. He transplanted into Hungary one of the graceful institutions of Western Europe, that of chivalry. Knights there were in the country, but they were not numerous and had not proved to be enthusiastic adherents of the king. Charles understood how to win the affections of the great lords; he distributed coats-of-arms and founded orders. In the wide courts of the castle of Visegrád, knightly tournaments became frequent, and the new knights, with their fresh heraldic devices, had an opportunity of meeting each other in armed combat in the presence of their foreign king. The king's court came to be the resort of noble youths, and boys of noble descent became the playmates of the royal princes. In order to rouse the warlike spirit of his great nobles, he allowed those of them who joined in a campaign with a certain number of soldiers, to lead their men under banners bearing their own armorial devices.

An event, however, of most tragic issue, which has furnished a fruitful theme to Hungarian poets and artists, almost overthrew the effect of the king's wise policy and endangered his life. The scene of the occurrence, which took place on the 17th of April, 1330, was the magnificent palace of Visegrád. The former palatine of Csák, Felician Zách, had become one of the king's chief councillors, and he, with his daughter Clara, one of the queen's maids of honor, a lady of extraordinary beauty, resided in the king's palace. Casimir, the King of Poland, and the queen's brother, was at the time a guest at Visegrád, and during his stay there, behaved improperly towards Clara Zách. The infuriated father, on learning this, broke in upon the royal family sitting in the dining-hall, and intent upon avenging the affront offered to his daughter, threatened every one in his way. He fell with sword drawn upon the royal children and their parents. The children remained unhurt, but the king was seriously wounded, and the queen had four of her fingers cut off. John Cselényi, the queen's treasurer, finally rushed to the rescue and felled the exasperated father with his bronze pole-axe to the ground, and the alarmed servants, who had meanwhile hastened to the hall, gave the miserable man, in presence of the royal family, the *coup de grace*. A frightful and most cruel punishment was inflicted, for her father's bloody act, on the unhappy Clara and all the members of the Zách family. The maiden's ears, nose, lips, and hands were cut off, and in this condition she was tied, together with her brother, to a horse's tail, and dragged through the land until both died a miserable death. The Zách family were exterminated to the third degree, and the remoter kinspeople doomed to slavery. Such a sentence upon those who had committed no crime was a most vindictive and savage one, and the people saw the avenging finger of God in the results of the unhappy campaign of that year against the Wallachians. One of the chronicles, referring to the disastrous issue of the war, says: "The king had hitherto sailed under favorable signs, and cut, according to his heart's desire, through the stormy waves with the ship of his fortune. But changeable fortune had now turned her back upon him.

His army had been defeated, and he himself is suffering tortures from his gouty hands and feet."

Ban Michael Bazarád, then the ruler of Wallachia, dared to ignore his dependence on the crown of Hungary. Charles eagerly seized the opportunity to punish the traitorous vassal, and hoped, at the same time, that the indignation of the people against him for his cruelty would subside at the news of a victorious campaign against the Wallachians. Declining the offers of peace made by the repentant ban, Charles boldly advanced, with his spirited knights, over the impassable and unfamiliar roads of Wallachia. He had penetrated so far into the land that his further advance was rendered impossible by the absence of any road, and he was determined to retrace his steps. The Hungarian army was led astray by the Wallachian guides, and in retreating found itself quite unexpectedly hemmed in between steep and towering rocks from which there was no outlet. A shower of stones descended on their heads; the Wallachians who occupied the heights sent down dense volleys of rocks and arrows upon the doomed Hungarians. Charles himself owed his escape to the generous devotion of Desiderius Szécsi, one of his men, with whom he changed dresses. This brave warrior sealed his devotion with his life. The enraged Wallachians, mistaking him for the king, attacked him from every side, and after valiantly resisting, he finally fell on the battle-field. His sovereign escaped in safety, and Wallachia maintained her independence.

Charles, upon his return home, once more busied himself with the carrying out of his ambitious schemes for the aggrandizement of his family, and the results of his efforts gave ample proof of his political sagacity. He acquired for his family both Naples and Poland, although as yet on paper only. Poland became only under his son Louis the undoubted possession of the Hungarian king, while Naples never came under his control. In 1335 Visegrád resounded incessantly with the din of feasting and merrymaking; never before nor afterwards were so many royal guests harbored within its stately walls. There were Casimir, become King of Poland, the last descendant of the Piast family; John, the adventurous King of the Czechs, who subsequently died the death of a hero on the field of Crécy; his son Charles, the Margrave of Moravia, and subsequently Emperor of Germany; three knights of the first class belonging to the order of German Knights; the dukes of Saxony and Liegnitz, and numerous church and lay magnates. The entertainment of so many distinguished guests constituted a heavy draft on the royal treasury. A contemporary chronicler states that "fifteen hundred loaves of bread and one hundred and eighty flasks of wine were needed daily for the court of the king of Poland." Whilst the guests were feasting, Charles employed all his ingenuity in shaping the destinies of Eastern Europe. His negotiations with Casimir, the King of Poland, resulted in an agreement that Poland should descend, after his death, to Louis, the son of Charles. Two years later Charles had the satisfaction of learning that the Polish nation had confirmed the private arrangement, and had acknowledged the right of his son's succession to the throne of Poland. One of the finest monuments of Hungarian mediæval architecture, the cathedral in Kassa, owed its completion to this welcome news. Queen Elizabeth ordered it to be completed in her joy at the elevation of her son Louis. Charles had also tried to secure Naples for his son Andrew, by having him betrothed, at the age of six, to Joanna, the grand-daughter and heir of the king of Naples. In July, 1333, the young prince proceeded to Naples to take possession of his kingdom, as his father thought, but in reality, as subsequent events proved, to the place of his destruction. Charles died at a not very advanced age, having brought most of his plans to a successful issue in his lifetime.

Six days after his death the crown of Hungary was placed upon the head of his son Louis, afterwards surnamed the Great, who was then seventeen years old (1342-1382). The young king immediately proceeded on a pilgrimage to the tomb of St. Ladislaus, the most popular Hungarian king, at Grosswardein. There at his grave he made a sacred vow to govern the Hungarian nation after the example of his great predecessor. From Grosswardein he proceeded to Transylvania to receive the oath of fealty of the son of Michael Bazarád. Hardly returned to his palace at Visegrád, the young king received depressing news regarding his brother at Naples. The young Hungarian prince was looked upon with jealousy by the numerous Italian dukes at the Neapolitan court, who tried by every means to hinder his accession to the throne. His mother, the Hungarian queen, at once hastened, laden with treasure, to Naples, to rescue her son from the machinations of his enemies. The Hungarian money had its due effect at the papal court, whose vassal Naples was at that time. Queen Elizabeth obtained the assurance that her son Andrew would be crowned, but she returned to Hungary before the ceremony of coronation had taken place. At her departure her mind was filled with evil forebodings, which were but too well justified by coming events. The queen's departure was the signal for fresh intrigues at the Neapolitan court. Philip and Louis of Taranto, the sons of Catharine of Valois, openly insulted the young prince. Joanna wickedly turned from her husband and sided with his enemies. At length the day of the coronation was approaching. Andrew, relying on the power he was soon to wield, warned his enemies that he would avenge the affronts that had been heaped upon him. His enemies were seized with terror upon seeing, at the tournament which took place shortly before the coronation, the axe and noose depicted beneath the arms of Andrew, floating on high on his banner. The imminent danger rendered the intriguing dukes desperate, and they at once determined to put Andrew out of the way. His assassination was resolved upon, and, Joanna giving her assent to the nefarious plan, the young prince was doomed.

On the 18th of September, 1345, the whole court, and amongst them Joanna, proceeded to Aversa, to indulge in the merry pastime of the chase. Andrew was accompanied by his faithful Hungarian nurse, Izolda, who, poor creature, little dreamed that her ward was to be the object of the chase. In the evening the whole company took up their quarters at the convent of St. Peter. Andrew had just retired to his chamber when a familiar voice called him into the adjoining room, in order to discuss some grave questions. The unsuspecting youth, anticipating no evil, left his chamber, but no sooner had he crossed the threshold when the door was locked behind him by his secretary. The assassins lying in wait fell upon their victim at once and strangled him; his cries for help remaining unheeded. His dead body they then dragged to the balcony and precipitated it into the garden below. Whilst this bloody scene was enacted, Joanna slept soundly, undisturbed by the scuffle at her door, and cries of distress of her husband. She afterwards gave the explanation that she had been put under a spell by a witch.

There was mourning at the castle of Visegrád at the sad tidings. Louis swore dire vengeance, and the nation enthusiastically took up arms to support him. From abroad there arrived but voices of sympathy. The Italian princes offered his armies free transit through their territories; Louis, the excommunicated German Emperor, entered into an alliance with the king; Edward III., the King of England, while condoling with him, spurred him on to revenge; the Pope alone maintained an ominous silence. This time, however, the desire for revenge proved stronger with the king than his reverence for the Pope, and in 1347 the Hungarian army was ready to march. To punish a faithless woman and not to conquer Italy was the object of their expedition, and the Italian princes were glad to afford the king's army every facility to reach the proposed goal.

All the great lords of the realm rallied round the king. A large black flag was carried in front of the Hungarian army and on it was depicted the pale face of Andrew. On two occasions they were led by the king against Naples, and each time he was accompanied by the most distinguished Hungarian families. Michael Kont, Andrew and Stephen Laczfy, with Dionysius, the son of the latter, and a host of others, brought with them their armed trains, by whose mighty blows both Aversa, of mournful memory, and proud Naples were soon reduced. Queen Joanna, with her second husband, Louis of Taranto, escaped beyond the sea. Louis of Durazzo, one of the intriguing dukes who was suspected of having been an accessory to the murder, expiated his crime by being killed after a gay carouse and thrown down from the same balcony which had witnessed the foul deed of the conspirators. Four other dukes were carried to Hungary as prisoners. King Louis himself was always foremost in battle and received grave wounds on more than one occasion. But his chief desire—to punish Joanna—was not gratified and at length he entrusted the Pope with the sentence to be pronounced against her. The Pope, however, declared her innocent of the crime of murder, imputed to her, but mulcted her in a fine of 300,000 ducats as a restitution of the expenditures of the campaign. The chivalrous king spurned the blood-money and left the punishment of guilty Joanna to a more upright judge—to Providence. And Providence dealt more severely with the queenly culprit than the successor to St. Peter's see had done. Charles of Durazzo, called also Charles the Little, son of Louis of Durazzo, having conquered the throne of Naples, ordered Queen Joanna in 1382, thirty-seven years after the commission of her crime, to be thrown into prison, where she met her death by strangling.

During the Italian campaign Hungary was also called upon to meet another enemy in the East. Roving populations were making constant inroads on the eastern border, harassing the Hungarian inhabitants, who had by this time become accustomed to the peaceful avocations of the husbandman and tradesman. The victorious arms of King Louis soon put an end to those lawless incursions. But one of the most beautiful legends of Hungarian history is connected with one of the campaigns against these marauding populations. Kieystut, the Prince of Lithuania, after having been defeated several years before, broke into Transylvania with an army considerably swelled by the accession of a numerous body of Tartars. The king sent Louis Laczfy, the vayvode of Transylvania, against him, and the brave Székely people followed in his train. But the Hungarian army was small and the issue of the battle remained for a long time doubtful. The legend tells that the news of the peril threatening the Hungarian arms reached Grosswardein, where St. Ladislaus lay buried, and that the heroic saint, leaving his grave, bestrode the bronze horse of his own statue, which stood in the centre of the public square, and hurried off to the relief of his distressed countrymen. The Tartars were struck with the apparition of a warrior "who towered over them head and shoulders," and above whom was visible the holy Virgin Mary, the patroness of Hungary. The pagans were seized with terror at this sight, and the battle ended in a brilliant victory for the Hungarians.

The arms of the king were no less successful in Servia where he was about "to kindle the light of faith." But the most glorious of his wars was the one carried on against proud Venice, which continued during the greater portion of his reign. Her enemies, especially Genoa, willingly sided with the king of Hungary, and the ultimate result was the utter humiliation of the city of St. Mark. At last, in 1381, one year before the king's death, peace was concluded between the two belligerents, a peace of which the Hungarians had every reason to be proud, for by its terms Dalmatia was unconditionally annexed to Hungary, and Venice herself had to send the Hungarian king, annually on St. Stephen's Day, the 20th of August, a tribute of 7,000 ducats. As an indication of the high esteem in which the name of Hungary was held at that time, it is interesting to learn that foreign rulers sent their children to the Hungarian court to be educated, and the inference is not a strained one that the court of Louis must have been a centre of the European culture and refinement of that day. The spouse selected by the king, Elizabeth, the daughter of Stephen, the Prince of Bosnia, had herself been sent to the court to be trained in courtly accomplishments. At the Hungarian court also, Charles IV., the Emperor of Germany, wooed Anna, the Duchess of Schweidnitz, his future empress. These two rulers were united by ties of close friendship, until the discontent of the Germans with "the stepfather of their country," as they called Charles IV., ripened a scheme to transfer the German crown to the Hungarian king. Although King Louis refused to accept the crown proffered to him, the sting remained, and his imperial friend became his deadly enemy. The emperor persisted in indulging in his unfounded suspicions of the king's good faith, and so far forgot himself as to speak insultingly of the king and his exalted mother. The Hungarian ambassadors at the emperor's court, incensed at the affront done to their master, challenged the emperor to mortal combat. But he cravenly declined to accept the challenge, whereupon they declared war in the name of their king. Louis, who almost worshipped his mother, approved of the proceedings of his ambassadors, and sent the emperor an insulting letter, in which he declared that nothing better might be expected from a drunkard. Very soon a large army of Kuns devastated Moravia, until, at length, after a warfare of several years, the humiliated emperor begged for peace, obtaining the Pope's intercession in his behalf. Peace was at last concluded, and matrimonial alliances were to make it doubly sure. Sigismund, the emperor's son, was betrothed to Mary, the king's daughter.

In the latter half of the fourteenth century Christianity in Europe was threatened by a new foe. The warlike followers of Osman had, by the capture of Adrianople firmly laid the foundations of their powerful empire in Europe. Youths, forcibly taken at a tender age from their Christian parents, and educated afterwards in implicit obedience to the behests of the Sultan, were rigorously trained as soldiers after the most approved fashion of the day, and the troops thus obtained were destined to become the most formidable aid in the building of the Ottoman power in Europe. The Eastern empire had sunk too low, at that time, to be able, single-handed, to resist such a power, and she lost her strongholds, one after the other. In this strait her ruler resorted to one of those deceitful devices characterizing the policy of the Eastern court. John Palæologos, the Eastern emperor, proceeded to the court of the king of Hungary, at Buda, and, promising to give in his adhesion to the Western Church, he asked the aid of Louis against the savage enemy. The "Banner-bearer of the Church," as the king of Hungary was styled by the Pope, deemed it his duty, under these circumstances, to come to the rescue of the distressed emperor, and shortly afterwards the two kindred nations, the Turks and the Hungarians, met in hostile array on the banks of the Maritza. This was the first warlike contest of the two nations. It resulted in the victory of 20,000 Hungarians over a Turkish army four times as large, a victory commemorated to this day by the treasures and appropriate inscriptions still to be seen at the church of Mariazell in Styria.

Casimir, the last Polish king of the house of Piast, died on the 5th of November, 1370. His death was caused by an injury contracted in falling from his horse during the chase.

On the 17th of the same month Louis was crowned King of Poland, at Cracow, by the Archbishop of Gnesen. At the very moment when he was about to reach the goal of the highest ambition of his predecessor, and of himself, Louis seemed to waver, and to doubt the expediency of accepting the crown. He could not help reflecting that governing two nations, which were united by no other tie except his own person, and defending them against their enemies, might prove a task to which one king was not equal. He nevertheless accepted the crown, but his sinister presentiments were fated speedily to be confirmed. The Polish lords were not used to an energetic rule. The nobles of Little and Great Poland were eager, each for themselves, to secure the offices of state, but both equally hated the queen-mother sent there to rule. The country soon fell a prey to internal dissensions and strife, compelling the queen to fly from the land, in which a new pretender had appeared. This pretender to the throne was a kinsman of the late king of Poland, and had retired to a convent in France in the lifetime of Casimir. His ambition made him exchange the cassock for armor, and a large portion of the people of Poland very soon acknowledged him to be their king. But his royalty was of short duration; the army of the adventurer was scattered by the adherents of King Louis.

The Lithuanians, whom we have before mentioned as being driven back by Andrew Laczfy, now took advantage of the disorders prevailing in Poland, and succeeded in securing such a foothold in that country that one of their dukes, Jagello, who was converted to Christianity, and subsequently married Hedvig, the daughter of King Louis, became in the course of a few years the founder of a new Polish dynasty, the Jagellons, a dynasty of mournful memory in the history of Hungary.

The last days of Louis were embittered by the disorders in Poland. He who had succeeded everywhere else failed there. Disappointment shortened his life; upon returning to Tyrnau on the 11th of September, 1382, from attending the Polish diet convened in Hungary, he was taken ill, and breathed there his last. The Hungarian nation lost in him one of their greatest kings. His reign was stormy but glorious. The Hungarian banner floated always victoriously on his numerous battlefields, and he humbled the enemies of the nation. In spite of his many wars, Louis found leisure to devote his time to the cultivation of the arts of peace. He gave laws to his country, which secured her permanence, and remained in force up to the most recent ages. He brought order into the affairs of the Church, and into the administration of justice. He was a zealous patron of learning, and established a university at Fünfkirchen (Pécs). His court, the seat of which he fixed at Buda, was brilliant; the Western customs, brought over from Italy, prevailing there. In times of peace magnificent tilts and tournaments at home took the place of the bloody game of war abroad, and the distribution of arms and knightly distinctions introduced by his father continued during his reign on even a larger scale. On all occasions Louis showed himself to be a brave, wise, and pious king, whose long rule is described by an eminent Hungarian historian as proving "a continued blessing" for his nation.

Dark days succeeded the glorious reign of Louis. The Hungarian nation was eager to testify their gratitude to their great king by a concession made to his dynasty—notwithstanding its foreign origin,—which they had refused to make to the glorious dynasty of the native Árpád family. After the king's death his daughter Mary was proclaimed queen and the crown conferred upon her. But the crown brought little joy to Mary, for the festivities of the coronation were hardly finished when she was menaced by dangers coming from two sides. The Poles hated Sigismund, to whom Mary was affianced, and insisted also that their ruler should live amongst them. Elizabeth, the queen-mother, in order to conciliate the opposition of the Poles, and not to risk the loss of Poland, offered them, as a substitute for Mary, her younger daughter Hedvig. The Poles agreed to this compromise, upon the condition that they should select a husband for Hedvig, their queen. It was a great trial for Hedvig to part from William, Duke of Austria, to whom she was betrothed, but her choice lay between him and the crown of Poland. The allurements of the latter prevailed, and in February, 1386, the Polish nation celebrated the nuptials of their queen with the Lithuanian duke, Jagello, recently converted to Christianity, whom they had chosen for her husband. This marriage put an end to the union of the two countries, and Poland had once more a ruler of her own.

There was greater danger threatening Hungary from the south. The nobles of Croatia were dissatisfied with female rule. There were some ambitious men who were incensed to see themselves excluded from the royal court, whilst a man of low descent, like Garay, the palatine, took the lead there. They were intent upon destroying the government in order to remove the queen. In Charles of Durazzo, who owed the throne of Naples to Louis the Great, they found a man who was willing to become a candidate for the throne of Hungary. The traitors, however, on the appearance in their midst of the energetic Garay, accompanied by the queen and the queen-mother Elizabeth, kept quiet for a while. But no sooner had the royal party left Croatia, when these men, who all owed their honors to the favor of the late king, resumed their machinations, and prevailed upon Charles of Durazzo to perjure himself and to break the oath he had pledged to the late king not to disturb his daughter Mary in the possession of her throne. In 1385, undeterred by the warnings of his wife, he arrived in Croatia.

Meanwhile the marriage of Mary and Sigismund had taken place. The latter, in order to collect an army with which he should be enabled to oppose the advancing enemy and defend the rights of his royal spouse, hypothecated a portion of the country to raise the necessary funds.

This ill-timed transaction increased the chances of his opponent, for the nation saw with indignation that Sigismund, in the capacity of "the guardian of the realm" only, without possessing any royal rights, began his guardianship by thus disposing of Hungarian territory. Such a disgraceful transaction was unknown in the history of the country, and it was not long before Charles could enter Buda, without let or hindrance; disguising, however, even then, his lawless aspirations, by pretending to have only come to make peace between the nation and her queen. But Charles was not long in showing his true designs. On the 31st of December, 1385, the cathedral of Stuhlweissenburg witnessed a most moving scene. The coronation of the usurper Charles was to be solemnized; the church was crowded, to its remotest corner, with sumptuously dressed lords. The widowed queen and her daughter Mary were also in attendance. The customary question was asked of the magnates of the land, by the Primate of Hungary, whether they wished Charles to be their king. The enthusiastic acclamations of assent became, at the Primate's third appeal, feebler and feebler as the piteous sobs of the two queens, who had sunk upon their father's and husband's grave, resounded in the church. The coronation proceeded nevertheless, and whilst the archbishop sent up his prayers of grace to heaven, the widowed queen was silently vowing desperate vengeance at the grave of her husband. Bad omens followed the pageant; during the solemn procession the banner of St. Stephen split into pieces, and as the new king entered the gates of his palace at Buda, its walls were shaken to its very foundations by a tremendous thunder-storm. Charles had occupied the throne thirty-nine days only, when he was summoned by the widowed queen, residing under one roof with him, into her presence to settle some grave matters of state. The king obeyed the summons, and was humbly received by Garay the palatine, Blasius Forgách the lord cup-bearer, Thomas Szent-Györgyi, the ban of Croatia, and the other lords present. The council had hardly commenced when, at a hint from the palatine, Forgách got behind the king and struck him on the head with his pole-axe. The blow inflicted a mortal wound and the king fainted away. The assassins had made careful preparations for the bloody event. Whilst Forgách was doing away with the king in the council-chamber, his Italian soldiers, in the palace, were disarmed by Garay's men. Charles was taken to Visegrád, where he was thrown into prison and afterwards strangled.

The news of the king's assassination stirred up fresh discontents in Croatia, where his party had been most numerous. Garay imagined he could quell the rebellion again by appearing amongst them. The two queens approved of his scheme, and proceeded, in his company, to Croatia. This time, however, their going to Croatia was to prove fatal to them. The queens, travelling with a small escort, were surprised by John Horváthy, one of the rebels, near Diákovár, and a mortal struggle ensued between the rebels and the queen's escort. Garay and Forgách fought with exasperation in defence of the queens. Garay, pierced by arrows, set his back against the coach, valiantly selling his life, and not allowing the enemy to approach his royal charges except across his dead body. All this heroism was wasted in the face of the overpowering number of the rebels, and the dreadful spectacle was soon presented to the queens of having the heads of their faithful defenders cut off before their very eyes. The queens themselves were placed in confinement at Novigrad, on the sea-shore. The long series of deaths by violence, which appeared to persecute the Anjou race like a curse, was destined to have one more added to it at Novigrad. The widow of Louis the Great was, after a short imprisonment, strangled by one of the rebels before the eyes of her unfortunate daughter.

The disorders had now reached their climax; one of the crowned rulers of Hungary, Charles, had been assassinated, the other, Mary, was a prisoner at Diákovár. The rebels were preparing to bring the son of the usurper Charles into the country, while another party had cast their eyes upon Ladislaus Jagello, the husband of Hedvig, as an available aspirant to royal honors. The Prince of Servia was arming to attack Hungary from the south, and Poland was preparing to invade the country from the northeast, whilst the princes of Wallachia and Moldavia, vassals of Hungary, declared their independence. So many disasters demanded a prompt remedy, and the nation, in their distress, decided to accept as their ruler Sigismund, the queen's husband. He was acknowledged as king, and the crown of St. Stephen was placed on his head by Benedek, the bishop of Veszprém, in March, 1387, and his reign lasted until 1437. To these melancholy circumstances did

Sigismund, of the house of Luxemburg, owe his elevation to the throne of Hungary. It was a heavy burden that he had taken upon his shoulders, the task of bringing order into the affairs of the distracted country. His first and foremost duty was to liberate his august wife from her imprisonment, but it must be reluctantly admitted that he exhibited little zeal in the accomplishment of this. While he was travelling leisurely from place to place without seemingly heeding the danger of delay, Venice came to the rescue. The statesmen of the city of St. Mark had watched with jealousy the union of Naples and Hungary in the hands of one ruler, and to obviate this danger to their own city, they sought the friendship of Sigismund, and sent vessels of war against his rebellious subjects. John Palisna, in whose charge the imprisoned queen had been placed, readily delivered her up to John Barbadico, the captain of the republic, stipulating only for himself the right of leaving without molestation. In July, 1388, husband and wife met near Agram (Zágráb), and Sigismund made up for his former laxity by sumptuously rewarding the Venetians who had liberated his queen.

The newly elected king had on the very threshold of his reign a twofold difficulty to face. He had to quell the rebellion, which in the southern part of his dominions was still active, and to arrest the encroachments of the Turkish power. He succeeded in putting down the rebellion. He marched into Croatia and Bosnia, pursuing the rebels to their mountain fastnesses, and after many years of varying fortunes of war he reduced them to obedience. The survivors of the scattered rebels sought refuge in the wild forests of Syrmia. A small band of thirty men rallied round Stephen Kont of Hédervár, the son of the famous palatine Michael, a man noted for his bravery. Sigismund charged Vajdafy, one of his trusty men, with the reduction of this band. He found it, however, impossible to get near them, and finally resorted to a stratagem. Vajdafy promised them a free pardon from Sigismund if they surrendered and came up to Buda with him. The thirty one warriors accepted this proposal, but on their way the treacherous Vajdafy ordered them to be placed in chains. They were so incensed at this disgraceful treatment, that they determined not to do homage to the king when brought into his presence. They refused to bend their knees before him. The king did not reflect long, but ordered the thirty-one gallants to be taken to St. George's Place in Buda, where they met their death at the hands of the executioner. Kont was the last to lay his head on the block. His faithful page Csóka burst into tears at the bloody sight. Sigismund comforted the youth, telling him he would be a better master to him than Kont was. "I shall never serve thee, Czech hog," was the boy's reply, a reply which cost him his life, for he was immediately executed. This barbarous and illegal act of the king would no doubt have provoked, in ordinary times, a rebellion in the country, but the general attention was just then absorbed by the encroachments of the Turks.

Servia had already become a vassal state of the Turks, and was compelled to swell with her army the power of the mightiest foe to Christianity. The last victory won by the Servians over the Turks was in 1387, when they mowed down two thirds of the Turkish army, numbering 20,000 men. Sultan Murad invaded Servia in 1389 to avenge the disgrace of defeat. He was met in June by Lazarus, the last independent Prince of Servia, on the Kosovo (blackbird) field, called in Hungarian the Rigómező. The engagement was a bloody one, and disastrous to the rulers on both sides. Sultan Murad received his death wound from the dagger of a Servian soldier, whilst Prince Lazarus was delivered by his own son-in-law, Vuk Brankovitch, into the hands of the Turks and into the jaws of certain death. With Lazarus was lost the independence of Servia, and his scattered army fled in dismay from the ill-fated battle-field. This victory had brought the Turks one step nearer to the borders of Hungary, and added further to the fear of their victorious arms in that Bajazet, the successor of Murad, surnamed the

"Lightning," was known to be eager for new conquests. Two years after the battle of Kosovo we find the Turks already on Hungarian soil. Sigismund tried, at first, negotiations. Viddin, Nicopolis, and Silistria, which belonged to Hungary under Louis the Great, had recently fallen into the hands of the Turks. Sigismund sent an embassy to Bajazet calling upon him to surrender these cities to their rightful owner. The sultan received the embassy at Brussa, and, conducting them into a hall ornamented with arms and weapons of every description, he pointed at these, saying: "Go back and tell your king that, as you see for yourself, I have a good enough title to these lands." Sigismund rightly understood this to be a declaration of war. He at once summoned the chivalry of Europe to take part in a crusade against the infidels, and entered into an alliance with Manuel II., the Emperor of the East. Many knights from England, France, and Italy responded to the call.

Meanwhile, Mary, the wife of Sigismund, died in 1395. It was to her that Sigismund owed his throne, and now that she was no more, there was nothing to keep up the ties of affection between the people and their restless and inconstant king. Sigismund hoped to dazzle the nation by the glory of a successful war. In 1396 he marched the assembled crusaders to Nicopolis against the Turks. The king, surrounded by the chief captains of the army, was merrily feasting when the news was brought that Bajazet, the "Lightning," was approaching. Both armies were eager for the contest. The French knights, in spite of Sigismund's protests, claimed the privilege of the first attack. Ignorant of the Turkish system of fighting, which consisted in sending the weakest and least-disciplined troops to the fore, to bear the brunt of the first attack, the French rushed with their united strength upon the enemy. The attack, as usual, was favorable to the French arms, but hardly had they dispersed the inferior troops when they found themselves face to face with the serried ranks of the Spahis and Janissaries. The hot-blooded Frenchmen were no match for these incomparable soldiers, and a large portion of them fell on the battle-field while the remainder were taken prisoners. This discomfiture had a depressing effect on the other crusaders, and their army scattered in disorderly flight. Sigismund, himself, escaped only with great difficulty, and took refuge on a ship on the Danube which brought him to Constantinople.

This unlucky campaign proved a fresh source of trouble to the country, for the king, keenly feeling the disgrace of his defeat, stayed away from Hungary for over half a year. The southern part of Hungary was again in rebellion and many, believing in the false report of the king's death, were desirous of proceeding to the election of a successor. The king, apprehensive of losing his throne, came back and, in his own fashion, rewarded his friends and punished his opponents.

In order to add to the number of his adherents he distributed amongst them, in defiance of an ancient law, the crown-lands. He filled the highest positions in the state with foreigners. This was more than the Hungarian lords would submit to, especially after the disgraceful defeat the king had just suffered on the battle-field. The impatient magnates, weary of his inglorious rule, entered upon a conspiracy to overthrow the king. On the 28th of April, 1401, a number of the great lords of the land assembled at Buda and requested the attendance of the king, in order to take counsel on affairs of state. The Garays, the unflinching adherents of the king, knew what was going to happen, but did not dare to divulge or oppose the plans of the conspirators. Sigismund appeared among the assembled magnates, but only to find out, too late, that he was, in fact, their prisoner. He was taken to Visegrád and confined in its castle. Another king had now to be elected. Three claimants were on the field—Ladislaus Jagello, William of Austria, and Ladislaus, the son of Charles the Little. It was fortunate, however, for the king that no election could be agreed upon; and, while the magnates were taking counsel with each other, the Garays succeeded in liberating the king and took him to Siklós, one of their own fortified castles. His followers, meanwhile, took up arms in his cause and succeeded in placing him again on the throne, after he had been a prisoner for four months. But before doing so they obtained his promise not to punish or molest the conspirators. Michael Garay was generously rewarded for his exertions on behalf of Sigismund; he received annually a pension of one thousand ducats, and was appointed to the dignity of a palatine. The severe lesson was of benefit to the king. He appeared totally changed after his experience in prison. He faithfully kept the promise he had given, and did not molest the rebellious lords, but rather sought their friendship, and, making union with them, seriously endeavored by legal means to improve the government of the country.

He had hardly seized the reins of government with firm hands, when the cry of battle called him again away. Having no son, Sigismund tried to secure the throne for his daughter Elizabeth. She was affianced to Albert of Austria, and the king prevailed upon one hundred and ten lords to sign a document by which his daughter's husband would, after the king's demise, become entitled to wear the crown of St. Stephen. The Neapolitan party was roused into rebellion by this arrangement, and Ladislaus of Naples penetrated into the interior of the country. The primate of the realm, the archbishop of Gran, sided with the rebels and placed the crown of Hungary upon the head of the invading foreigner. Sigismund, who was just then amongst the Czechs, whose crown he coveted, hastened home upon learning the peril with which he was menaced. The followers of Ladislaus were soon put down, and, being assured of the king's pardon, they all gave in their submission. Ladislaus, fearful lest the fate of his father, Charles the Little, should overtake him, left the country, and henceforth dared not to question the right of Sigismund to the crown. In the course of the years that followed some wise measures were introduced concerning the privileges and franchises of the cities, and regulating the relations of the Church of

Hungary to the Vatican. The Pope having been the most zealous partisan of Ladislaus of Naples, a law was enacted putting an end to the Pope's right of interference in the affairs of the Hungarian Church.

The king formed again new marriage ties, and took Barbara, the daughter of Count Arminius Cilley, the powerful lord of the Styrian castle of Cilli, for his wife. The new queen added but little to his happiness. The king established the order of the dragon in commemoration of his wedding. The insignia of the order were a red cross with a gold dragon who twisted his tail in a circular shape around his own neck. The membership was confined to twenty-four, who bound themselves to defend the Christian faith against the Turks. The king and queen were the first members of the order, the remaining members were selected from among the highest dignitaries of the land. A high distinction fell to the lot of the king of Hungary on the 20th of September, 1410. Ruprecht, who had been elevated to the imperial throne of Germany, after the deposition of Wenceslaus the drunkard (the half insane brother of Sigismund), was now dead. Wenceslaus was now striving to regain the lost dignity, but in this he was opposed by his own brother Sigismund. The electoral princes voted for the latter. This was the first time that a similar distinction had been conferred upon the wearer of the crown of St. Stephen. The nation felt proud of the exaltation of their king, but the nation as well as the king found subsequently ample reason to regret their premature rejoicing. Indeed the fears of St. Ladislaus and Louis the Great, who had declined the imperial crown lest they might, accepting it, be caused to neglect the affairs of Hungary, proved but too well founded. The business of the emperor required his presence elsewhere, and while he was absent for years from the country, matters at home visibly went to rack and ruin.

The emperor-king could not spare time to attend to the most important duty of his reign, the driving back of the Turks, and, there can be no doubt, that it was owing less to the civil wars of that period than the lukewarmness of Sigismund in the face of the Ottoman advances during the last years of his reign, that it became possible for the Moslem power to obtain possession, a century later, of the stronghold of Christianity. The signs of the coming life-and-death struggle became already apparent—and once the struggle begun there was no way to destroy the Ottoman power, nor could a favorable opportunity, once missed, return again.

The fortunes of war were once more propitious to the Hungarians—in their war against Venice—but for several years afterwards history records nothing but a long series of uninterrupted disasters. The war with Venice was carried on to get possession of the littoral islands and cities. Venice was shamefully beaten, and the peace-suing ambassadors of the proud city of St. Mark had to undergo the humiliation of seeing before their very eyes nineteen of their flags torn to pieces in the streets of Buda. But the new banners of Venice were soon destined to be victoriously planted on the Hungarian littoral territory, and Sigismund was compelled to sign a peace by which the nation lost her seacoast possessions. And while the power of Venice was curtailing the country in the south, the richest towns in the north were being lost through the recklessness of Sigismund. In order to extricate himself from financial embarrassments he hypothecated to Ladislaus, the king of Poland, thirteen of the wealthiest cities of the Szepes country, which was largely settled by German merchants and tradesmen. These places remained hypothecated until the first partition of Poland, 1772, when Hungary was reinstated in the full possession of the mortgaged towns. After arranging these affairs the king went abroad, where he remained for six years. During his absence the country, owing to the despotic rule of Barbara, his queen, became a prey to disorder. It would cover pages unprofitably to give a detailed account of the private affairs of the wanton queen, and, passing over these, we shall accompany her royal husband on his journey to the Council of Constance.

The condition of the Church of Rome was at that period a most lamentable one. The question of reforms within the Church became from day to day more pressing. Wycliffe, the Englishman, had the boldness to assume the rôle of a heretic. John Huss, the rector of the university of Prague, soon became a zealous propagator of his teachings. The majority of the inhabitants of Bohemia embraced the new tenets, assuming, after their leader, the name of "Hussites." One of the chief objects of the Council of Constance—1414-1418—was to extirpate heresy, and to exterminate its votaries. Numerous ecclesiastical and lay lords gathered at Constance to advise together under the guidance of the emperor-king, who presided. The attending Hungarian magnates deemed it due to their fame and dignity to indulge in the most extravagant luxury. The emperor-king felt constrained to eclipse his subjects in sumptuous display on such an occasion, and, in order to accomplish this, he had to sell Brandenburg to Frederick of Hohenzollern, and there can be no doubt that through this sale he unwittingly contributed to the future greatness of the present imperial dynasty in Germany. We will not attempt to describe here the Council of Constance, but need only mention that it was the treachery and bad faith of Sigismund which caused the tragic end and martyrdom of John Huss. His disciples vowed vengeance, and Hungary, of all the dominions of the emperor-king, was, during many years, most exposed to their cruel devastations.

After an absence of six years, during which Sigismund had visited Germany, France, Italy, and England, he at length returned to Hungary. He found the country unsettled, and menaced on two sides by powerful enemies. Having sent his wife, the cause of the internal disorders, to prison, he led an army against the Turks, who were threatening the southern portion of the country. Before describing the events of that campaign let us cast a rapid glance at the condition of the Moslem world in Europe. A dreadful blow had fallen on the Ottoman empire in July, 1402. Timur, the Central-Asian conqueror, destroyed the Turkish army near Angora, and captured the person of the redoubtable Bajazet himself. The impaired power of the Ottoman empire was still more weakened by the internecine strife between Bajazet's sons. Mohammed I. emerged at last as the victorious sultan, and in his person the warlike qualities of his ancestors reappeared once more on the throne of the Osmanlis. The rulers of Servia and Moldavia very soon acknowledged his sovereignty. Hervoja, the Bosnian boyar, followed their example. The three captains of Sigismund, John Maróty, John Garay, and Paul Csupor, marched against the latter. The engagement resulted in the victory of Hervoja. Csupor was taken prisoner, while his fellow-captains sought safety in an ignominious flight. Csupor, years ago, had scoffingly greeted Hervoja, when at the Hungarian court, by bellowing like an ox, and the victor, now remembering the affront put upon him, revenged himself by having the ill-fated captain sewn into an ox's skin, and telling him: "Now thou canst bellow as much as thou likest; thou hast also the shape of an ox." He caused him to be thrown into the water, where he was drowned.

Meanwhile Stephen Lazarevitch, the Prince of Servia, became weary of the Turkish alliance, and with a view to securing to his nephew, George Brankovitch, the succession in Servia, he sought the aid of Sigismund, offering to surrender to him several important fortified places along the Danube for his services. The Prince of Servia died in 1428, and Sigismund claimed the possession of the places promised to him. The Servian commander of Galambócz, one of the strongest of these fortresses, however, treacherously allowed it to pass into the hands of the Turks. It was to re-possess himself of this fortress, which he could not permit to remain in Moslem hands, that Sigismund marched against the enemy. He had nearly succeeded in capturing it, when news reached him that Sultan Murad II. was approaching. Sigismund did not dare to engage in battle with such overpowering numbers, and having stipulated for himself and his army free passage, he pusillanimously gave up the siege. Yet the Hungarians were just beginning to cross the Danube, when the Turks, breaking faith, attacked them. Sigismund himself was in great danger, and he owed his escape only to the heroism of Cecilia Rozgonyi, the wife of the captain-in-chief, who facilitated his flight in a galley steered by herself. This was Sigismund's last armed encounter with the Turks, and its issue did by no means add to his laurels.

The remaining years of Sigismund's reign were taken up with the organization of the defences of the country and with continual warfare against the Czech Hussites in the north. Wenceslaus, the king of Bohemia, died in 1419, and Sigismund endeavored to obtain his brother's crown. The Czechs hated the executioner of their beloved spiritual teacher, and conceded to Sigismund the Bohemian crown only after a hard and protracted struggle. Hungary had to suffer for the ambition of her king, for, during these struggles, the exasperated Czechs, on more than one occasion, laid waste her territories in the north-west. Sigismund, however, did not allow himself to be deterred from pursuing his aim. Acting upon the principle of *divide et regna*, he very sensibly conciliated a portion of the Czechs by granting them religious reforms, and whilst the people were desperately fighting among themselves he succeeded in securing the crown of Bohemia.

Sigismund may be said to have reached the goal of all his wishes. He united on his head the crowns of imperial Germany, Hungary, and Bohemia. Yet, on the whole, he was not a happy man. His wife Barbara had regained her freedom and was embittering the last days of the sickly monarch. This ambitious woman coveted the crown of Hungary, and in order to obtain it she was scheming, first of all, to hinder the succession of Albert, the son-in-law of the emperor-king. With this view she entered into negotiations with Ladislaus III., the king of Poland, the purport of which was that he should marry her after Sigismund's demise, and thus unite the dominions of the king of Hungary with Poland. The arrangement was nearly concluded when these intrigues were discovered by Sigismund. He deprived his wife once more of her liberty, and hastened from Bohemia to Hungary to prevail upon the Estates to accept Albert's succession, and then to turn his steps towards Transylvania to put down the rebellion that had broken out there. The peasantry of Transylvania, having a leaning towards the teachings of Huss, were exposed to constant persecutions. They were also oppressed by burdensome taxes, and finally, goaded on by their unhappy condition, they rose in arms against their tyrants. The massacred nobility and burning villages bore witness to the exasperation of the peasantry. Fate prevented Sigismund from either meeting the estates or quelling the Transylvanian rising. He was overtaken by death at Znaym, in Moravia, in December, 1437. His dead body and the captive queen arrived in Hungary one week later. His remains were conveyed from Presburg to Grosswardein to be placed there by the side of his first wife, Mary, and at the feet of St. Ladislaus. It is rather saddening to reflect that, after a reign of fifty years, his funeral procession should have been lighted by the glare from the burning villages of Transylvania, set on fire by her own peasantry.

CHAPTER IX.

JOHN HUNYADI (HUNIADES), THE GREAT CHAMPION OF CHRISTIANITY. 1456.

VERY little, if any thing, is known of the father of John Hunyadi, or of the pedigree of his family; indeed, the very circumstances of his birth are shrouded in dim legendary light, and yet he looms up all at once in the proud position of governor of Hungary, the adored idol of his country, and the admiration of all Christian Europe. It was owing to his exertions that his family became great, rich, and powerful, but, at the same time, he guarded Hungary against the evils of domestic war, and saved her from Moslem rule. He served his country in the capacity of a brave soldier, an eminent general, and a cautious and energetic statesman, lending her the aid of his strong arm, his undaunted courage, and his clear understanding.

In his time, during the fifteenth century, through all Europe, and especially in Hungary, that man was most respected who had earned the repute of a distinguished soldier. If any one wished to become conspicuous amongst his countrymen he had to be, first of all, an able general and a military hero. According to the views of that day, only he was looked upon as a true man who was a free man, or, in the nomenclature of that period, a noble man, but every noble was a born soldier, and soldiering was both his duty and privilege. Martial merit was recognized as the only real merit, and military service as the only honorable occupation. By this means every man had the chance of becoming the possessor of land, and of acquiring nobility, for bravery was rewarded by the king with a grant of lands, and with the rank of a noble. As a consequence wars were longed for by many. The common man (or as he was then styled, the bondman) hoped to acquire land and to be created a noble, the noble to add to his landed estate, and to rise in rank. The more land a noble owned, and the greater the number of his bondmen, the larger the number of the soldiers he was able to equip, and the greater the military power wielded by him, the better his prospects of promotion to a higher position in the state, in society, and about the person of his king. The first games of childhood were martial games, and the first tasks of youth were military tasks.

Such, no doubt, had also been the early training of John Hunyadi; by such means he rose, acquired a large fortune, and was able to support a great army. In truth, however, there is no information whatever extant as to his early education, for when he first entered upon the stage of war, in 1437, he was already an accomplished general. In this year the Turkish sultan, who was constantly attacking, harassing, and laying waste the vassal states of Hungary, Bosnia, Servia, Wallachia, and Bulgaria, turned his arms against Servia. The general of the Hungarian king met the enemy near the fortress of Semendria, where the decisive battle was to be fought. During this engagement a knight with a coat of arms, familiar to no one, made his appearance. A black raven, holding a gold ring in his beak, was painted on his shield. Never before had they witnessed fighting as gallant as that of the Raven Knight at the head of his small troop. He was seen now in one place, now in another, but wherever he showed himself the enemy either fled before him or was slain. To the Hungarians it seemed as if the god of war himself had descended to fight under their banners, and they were seized with wild enthusiasm. The Turkish general, with the remnant of his army, fled in dismay, and from this day forward the name of the raven knight continued to be the terror of Turkish warriors. This mysterious knight was John Hunyadi. To be sure, men like Pongrácz, Szentmiklóssy, Thalloczy, or Maróthy, had before this day proved themselves heroes in the many struggles against the Turks. After this memorable battle, however, the splendor of Hunyadi's name dimmed the glory of all. With the people, whose chief delight was martial exploits, and in whose eyes the Turks were the most dreadful enemy of their country, his prestige increased from year to year. For Hunyadi, like his powerful antagonist the Turk, never knew what it was to rest. No other enemy was like this one he had to cope with. The Turkish state was so organized that it could not exist without fresh conquests and incessant wars. The Janissaries wanted occupation and glory, the mounted Spahis new lands, the immense hordes which marched at the distance of a day's walk in advance of the Turkish army were hungry after booty, and the sultans themselves longed to win fresh conquests and military glory against the infidels, as the followers of the cross were styled by them.

An enemy like this was a most dangerous neighbor. It is true that Hungary was divided from the Turkish empire by her vassal states, Bulgaria, Wallachia, Servia, and Bosnia, but the Turkish sultans already looked upon these territories as their own, and were constantly organizing inroads into Hungary from them. Hunyadi had passed his early life near the border; and, accustomed to the perpetual fighting going on there, he was also familiarized with the magnitude of the danger. With an iron will he determined to devote his whole strength to the struggle against the Turks. By his gallantry he gradually acquired the fortune necessary for this purpose, for the kings were lavish in granting to him again and again large estates as a compensation for his bravery. Nor was he wanting in opportunities against the Turks, for, having been successively created Count of Temes, ban of Szöreny, and vayvode of Transylvania, it became his duty to defend the border with the money and army placed in his hands. If the Turks appeared at any point on a marauding expedition, or to provoke hostilities, Hunyadi was quick to meet them at once, and did not rest until he had achieved victory.

In one such expedition, Ishak, the pasha of Semendria, fared badly. This overbearing Turk, issued from the fortress of Semondria, and, having overrun the country, left behind him nothing but desolation and the tears of widows and orphans. Hunyadi, with a small troop, started in his pursuit, and, coming up with him, he took away from him the prisoners and the booty he had captured, and drove him and his army back to the very walls of Semendria. The sultan, upon hearing the news of this defeat, at once despatched Mezid Bey with an army of 80,000 men against Hunyadi. Orders were issued to destroy every thing—property and human life alike; neither the young nor the old nor the women were to be spared. Hunyadi was well informed as to the enemy's movements. He knew that in this campaign the special aim would be to kill or capture him, for his person stood almost alone in the way of the Sultan's conquests and glory. The Turkish commander offered, on the eve of the battle, an enormous reward to the soldier who would succeed in capturing Hunyadi. This critical occasion showed not only the importance attributed to Hunyadi's person by the Turks, but also the great love with which he was surrounded and the degree to which he was idolized by his soldiers and comrades. One of the latter, Simon Kemény, who knew of the intentions of the enemy, urgently begged his leader to exchange with him horses and accoutrements. Hunyadi at first refused, but finally yielded to Kemény's entreaties and handed him over his military equipments.

But he built his plan of battle upon this ruse: He ordered five hundred distinguished soldiers to be stationed near the person of the devoted officer, and he himself withdrew with his reserve and took up a position in a remoter spot. The following day the two armies engaged in battle. Every Turkish warrior sought the famous Hungarian hero; all were eager for the glory of capturing and killing him, and anxious to secure the prize set on his head. They all knew his face—which strikingly resembled that of Simon Kemény—and his accoutrements, which had been minutely described to them by their comrades. They at once made a rush on Kemény, the pretended Hunyadi. This gallant hero, with his five hundred men, stood the brunt of the onslaught with superhuman courage; the enemy were literally mowed down by their swords, but, at last, they had to give way to superior numbers, and their brave leader laid down his life on the battle-field. The Turkish soldiers precipitated themselves eagerly and with shouts of triumph upon his inanimate body, when suddenly Hunyadi broke upon them—the real and living Hunyadi whom the enemy had already thought dead. At this sight, the enemy, who, a few moments ago, felt sure of their victory, were seized with a panic, and sought safety in flight. Their leader, Mezid Bey himself, and his son lay lifeless, with battered skulls, on the field of battle.

The entire Turkish camp, with immense treasures and its military stores, as well as numerous prisoners, fell into the hands of the victorious Hungarians. Many a brave Hungarian warrior, it is true, had lost his life, and the devoted Simon Kemény had found the death he expected, but the country was saved, and the Hungarian losses were as nothing compared with the losses of the Turks. The devout Hunyadi afterwards caused a chapel to be erected from the proceeds of the Turkish booty in memory of his martyred comrades.

The news of the ignominious defeat reached Sultan Murat at Adrianople; he was greatly incensed, and swore dire vengeance against the Hungarians. He summoned before him his brother-in-law, entrusted to his command eighty thousand men, and ordered him to invade Hungary, to lay every thing waste with fire and steel, and to annihilate Hunyadi and his army. The Turkish commander, letting loose his Tartars, entered Hungary quite suddenly through Wallachia. The frontier is here formed by gigantic mountains, and but narrow passes lead from one country into the other. Through one of these passes, the Vaskapu (Iron Gate), the Turkish army passed into Hungary. The invaders had hardly time to rest from their fatigues, when Hunyadi with his army appeared before the unsuspecting enemy, ready to give battle. Abedin was surprised and disconcerted; he thought the Hungarians would fly before him, and they were facing him. Hunyadi entrenched his foot soldiery in a wagon-camp, whilst he himself with his horse attacked the Spahis (Turkish cavalry). After scattering the latter, he turned against the Turkish infantry, the Janissaries, in the rear, but the attack was only a feigned one. As if fearful of being surrounded, he suddenly began to retreat with his army to that portion of the valley where the wagon-camp was stationed. The Janissaries, leaving their protected positions, started with wild exultation in pursuit of the Hungarians.

Hunyadi, having taken up his position at the fortified place in the narrow valley, directed a side attack against the Turkish horse and drove them back upon the fighting Janissaries, whose storming of the wagon fortress was attended with as little success as that of the waves beating against the solid rock. The Turkish army could not display its strength, and confusion and wild disorder soon seized the troops. Their commander, perceiving that it was impossible to save his army, mounted his horse and galloped away. Fifteen thousand Hungarians were opposed, on that occasion, to eighty thousand Turks, inured to war, well trained, and accustomed to victory. The Turkish Janissaries, whose impenetrable line never broke, were annihilated; the cavalry, the far-famed Spahis, were scattered; and the whole Turkish army was in part massacred and in part put to disorderly flight. The meanest portion only saved themselves by running away; the best of the warriors perished, for the Turkish troops were by no means lacking in personal courage. The principal difference between the opponents was that the Turkish army was usually too confident of victory, and was often led by incompetent generals, while among the Hungarians discipline prevailed. Hunyadi, furthermore, not only gave battle according to plans concerted by his military genius, but understood also, during the tumult and confusion of the battle, how to execute with his troops rapid and precise movements. These qualities had decided the present battle, and were also the secret of his future triumphs.

All Europe hailed with joy and admiration the splendid victories of the Hungarian arms, for the whole Christian world had witnessed with alarm the extension of the power of the dreaded Osmanlis. Not only Hunyadi himself, but all his companions in arms, felt that, in inflicting such heavy losses upon the Turks, they were not defending Hungary alone, but saving all Christendom from that Turkish rule which had exhibited a boundless appetite for continental extension. Aware of this state of things, Hunyadi initiated a policy exceeding in boldness the one hitherto pursued by him. He appealed to all the rulers of Europe—to some personally, to others through the king and the pontiff of Rome—to lend him their aid, and he declared that, if they responded to his appeal, he was ready to begin an offensive war against the Turks.

All Europe received with satisfaction both his plan and request, but all he could obtain was gracious words and fair promises; aid in any tangible shape was flowing in but thinly. The Poles (the Hungarian king Uladislaus being also their king) sent a tolerably large contingent; in Germany, France, and Bohemia, too, there were many ready to enlist in a holy war against the unbelieving Turks, as had been formerly done in the time of the crusaders, and these joined Hunyadi's camp. The southern vassal states sent also some forces. The principal army, however, was still composed of Hunyadi's Hungarians, which was joined by the king's own troops. They may have numbered altogether forty thousand men. The king himself joined in the offensive campaign (in July, 1443) and placed himself at the head of the motley army. His leadership proved an injury rather than an advantage, for the discipline would have been far more perfect in the army if Hunyadi in person, with his own men, had taken the lead. The Hungarian general, nevertheless, defeated the Turks in their own country in four smaller engagements and in two larger battles. When the Hungarian army approached the Balkans—the heart of the Turkish empire in Europe—they were already wading in snow. They nevertheless marched on, undaunted by the enormous mountains and the impracticable and narrow passes. But the Turks had already taken up their positions along the difficult passes, on the mountain tops, and in the passes themselves, in such a manner that they had made sure of every advantage. Hunyadi quickly perceived that the position of the sultan behind such entrenchments and bulwarks was impregnable. Being, therefore, foiled in his desire to aim an offensive blow at the enemy, he endeavored to entice him into the plain. In this he succeeded. As he was retreating from the Balkan passes, slowly and cautiously tracing his way back, the Turkish army quickly started in his pursuit. The sultan reasoned that the Hungarian army was, by this time, exhausted with cold, the fatigues, and the extraordinary exertions, and that it would be an easy matter to catch them now in their own trap. But he counted without Hunyadi. When the latter thought the time had come for it, he turned and faced the enemy. He selected a vantage-ground where the Turkish army could at no time bring all their forces into play, and must therefore offer to the Hungarians a chance of beating them in detachments. The struggle was protracted, for the Turks could afford, to wait. As soon as one of their generals was defeated, the sultan had him strangled on the spot, and despatched in his place another general and another army. The contest went desperately on by the light of the moon. Every one took part in it; King Uladislaus himself was wounded. The exasperated Turks, after their ranks had been broken up, did not attempt to fly, but perished fighting. The commander-in-chief of the sultan's army was taken captive.

The Hungarian army returned in triumph to Buda. Close upon their heels followed the sultan's envoy, begging for peace. All he now asked for was to be let alone in his own country, and he in turn would not molest Hungary. This was an important concession, for the faith of the sultans had heretofore been held to forbid them to enter into a parley with, and still less to entreat peace of, the infidel Christians. But the sultan had just now a special reason for peace. Half of his empire had risen in arms against him—the Albanians in Europe and Mohammedan rebels in Asia. As usual with states based upon violence, the discontented rose on all sides at the news of the first lost battle. This was the effect of Hunyadi's campaign.

The terms of peace offered by the sultan were of the most flattering and tempting nature. He promised a great deal of money, territory, mines, and captives. Hunyadi was now in favor of peace; he felt that he must gather strength. Peace was therefore concluded, the king swearing by the Gospel and the sultan by the Koran. The ambassadors of the sultan had hardly left Hungary when Cardinal Julian, the pope's nuncio, arrived in the country and declared, in the pontiff's name, the oath of Uladislaus, the Hungarian king, to be null and void, adjuring him, at the same time, by all the saints, to hasten and make use of this opportunity to annihilate the Turks, and insisting that one so favorable would never occur again. All Europe's eyes were upon them, he added, and all Europe wished to take part in the struggle. And, indeed, the Christian princes hastened to protest against the peace, and offered money and soldiers in abundance to continue the war.

Meanwhile news arrived that the Italian naval squadron had appeared in the Turkish waters to intercept the sultan's crossing over from Asia to Europe. It was urged that now had come the time to fall upon the Turkish empire, which was without a master. The papal nuncio summoned all his eloquence to prove that the peace concluded with the Turk was not valid, for the word given to an unbeliever was not binding, and God did not listen to an oath deposited into pagan hands. "All Europe," he continued, "scoffed at this peace, and the honor and martial glory of the Hungarian nation will be like naught if she persisted in keeping it. It will disgrace her heroic name."

There was no occasion for adding more; the Hungarians had no wish to be thought cowards, and to this they preferred perjury. They enthusiastically resolved upon war. Hunyadi alone remained cold; he had no faith in big words and promises. But he was compelled to obey the commands of his king. He collected about 20,000 men, and with these he again marched into the Turkish empire. The famous European contribution had dwindled down to a few hundred soldiers and a few thousand florins, but it was hoped that many of the discontented would join them on their march. And, indeed, the vayvode of Wallachia joined them with about 10,000 men, but he could not help remarking to the king with regard to the forces of Sultan Mura, that the latter was in the habit of surrounding himself when on a hunting expedition with a retinue more numerous than the entire Hungarian army. It was, however, too late to think of drawing back.

And now bad news came crowding in; it seemed as if good fortune had altogether deserted the Hungarians. The Prince of Servia refused to join them. The Albanians failed in their attempt to cut their way to the Hungarians, and what seemed most incredible of all, the Italian naval squadron, whose task it was to have been to hinder the sultan's crossing over to Europe, had itself carried over the Turk for good money. The Hungarians were left alone and forsaken in the foreign country. There was reason enough now for retreating, and there were some who counselled retreat. It was Hunyadi's turn now to interfere. He declared that he did not fear the Turks under any circumstances, and if they had got so far they were bound to engage them in battle by beginning the attack themselves. As soon as Hunyadi came to the fore, confidence was at once restored; his person inspired the army with courage, and they continued their march against the Turks. The two opposing armies met near Varna, on the 10th of November, 1444. The sultan had pitched his tent on the top of a hill, and near it he had the document, upon which the treaty of peace was written, hoisted on a pole. He had with him more than 100,000 men ready for the fray. But the order of battle of the Hungarian army was again most admirable, such as could only be suggested by the lofty genius of Hunyadi. To every man was assigned his part and place, nor was any exception made in this respect in favor of the king. He obtained a post where no danger could reach him, and Hunyadi solemnly engaged him not to leave his place until he himself would call upon him to do so.

The battle now commenced. Hunyadi with his reserve horse-troop went wherever there was most danger, assisting, encouraging, and commanding. The first set-to took place between the cavalry. The struggle did not last long; the brilliant Turkish cavalry was put to flight in disorder. At this desperate sight the sultan put spurs to his horse, and turning its head was about to leave the battle-field, but the commanders near him seized the bridle of his horse, and menaced him with death if he did not go on with the battle. The sultan, taking courage again, ordered fresh troops into the fight, and the battle began to rage with renewed fury. In the midst of the sanguinary contest the two hostile leaders met face to face. Karafi Bey, his eyes sparkling, fell upon Hunyadi, and lifted his sword, but before he could strike a blow he slid from his horse pierced to the heart. The fall of their leader was the signal for the wild flight of the Turkish horse.

The Polish banner-bearers, surrounding the king, were envious witnesses of Hunyadi's victory, and urged Uladislaus, who was hardly able to restrain his youthful ardor, to participate in the engagement, by representing to him that victory was already assured, that he should not leave all the glory to Hunyadi, and that he should, at least, draw his sword and show himself a hero worthy of the double crown.

The king, forgetting his promise, accompanied by the banner of the country, made straight for the Janissaries, who had, as yet, hardly been in the fight. Hunyadi immediately saw the king's movement, and followed him as swiftly as he could. Upon this the king penetrated more deeply still into the ranks of the Janissaries, Hunyadi being unable now to cut his way to his sovereign. The king's companions succumbed one after the other. At last a Janissary succeeded in creeping up close to the king's horse, and striking at the horse's feet with his sword, he brought it down. Horse and rider fell, and the king was instantly despatched. The mad fray lasted a few minutes longer, when suddenly the pale head of the king, in his silver helmet, stuck on a pike, became visible. At this sight the Hungarian army and their leaders lost their senses, and the campaign came to a sudden end. The victorious Hungarians became fugitives, and Hunyadi himself returned to his home a lonely wanderer. The sultan, in surveying the bloody battle-field, exclaimed: "I wish my enemies only a victory like this." The Turks were not in a condition to pursue the defeated Hungarians.

The discomfited army crept back to their country, bringing with them the news that Hungary was without a king. The uppermost question now was who should be elected king. The plight of Hungary at that time was a sorry one, indeed. The king had left no children behind him, and yet there was an heir to the throne. When Albert of Hapsburg, the predecessor of Uladislaus, died, in 1439, his widow was *enceinte*, and she afterwards gave birth to a boy. The partisans of the late queen caused this her son, Ladislaus, to be crowned at once. The great majority, however, and Hunyadi with them, wanted on the throne a man who would be able to be their leader in the struggle against the Turks.

The result was the election of Uladislaus, the Polish king, in 1440.

The widowed queen with her son repaired to the court of the Duke of Austria, and from there she caused Hungary to be devastated by the Bohemian, John Ziska.

It was quite natural that after the death of Uladislaus the whole nation should look to the child Ladislaus as the future king. But the Austrian duke claimed a large sum under the title of the expenses of education of the young prince, a sum which the Hungarians were neither able nor willing to pay. Whilst this matter was being discussed, Hunyadi, being the captain-general of the country, was temporarily entrusted with the conduct of the principal affairs of state. Two years later he was elected governor of the country, with powers that but little differed from those of royalty.

As governor he deemed it his paramount duty to resume hostilities against the Turks. His mind was busy again with the plan to which he had devoted his life and fortune—namely, to attack the Turks and to drive them from Europe. In 1448 the sultan, at the head of an army of 150,000 men, invaded Albania, a country with which Hungary, owing to their community of interests, deeply sympathized. Hunyadi thought this an opportune moment to carry out his plan. From abroad he received again assurances of aid, but in the end they turned out to be, as before, empty promises. Putting his trust in God and himself, he started with 24,000 men. It was his purpose to unite his forces with those of Scanderbeg, the commander-in-chief of the Albanians. But as soon as the news of Hunyadi's advance reached the sultan, he left the Albanians and marched against his old and most implacable enemy. He offered him peace, but Hunyadi replied by drawing up his army in battle array. The battle was fought with great desperation, the fight continuing for days, and although the Turkish army outnumbered five times the Hungarians, the strategy of Hunyadi rendered the issue doubtful for some time. At the last moment, however, it was decided in favor of the Turks. Treason had turned the scale; the Wallachian vayvode, losing confidence in the wearied troops of Hunyadi, deserted with 8,000 men and joined the sultan. When the Hungarians saw this, they refused to listen any further to their commanders, and, scattering, they fled. Hunyadi himself escaped with great difficulty only. Whilst wandering towards his country on foot, unarmed, and through impassable roads, he fell into the hands of two Turkish marauders.

They little knew what a distinguished person they had captured, but there was no mistake about the golden cross on his breast. Luckily for Hunyadi they both coveted the cross and began quarrelling over it, and finally fell to fisticuffs. During their fight Hunyadi suddenly drew the sword of one of them, slaying him with it; the other, on seeing this, took to his heels. He had hardly escaped one danger, when another was in store for him. On his way he had hired a guide, who, instead of taking him to his own country, brought him to Brankovitch, the Servian prince, the man who, since the campaign of 1443, had been constantly crossing his plans. The treacherous Servian, who was licking now the hands of the Hungarians, now of the Turks, entered into negotiations with the Turkish sultan concerning Hunyadi's head. The latter, however, esteemed, even in his enemy, the pure-minded hero, and refused to entertain so base an offer.

Hunyadi returned to Hungary, and hastened to forget the injury done to him by the Servian prince; but the Turks he did not forget. In his most desperate straits he steadily kept before his eyes—the main object of his life—the ruin of the Turks. In 1453, the child-king, Ladislaus V., began his reign; but, although Hunyadi then relinquished his position as governor of Hungary, he still remained the captain-general of the country, the commander-in-chief of the army, and as such he missed no opportunity to injure his arch-enemy.

This same year, 1453, witnessed a most remarkable event in the history of Europe. Mohammed II., the new sultan, took Constantinople, the capital of the Greek empire and the gate of Europe, and made it the capital of his empire. "There is one God in heaven, and one Lord on earth, and I am that Lord!" exclaimed the sultan on entering Constantinople. All Europe trembled; Hunyadi alone remained calm and prepared for war. After a few minor engagements, Turks and Hungarians stood face to face again near Belgrade in 1456. This fortress was the gate of Hungary, and the great sultan wanted to get possession of it. For this purpose he determined to make a supreme effort, feeling that the seizure of this fortified place would decide the fate of generations to come. He led over 150,000 men under the walls of that famous fortress, and hastened to station his ships on the Danube, on which Belgrade lies, in order to cut off the communication between the Hungarian army and the garrison, and thus to isolate the latter. The Hungarian army itself did not number, even now, over 15,000 men, hardly more than those whom Hunyadi had been able to collect by his own exertions. Only this time, however, the great captain did not stand alone, but received great help from another quarter. A monk of magic eloquence, John Capistrano, who was sent by the pope to the country to preach a crusade, had, by the irresistible power of his appeals, collected 60,000 crusaders to assist Hunyadi. These men were armed with scythes and pole-axes only, and were led by the sound of bells instead of words of military command; but their fanaticism was quite equal to that of the Mohammedan Turk.

With an army composed of such warriors Hunyadi engaged in the great contest. His first effort was directed to the river, in order to relieve the garrison of the fortress. After an engagement of five hours, the great naval squadron of the Turks was scattered by the small galleys which had been the objects of the enemy's ridicule, but which were led to the attack by fanatic crusaders under the captaincy of Hunyadi. This restored the communication of the Hungarian army with the Hungarian garrison. Still Mohammed looked with scorn at the rabble collected on the opposite bank, the leaders of whom were largely monks, and he swore an oath that in two months' time, he would plant the proud crescent on the walls of Buda, the capital of Hungary. For eight days and eight nights the Turkish guns roared against Belgrade, and on the ninth day Mohammed ordered a general assault. The assault was renewed three times, and three times were the Turks repulsed. At the last moment, when the strength of the besieged seemed ready to give way, the Hungarian commander ordered the fascines soaked with oil and pitch, which were piled up in the ditches, to be set on fire and to be hurled at the storming men. Confusion seized the assailants, and each sought safety for himself, for he who did not escape met with a miserable death in the flames. Meanwhile the defence was rapidly changing into an attack along the whole line; the crusaders, mad with the excitement of the struggle, rushed forward, while Hunyadi directed an orderly attack against the Turkish camp. The engagement now became general, and the sultan himself received a wound. Dismayed, he took to flight, his troops following. Nothing could keep them longer together; the immense army was scattered to the winds, leaving behind them, under the walls of the famous fortress, 40,000 killed and 300 cannon.

At that most glorious moment of Hunyadi's life, when the Turks were put to flight by the bare mention of his name, this Christian hero, suddenly and without any premonition, breathed his last. He did not live to hear the panegyrics and felicitations of all Europe, the grateful recognition of his services by his own nation. His mighty frame sank under the weight of the fatigue of war, and, after a brief agony, he expired. His inveterate enemy, the great sultan himself, expressed grief at the news of his death, pronouncing him to be the ablest general in Europe.

Many there were, however, who rejoiced at his death. For, like all great men, he too had enemies against whom he was engaged in a life-and-death struggle as much as against the Turks. He had his envious rivals from the moment he had struggled into fame and had acquired a fortune. These men cared little to remember that he was indebted for both to his talents and courage. Some of the great lords, who were able to trace back their pedigrees to past centuries, looked upon him, the son of a simple noble, as an upstart. When he afterwards became captain-general and governor, they refused to obey him, but he made them obey by force of his arms. They were only silenced, however; in their innermost hearts they both hated and feared him. Among these were Garay, Brankovics, and Czilley, all of them connections of the royal house. The latter, Ulric Czilley, a wily and base man, who, though a foreigner, had pushed himself into the first place near the minor King Ladislaus V., was unremitting in his intrigues against him. He and his companions made the shallow-minded young king believe that Hunyadi and his two sons, who were growing into manhood, were ambitious of the crown, and, under this pretext, but without the king's knowledge, they laid traps for him. The fearless hero faced all such base machinations with the loftiness of a truly martial spirit. The secret attacks he met with caution and straightforwardness, and the slanderous insinuation that he coveted the throne he refuted by the simplicity of his life. Rich enough to have at any moment ten thousand men at his back, he was always as modest and unselfish as a monk. His detractors reflected on his great wealth, forgetting that his entire income was spent in armaments against the Turks.

He lived and died like a true knight, and in Hungarian history he will live forever as their grandest hero. If he did not achieve his most ardent wish, the expulsion of the Turks from Europe, his will always remain the merit of having made the arms of Hungary respected and feared by the Turks, and they no longer dared to look upon his country as an easy conquest. Over sixty years elapsed before a Turkish sultan again ventured to threaten Belgrade.

CHAPTER X.

KING MATTHIAS.
1458-1490.

MATTHIAS, the son of Hunyadi, was indebted for his elevation to the throne to the prestige of his father, who was the idol of the nation, but it was through his own genius alone that he strengthened the throne and became famous, mighty, and, perhaps, the greatest king of whom his country could boast. He excelled alike as a soldier and leader of armies, as a statesman and diplomatist, and as a man delighting in science and art. In those warlike days it would not have been possible for him to become conspicuous among his contemporaries and to become a powerful king, unless he had, in the first place, shown ability as a soldier. Matthias inherited the courage and soldierly qualities of his great father, and, following in his footsteps, became the foremost general of his age, combining rare personal gallantry with a remarkable capacity for military organization. The splendid example of his father had been before his eyes since his most tender years; it was his father who initiated him into the skilful handling of arms and into the secrets of strategy, and both his father and his famous mother, Elizabeth Szilágyi, vied with each other in inuring his body and mind to the struggles and dangers of which, since his earliest childhood, so large a share had been his lot.

Trained amid warlike games, he very soon had to face serious struggles, for the men who had looked upon John Hunyadi with envy and jealousy extended their ill feeling to his two handsome boys, Matthias and his elder brother, Ladislaus. No secret was made before the youths of the dangers that surrounded them; they were taught rather to brave than to avoid them. Ladislaus, less fortunate than his brother, soon fell a victim to the machinations directed against both.

Ladislaus was threatened with assassination in his own castle at the hands of Czilley, who was a foreigner and the guardian and friend of the boy-king. His men, attracted by the noise of the scuffle which ensued, rushed in and killed the would-be murderer. The king vowed that he would not molest Ladislaus for this act of self-defence, but he had him afterwards seized, thrown into prison, and executed without warrant of law or judicial sentence. This was the work of the enemies of the house of Hunyadi, but very soon they had to pay the penalty of their iniquity. The mass of the nation was roused, and upon the sudden death of Ladislaus V. in his other kingdom, amongst the Czechs, Matthias, the surviving son of Hunyadi, was proclaimed king of Hungary.

Although but fifteen years old when he ascended the throne, he both knew and was accustomed to the dangers that lurked around him, and it was not long before he proved that he could cope with them. Indeed his natural disposition and early training rather led him to seek danger. From his earliest childhood he worshipped heroes, and nothing delighted him more than the ballads, legends, and heroic songs glorifying the gallant deeds and wonderful performances of such leaders of men, as Attila, Alexander the Great, Roland, the French Knight, or his own father. He could listen to these stories all day long, forgetting both hunger and thirst. As he grew to manhood and became king, he had opportunity himself to perform the great deeds he had admired in others. His personal courage knew no limits, and his reckless daring frequently confounded his own men, who, not without cause, feared for his life.

There was one remarkable trait which particularly characterized his valorous deeds as well as his other acts, and that was his love of justice. To this might be traced, in most cases, his boldest actions. Nothing afforded him greater pleasure than to unmask the hypocrite, and to shame the bully and braggart. On occasions like these he would often risk his life to make the truth triumph. Many an instance of this kind is related of him. On one occasion, a German knight, by the name of Holubar, came to Buda, the capital of Hungary. He paraded everywhere his gigantic frame and extraordinary strength, and was indeed thought to be invincible in the tournaments where mounted knights rushed at each other, lance in hand, for he invariably precipitated his adversary to the ground. King Matthias, anxious to measure arms with the big-bodied German, challenged him. The latter declined the challenge, fearing lest he might do some harm to the king, and be in consequence exposed to ill treatment. But the king insisted, and Holubar finally consented. He was determined, however, to slide from his saddle at the slightest thrust from the king. Somehow the king heard of his determination, and immediately caused him to be summoned to his presence. He there vowed, by all the saints, that if he perceived Holubar doing this, he would have him executed, and at the same time made him swear that he would fight with him as if he were the knight's mortal enemy. The contest took place in the presence of many thousands, and many doubted the king's success, comparing the German giant with the middle-sized Matthias. The two combatants rushed at each other with tremendous thrusts; the steeled muscles of the king proved superior to the heavy bulk of his adversary, who reeled from his horse, struck by a heavy blow on the forehead, and lay with his arm broken and fainting on the ground. The king, too, staggered by his adversary's thrust, had to slide off the saddle holding on by his horse's bridle. The king, having humiliated the bragging foreigner, sent him away with presents of horses, splendid dresses, and a large purse of money. This happened shortly after his elevation to the throne, showing that he then already was a practical master in the use of arms. Matthias was of middle size, but the trunk of his body tall in comparison with his legs, which were rather short, and it was owing to this freak of nature that when on horseback he always overtopped his fellow-riders. He was broad-shouldered, deep-chested, and his limbs were as hardened as steel. On this solid frame rested a massive yet finely cut head, and his eyes were as sharp as those of the falcon.

He was able to concentrate his strength and will on one point, never losing his self-confidence, never wavering, and full of endurance. He never vacillated, and sure of the present and of the coming moment, was always ready for action. He possessed an even nature, and was equally unruffled and steady in single combat and on the battle-field, in his private and his public life. He at all times produced the impression of a man full of power and determination, and of a mind of large culture and many-sidedness.

We shall now speak of him as the soldier, for he will appear before us during most of his career in wars and battles. He waged war, on several occasions, against his neighbors on the north, the Poles and Czechs, defeating them often, and finally becoming the king of the Czechs. On the south he fought numerous smaller battles, but almost without cessation, against the sultan. His most inveterate enemy, however, was Frederic, the envious and avaricious emperor of Germany, his western neighbor, who incessantly harassed him. Matthias was engaged in four great wars against him, and finally captured, in 1485, Frederic's capital, Vienna, compelling the German emperor to go begging from convent to convent, seated on a wagon drawn by oxen.

Hungary was, at that period, beset by many troubles and enemies, but her name was honored and respected everywhere. The sword was in everybody's hand, and it almost seemed as if men were born with it. It was the prevailing characteristic of European society, in that age, that all men went about armed, and were ready to draw their swords on the least provocation, and in Hungary especially, where fighting against the neighbors was constantly going on, this fashion was more prevalent than elsewhere. King Matthias was well aware that the rash, passionate, hot-headed, free, and soldier-nation he ruled over would but reluctantly submit to restraint. He was, nevertheless, determined to introduce discipline amongst his soldiers. It was an exceedingly difficult task, considering that the armies of Europe in general were, in those days, undisciplined, loosely organized, composed of motley elements, and not subjected to uniform military training. But Matthias was not at a loss for a remedy, being a man to inquire, to observe, to learn from others, and to put to use what he had learned. He remembered the example of his father, who had drilled his own soldiers, the lessons derived from the study of ancient Roman generalship and from conversations with the most renowned contemporary captains, and finally he did not spurn to profit by the example of his enemies, the Turks. The Turkish Janissaries, the most famous foot-soldiery in the world, were well-disciplined troops, forming a permanent and standing nucleus for the Turkish forces.

A similar standing body of soldiers was now organized by King Matthias. He employed his genius in their training, kept them together, supported them by his own means, and established discipline amongst them by the force of his character. This was the famous *black troop*, one of the corner-stones of his power, and, next to the French, the earliest standing army in Europe. These soldiers he attached to his person by the strongest ties. He lavishly bestowed upon them both pay and booty, and made them sharers of his triumphs. But it was, above all, the rare charm of his personal qualities which won for him their affections. They were not only faithfully devoted to him during his life, but fondly cherished his memory after his death. He himself trained and instructed them, sparing neither time nor trouble to accomplish his purpose. He set them a bright example in all soldierly duties. He shared with his soldiers all the hardships of war; suffered with them cold, hunger, and thirst, and the fatigues of forced marches. He did not shrink from the most exposed position on the battle-field whenever his presence was needed. At sieges, he was often seen walking to and fro amidst a hail of bullets and arrows, a recklessness to which numerous lesser and larger wounds on his body abundantly bore witness. He paid particular attention to the ferreting out of the weak points of fortresses. He employed clever spies for that purpose, paying them liberally, but never placed implicit trust in them, for he himself was a cleverer spy than any of them. It particularly gratified him to hoodwink an enemy by discovering his plans, even at the risk of his life, and thus frustrating them.

In 1475 he laid siege to Shabatz, situated on the southern border of the country. He was exceedingly anxious to take the place, but knowing nothing about its defences, he undertook in person the spying out of the plan of the fortifications. At night he got into a boat in company with a trusty attendant and an oarsman, who was to row him around the walls. They were hardly half way, when the Turks discovered them, and hailed them with a volley of shots, which, in spite of the darkness, struck his attendant. The king, defying death, continued his investigations, undaunted by the heavy fire, until he had finished the inspection of the fortress. The bold venture, moreover, was not thrown away, for shortly after the place was captured. Some of his expeditions were more amusing, but not less dangerous.

At the siege of Vienna, in 1485, he frequently walked all around the walls, unattended, or, at most, followed by a page. On one occasion, he stole into the city in disguise. Dressed in the shabby dress of a country boor, with a basket containing butter and eggs on his back, he traversed the city in every direction, selling his wares, and at the same time spying out the condition of the fortifications. He lounged about in the market-place, listening to what the people talked about, and what they were planning. He made his escape in safety, and, making good use of what he had seen and heard, the city shortly afterward fell into his hands.

Upon another occasion, his forces being stationed opposite the Turkish camp, he assumed the disguise of a Turk, and mixing with the country people who entered the camp to sell their provisions, he succeeded in passing in with them. Once there, he had the hardihood to seek out the sultan's tent, and, settling down near it, he went on selling provisions and spying all day long. Upon his return to the Hungarian camp, he sent, on the following day, a letter to the sultan, conceived in these terms: "Thou guardest thy camp badly, emperor, and thou art thyself badly guarded. For yesterday I sat, even from morn until night, near thy tent, selling provisions. And lest thou doubtest my words, I will tell thee now what was served on thy table." The sultan, upon reading this letter, became frightened, and, together with his army, noiselessly left the neighborhood.

The king was particularly rigorous in the ordering of the sentry service. He used to rise at night and inspect the sentinels, to see if they were awake, and in their places. He was especially active during sieges, being constantly on his feet. He was never satisfied with reports alone, but was bound to look after every thing in person. Everybody marvelled at his incessant watchfulness. He awoke at the slightest sound, at the merest whisper. At the same time, he was famed for his sound slumbers amidst the din of battle. Upon such occasions, the shouts of the men, the roaring of the cannon, and the reports of the musketry seemed to lull him to sleep.

He was self-willed when it came to action. He would, it is true, call a council of war, and listen to the opinions of his captains, but in the end he nearly always acted on his own views. He was admirable in distinguishing idle reports from the truth, being as indefatigable and clear-headed in his investigations as he was quick and fertile in the concerting of plans. During the intervals of rest, he liked to mingle with his soldiers. He would joke and be full of mischief with them, and, especially in his younger days, would often eat and drink with them. He always had a kind word for the men in the ranks, just as, in civil life, he was anxious to impress people that he held the great lord, the poor noble, and the peasant in equal esteem, as long as they proved themselves worthy of it. This was truly a rare princely virtue in his age. Always gracious and affable, he loved to discover merit, and to reward it. He sought out the wounded, often even on the battle-field, inquired into their circumstances, comforted them in their troubles, and reassured and nursed those who were low in spirits.

He made it a point that his soldiers should be regularly and punctually paid, and rather than get into arrears with their pay, he would borrow or levy heavy taxes. On one occasion, however, during the Czech wars, he was completely out of funds. He had been just pondering how to raise money for his soldiers, when he was called upon by his captains to join them in a game of dice. The playing was kept up all night, and the king hardly threw any other numbers than those indicated by him beforehand. It was easy for him, with fortune thus in his favor, to win 10,000 florins, a sum which he at once distributed amongst his soldiers in the morning.

Full of sympathy for his soldiers, and princely in his rewards, he yet rigidly exacted discipline, especially in times of peril; and well might he do so, as he himself was amongst the first to submit to it. A comrade to his soldiers during the hours of rest, he became a most severe commander in war, and during the military exercises and drills. Disregard of discipline and disobedience were punished with death. At the tournaments, he often challenged (as was customary in Europe during the middle ages) his captains to combat, rigorously enjoining upon them not to spare his person, but the very person whom he thus distinguished was mercilessly punished if he offended against military discipline. At a tournament, he met in single combat, in sight of the whole country, Szvéla, one of his captains; yet, but a short time afterwards, he sent both him and his companions to the gallows for breaches of discipline and mutinous conduct. He was, however, never cruel to his soldiers, and readily forgave offences if he was convinced that they sprang, not from ill-will, but from awkwardness and lack of experience.

During the campaign against Frederic, the emperor of Germany, he sent against him one of his generals by the name of Simon Nagy. Nagy, otherwise a brave captain, was defeated, and returned home filled with shame at his disgrace. The king received him with a cheerful countenance, well knowing that the gallant captain had done all he could, and sent him back again at the head of an army to resume the campaign. The brave soldier, animated by his king's confidence and magnanimity, achieved such a triumphant victory that from that time Frederic never again ventured to send an army against Matthias. He was happy in the selection of his generals, and did not object to raising a man of merit, although of low degree, to the most exalted position. Kinizsy, his most distinguished captain, a man of mean fortunes, owed his elevation to the king. This man had been, in his youth, a plain miller-boy, endowed by nature with gigantic strength. As a miller, he was capable of lifting with one hand the heaviest mill-stone, and, on becoming a leader of armies, he rushed upon his enemy with a ponderous sword in each hand. Such was his enormous strength that, at a great feast held on the battle-field to celebrate his most renowned victory, near Kenyérmezo, he, the triumphant Kinizsy himself, stood up before the merrymaking crowd, and, holding the dead body of a full-grown Turk in his right hand, another in his left, and a third between his teeth, tripped the national dance. Captains like these contributed to the military prestige of the king, but he owed still more to his own royal qualities.

The impression made by these qualities upon his soldiers remained unchanged, for he continually demonstrated his soldierly virtues, his affability, his liberality, and generosity by deeds. Anecdotes in which the king always played a pleasant part went all the time from mouth to mouth. An old chronicler says of him. "Never was a prince more beloved and respected by his people and his soldiers than he, but, at the same time, everybody feared him as they would a savage lion." At the sound of the drums and the blowing of the horns, every one stood instantly ready for the engagement, and willing to meet death for his king. During the military drills, every eye was fixed on his person, and every ear listened to the sound of his voice only; he alone was the magnet that attracted and riveted the general attention of his soldiers. In this respect, Hungary stood alone amongst the nations of Europe, and it was with men like these only that he was enabled to achieve his wonderfully rapid and well-planned strategic movements. At a time when the armies of Europe were generally noted for their unwieldiness, this mobility constituted one of the chief advantages of the king's army, and to it he owed his most conspicuous military achievements.

The king, in his turn, placed the fullest confidence in his soldiers. In the camp and on the battle-field, as we have seen, he went about unattended, or, at the most, accompanied by one or two of his men. He bestowed no care upon the guarding of his person, although at that period immense sums were lavished by the rulers to insure their personal safety by surrounding themselves with a body-guard composed of picked men. He did not feel the necessity of imitating his royal neighbors in this particular; the love and respect of his soldiers proved a more powerful protection than any troop of body-guards he could have organized.

In summing up all we have said about Matthias as a soldier, we obtain an interesting, attractive, and by no means commonplace picture of him. Severe to others, he was no less severe to himself; active, energetic, enterprising, and crafty, he was most happy when actively engaged. Versed in military matters, he at times exhibited a knowledge of military science which reminds us of a modern tactician.

The general historian, as well as the chronicler of his own country, will always assign to him a conspicuous place, not only as a ruler and statesman distinguished in his own age, but also as an illustrious example for the world of royal power, dignity, and magnanimity. He entertained a high opinion of the functions of a ruler. Being ambitious and proud, he liked to give to the world the spectacle of a throne occupied by a king dignified, powerful, and splendid, who, nevertheless, paid tribute to all that was noble and virtuous in humanity. His mind was always busy with great affairs and bold schemes, and he was unwearying in seeking the means of accomplishing them. He never shrank from any task, nor was any task too trifling for him to engage in if there was a pressing occasion for it. He was as indefatigable in his study attending to diplomatic affairs as on the battle-field, unflagging in his activity, and thoroughly informed about every thing.

There was a great deal of work to be done, for Matthias took a large part in the political mazes of Europe. He kept up connections with all Europe, with a view to maintaining and increasing his power—a system which was at that time pursued by no other European ruler. The intercourse with the foreign countries was now of a friendly now of a hostile nature, but it never ceased. As soon as the campaign was at an end on the battle-field, the diplomatic contest was resumed and continued in the study. As the king grew older and more powerful, his troubles with the neighbors increased, for, owing to the enhanced weight of his word, more and more people sought him out and entered into relations with him. Foreign ambassadors were continually either arriving or departing from his court, while his own emissaries were either leaving on, or returning from, missions of lesser or greater importance concerning affairs of state or family. Upon such occasions, especially in the case of missions of greater importance, he felt the whole dignity of the royal position and spared neither pains nor money to surround it with stateliness. The ordinary embassies usually numbered from fifty to sixty members; the more brilliant embassies were frequently attended by as many as a hundred servants.

In 1487 Matthias sent a splendid embassy to the court of Charles VIII., king of France, a description of which will give an idea of the pomp displayed by the Hungarian king. He caused three hundred horses of uniform color to be selected, on each of which sat a youth clad in purple velvet. These youths all wore long gold chains on their sides, and upon entering a city each placed a braidwork mounted with pearls on his head. The contemporary chronicles speak with ecstasy of the beauty of the men, of the splendor of their dress, and of the rich harnesses of their horses, embossed with precious stones. The presents sent to the French king on that occasion, consisting of costly horses, horses' trappings, splendid robes, vessels and ornaments of gold and silver, amounted to a sum of no less than half a million of florins of the currency of our days.

The embassy sent by Matthias in 1476 to the king of Naples—whose daughter, Beatrice, became subsequently his wife—exceeded the last named in numbers, if not in splendor. It was composed of church and lay magnates, scholars, prelates, soldiers of high rank, nobles, knights, relatives of the king, his intimates and councillors. These again were attended by their secretaries, chamberlains, pages, grooms and forerunners. It was a wonderfully variegated sight, rich in coloring, this mounted army of men dressed in costly robes of various and glaring colors. The great lords were dressed from head to foot in gala costumes, brilliant with gold and silver and jewels, the nobles and knights in costumes of colored velvet, the pages and courtiers in colored satin—all of them mounted on high-mettled steeds. In their train followed the numerous jesters or fools, whom it was customary at that time for every great lord to have by his side, to make sport, or to tell the truth; musicians, especially, according to the fashion of the day, trumpeters, drummers, and harpists; and, finally, players and buffoons, all of them attired and bedizened in motley, parti-colored and tawdry costumes.

The horses' keep alone cost this embassy a million of florins, present currency. But not satisfied with carrying on their backs half of the current wealth of the country they came to represent, the members of the embassy had brought with them, besides, vessels of gold and silver, and jewelry of all kind, to be distributed as presents, or to be paraded about. Ostentation was the fashion of the day; objects of luxury were still a sort of novelty, and those possessing them were anxious to have the pleasure of their display. There was another feature about the pageant of this mission which made it almost unique; and with which Matthias created the greatest sensation. This was a band of Turkish prisoners of high rank, clad in costly caftans with golden turbans on their heads, who preceded the brilliant Hungarian procession upon their entering the Italian cities. These prisoners had just been captured by the king near Shabatz, and they were to serve as an evidence of Hungarian prowess. At that time half Europe stood in awe of the powerful Turks, particularly the Italians, who, although excelling in art and science, were wretched and pusillanimous soldiers. Both Matthias and his father, John Hunyadi, were known to the Italians as the most powerful and successful foes of the dreaded Turks, and the prestige of the names of these two warriors won greater respect for the embassy than all the wealth and luxury displayed by it.

Brilliant as were the embassies sent by Matthias to foreign courts, he was no less gratified by the arrival of missions to his own, which were looked upon as a sort of holiday event. The king himself was inclined to be liberal if he wished to do honor to any one. There were, besides, gathered about his person a motley crowd of Hungarian, German, and Czech magnates, prelates and nobles, attentive to every command of his. Then there were the court attendants amounting to many hundreds, and all these persons required but a nod from the king to devote themselves to the preparation of a brilliant reception. They were quick to don their sumptuous and costly dresses, they brandished their weapons inlaid with precious stones, they pranced on their steeds caparisoned in colored silk and velvet, and, attended by an army of courtiers and servants, clad in garments representing all the colors of the rainbow, the procession went out amid the blast of horns, to meet the ambassador and to escort him to the court. In 1487, John Valentini, the envoy from the court of Ferrara, in Italy, and in 1488, Melchior Russ, the Swiss envoy, were honored by receptions of this kind. In December, 1479, John Anagarini, the papal cardinal ambassador, was received with the greatest imaginable pomp, by the king in person, who, attended by his church and lay dignitaries, came out to meet him at three o'clock in the morning. Thousands of wax torches shed a light as broad as day over the dark and wintry scene. Three days after the arrival of the cardinal the solemn audience took place. The king appeared in his royal robes, surrounded by the highest dignitaries of the court, and by the church and lay magnates, all sumptuously dressed. The king well understood the art of astonishing and dazzling his visitors by the dignity of his presence and by the display of lavish pomp.

Upon one occasion he was staying at Visegrád, his splendid palace a short distance from Buda, when the sultan's ambassador arrived. It gratified the pride of Matthias to dazzle the eyes of the Turkish envoy, who was accustomed to the brilliant surroundings of the sultan, with the splendor of his own court. Visegrád, which was called by the contemporaries "an earthly paradise," fully suited his purpose. The envoy and his train were brought from their city quarters to the royal castle, in order to be admitted to the solemn audience with the king. As the gates of the castle were thrown open a gorgeous spectacle met their eyes. The king stood on an eminence of one of his hanging gardens. Around him, above and below him, were grouped the great of the land and his courtiers, clad in silk, velvet, gold, and silver robes, with shining arms. At this unexpected sight the envoy was struck with awe.

In confusion he drew nearer, but as his eyes met the proud look of the king he became so embarrassed that he lost the command of his voice, and was only able to stammer out, after a pause: "The padishah greets you, the padishah greets you." The king, perceiving his painful hesitation, had him led back to his quarters. After the lapse of a few days he was conducted again into the king's presence, who, after having bestowed upon the envoy rich presents, sent him back to his master with the proud message to "send another time an ambassador who, at least, can speak."

Of such a nature were the audiences granted to foreign envoys. The audiences granted to his own subjects lacked, of course, the pomp and pageant of the former, but the king was particularly careful and painstaking in the treatment of the matters thus brought before him. This was more especially the case during the beginning of his reign. His first wife, the daughter of the Czech king, whom he had married in 1458, died a few years afterwards, leaving him a widower, and the ceremonial of the court, in the absence of a queen, admitted of an unrestrained intercourse with his people. But he married again in 1476 the daughter of the king of Naples, Princess Beatrice. With her presence Italian etiquette and formality began to prevail in the royal court, and free access to the king's person became more and more difficult. In his youth the business of his doorkeepers was but scant, for the doors stood wide open for the petitioners, who were kindly received by the young king. Nor was the number of these small, for the king's fame as a friend to justice had spread all over the country. A whole army of petitioners, from the great lord to the simple peasant, frequently besieged the doors of the audience hall, for Matthias was known to treat them all with uniform affability. He attentively listened to and duly weighed the petitions and complaints of all. This was a matter of great importance at a time when a privileged class, the nobles, were the masters of the property of the numerous peasantry, and frequently held control even of their lives. The laws at that period were both loose and defective, and the judges could, with impunity, either misinterpret or distort their meaning to the injury of the suitor. Besides, in that age nearly every noble had a train amounting to a small army, and the temptation proved frequently irresistible to be his own judge and to treat the weaker party as he pleased. Such was then the condition of things all over Europe.

The most efficacious remedy for these evils was a king just and strong, who was not loth to inquire into abuses and was ready to lend the weight of his kingly command and of armed force against the recalcitrant. Matthias was a ruler equal to such a task. Many excellent laws were introduced during his reign, and he had both the sense of justice and the power to enforce them. The very knowledge of the existence of such a final appeal greatly improved the administration of justice, for every one was aware that the king was a man of his word, and that his threats were not empty utterances, but were sure to be followed by swift and severe punishment. He was as quick in disposing of the matters submitted to him as he was careful in their consideration. If he ever delayed affairs they were mostly connected with important questions of state, diplomacy, and finances, requiring caution in their management. On such occasions he was master in the art of keeping silent, and might have excited the envy of the craftiest Italian diplomatist by his wariness. His mind was not easily open to extraneous influences; he liked to get at the bottom of all complaints and accusations by personal investigation. He brought into the management of civil affairs the habits exhibited by him on the battlefield; he was always inspecting and investigating. It was a matter of frequent occurrence with the king to go among the people in disguise in order to study their characters and dispositions, to learn their complaints and troubles, and, if possible, to give at once a helping-hand. During these expeditions he strayed unknown into the villages, exposing himself frequently to the overbearing treatment of a village judge, a landed noble, or a constable, and even to occasional blows, but if he afterwards got hold of the guilty parties he showed them on his part no mercy. In his disguise he was indifferent to the scoffs and gibes levelled at him; he rather enjoyed the incongruous and comical plights he often found himself in, but at the same time he was apt to give and to take a joke. Of course the king always laughed last, when the disgraced culprits, after being punished, ruefully slunk away. He was, as a general thing, very fond of good-natured intrigues, and liked to season even graver matters with a bit of pleasantry.

To the secret denunciations of eavesdroppers the king, unlike many of his royal contemporaries, never listened, preferring to trust to his own eyes and ears only. This manly straightforwardness inspired all his actions, and was instrumental in causing him to arrive at the truth and to do justice, and obtained for him among the people, even in his lifetime, the name of "the just." The memory of his fame for justice has survived to this day in the current popular saying: "King Matthias is dead, justice has fled!" Although as a soldier and statesman crafty and full of expedients, and even loving disguise in contact with his people, he never was treacherous and deceitful. Poisoning and assassination did not enter into his catalogue of expedients as it did into the policy and practice of his contemporary, the French king, Louis XI., or the Italian princes, the Estes, Sforzas, the Borgias, and the popes themselves, who employed both as a favorite means for accomplishing political objects. All unclean means were repugnant to his frank and knightly nature, as was evinced by the following instance. While he was engaged in war, in 1463, against George Podiebrad, the Czech king, he was approached by a man who offered to take George's life in armed combat for a reward of five thousand florins. The king, knowing the difficulties of the enterprise, at once consented, promising even a larger amount in case of success. This man, after lurking for a long while about the person of King George, despaired of being able to carry out his fell design, for the king was surrounded by the finest soldiers of the period, and to attack him, under those circumstances, would have been equivalent to forfeiting his own life. He therefore proposed to King Matthias to remove the Czech king by poison. The king indignantly refused to profit by the assassin's offer, proudly exclaiming: "We are in the habit of fighting with arms and not with poison!" At the same time he sent a message to the Czech king putting him on his guard against the attempt to take his life by poison, and cautioning him not to partake of any food or drink unless it was first tested by one of his trusty men.

With views like these it was natural that King Matthias should not be accessible to any fear of poison or assassination. It was secretly intimated to him at one time that his courtiers intended mixing poison with his food. Upon hearing this he exclaimed: "Let no king ruling justly and lawfully fear the poison and assassin's dagger of his subjects." His capacity for government was particularly shown in the right selection and thorough appreciation of men, and in the independence which he always maintained. This trait of character became at once evident on his ascent to the throne. Being only fifteen years of age he was deemed too young for the burden of government, and a governor and state-councillors were placed by his side. But he felt equal to the duties of his royal office, and determined to take the reins of government in his own hands. In this scheme, however, he saw both his friends and his enemies arrayed against him. The former, the adherents of old Hunyadi, to whose services he owed his throne, wished to superintend his education, to guard him against dangers, and to maintain at the same time their influence over him. His enemies, on the other hand, true to the instincts of their inveterate hostility to the Hunyadi family, after having first opposed his aspirations to the throne and afterwards intrigued against him, were glad of an opportunity to balk him in his wishes, and therefore they now sided against him, and soon after openly declared for Frederic, the German emperor.

The position of the young king was an exceedingly critical one; his foreign enemies, too, the Turks, Germans, and Czechs, began open opposition and, what was most discouraging of all, the treasury was empty. But he surprised everybody by the independence and circumspect conduct with which he met both friends and foes, and also the difficulties threatening from abroad. His astute questions and ready replies in conversation were the theme of universal admiration. It was thought that, being a youth, he would busy himself with empty trifles, and give little thought to his royal responsibilities. His partisans had hoped to be called upon to instruct him in the art of government, whilst his enemies had anticipated that, unmindful of his kingly duties, he would very soon be ruined. But he disappointed both. In the council chamber he listened attentively when any of the lords spoke, but as soon as their views diverged and threatened to degenerate into a heated discussion, it was he, the youth, whom they had met to advise, who admonished them to be calm and to agree. His enemies saw that the youth was thoroughly conscious of the exaltedness of his position, which placed him above his adherents as well as his enemies, and they now tried every means to create dissensions between him and his partisans. In this they failed, for the king was on his guard. Knowing his difficult position, he took pains to conciliate his friends. In the treatment of them he was both determined and smooth. In conversation he first ascertained the views of those to whom he spoke, and then shaped his own remarks accordingly. He had the talent of persuading his antagonists without seeming to do so, and of getting them to share his views, and as he was quick to discover the opinions of others, he was not liable to being imposed upon. By slow degrees all opposition to him died out and both friend and foe were silenced.

After disposing of his domestic antagonists, he turned his attention to his enemies abroad, and, by dint of an active mind, knowledge of men, polished manner, and generosity, where it was needed, he soon succeeded in strengthening his throne against all enemies. One by one, the proud princes and oligarchs, who had only reluctantly and disdainfully accepted the sovereignty of the upstart, were conciliated by his royal qualities, and under the rule of Matthias, the son of Hunyadi, Hungary secured an wider influence and a higher degree of power than she had ever attained beneath the sceptres of the descendants of the ancient kings.

An account has been previously given of the splendor which the king's embassies displayed abroad, and we may add that Matthias was the wealthiest and most luxurious ruler in all Europe. He had enormous wealth at his disposal, composed in part of his own private fortune, and in part of the royal revenues. At that time there was generally no distinction made between the revenues of the king and those of the state. The king disposed of all the sums flowing into the royal treasury, whether derived from the state taxes or from any other sources. King Matthias was quite proficient in the art of turning to the fullest use these sources of income, and of adding fresh ones, in case of need. He introduced a more punctual and rigorous administration of the finances with most admirable results. He was himself also the possessor of a vast private fortune, inherited from his father. His domains extended for many miles, and he was the owner of mines of gold and silver, of great productiveness, in the richest mineral region of the country. None of his subjects could compare with him as to the extent of their private estates, although there were many amongst the church and lay magnates who could boast of immense wealth.

In his reign the royal revenues increased upon an unprecedented scale. The aggregate annual income of the Hungarian treasury amounted under King Ladislaus V. to only about 120,000 florins. Under

Matthias it increased, on an average, tenfold. His yearly income very soon exceeded one million, and not unfrequently reached even two million florins, and this at a period when the French king, who was supposed to be the richest sovereign, was unable to make his income reach one million. It is true Matthias stood always in need of a great deal of money to carry out his vast schemes, his soldiers and wars swallowing up enormous sums; while it may be said, he was also prone to indulge in all the luxuries of life.

The time had passed when men's whole lives were divided between war and prayer only. Until now these had been the essential characteristics of the middle ages. But all this was suddenly changed; people awoke to the consciousness of their wealth, and there were several countries in Europe offering a long list of varied enjoyments fit to tempt the most fastidious. The arts, painting, sculpture, and skilful working in precious metals, as well as the sciences, began to flourish; and people began to read books, books written by hand in elaborate manuscripts and richly ornamented with gold and silver and the most varied illuminated work. The classic authors of ancient Greece and Rome—long lost sight of—had been rediscovered, and scattered memorials of ancient art came to light, and were cherished by the finders with the fresh delight of childhood enjoying new playthings.

In this movement Italy occupied the front rank. From his early youth Matthias was drawn by all the fibres of his heart towards the awakening culture, the motto of which was to enjoy the beautiful. How thoroughly he entered into the spirit of the rising glory of the new civilization, is best shown by the fact that his Italian contemporaries praised him to the skies as the whole-souled patron of science and art. In the magnificence and the splendor with which he surrounded himself, Matthias certainly exceeded all his contemporaries, not even excepting the Italian princes, who were famous for their sumptuousness and their appreciation of works of art, and of whom Matthias had undoubtedly, learned a good deal. The example set by the king influenced his subjects, the chief prelates of the church, who had obtained immense endowments from the first kings of Hungary, and the proud and rich great lords. But none of them could approach the king in magnificence or in refined luxury. His court was the gathering place of scholars and artists not only from Hungary and Italy but from all Europe. To them he assigned the highest places in the state, in the church, and in the schools. From these scholars he selected his chancellors and vice-chancellors, his treasurers and sub-treasurers, the royal councillors, his son's tutor, men employed to read to him, his librarians, court historiographers and secretaries, all of whom were munificently rewarded for their services.

Nor was it necessary for a scholar to have a fixed position at court in order to secure a rich income; his very presence at court was supposed to give him a valid title to a compensation. Theologians, philosophers, poets, orators, jurists, physicians, and astronomers came to admire the renowned court, and remained there to add to its brilliancy, to amuse the king, and to be the recipients of his munificence. These men were treated by the king as his friends and companions and led a comfortable, and, frequently, a luxurious life. They had their abundant share in the good cheer of the table, and in the pastimes and honors. The frequent discussions of scientific and literary questions, which arose in such a circle, produced, especially when peaceful seasons intervened for a time, a busy scholarly life at court, of which the king, who was fond of taking part in the conversations, was the bright centre. He was himself proficient in the lore of his age. It is true that his youthful education had not been completed, for he had been left an orphan at a tender age, and had soon been compelled to exchange the games of youth for the cares of government, but his great talents, his quickness, and the keen interest he took in every thing, greatly contributed to make up for any deficiency in precision of knowledge. He had a retentive memory and rarely forgot what he heard in conversation, and probably a large part of what he learned came in this way. It was also the fashion at that time for scholars to prolong their discussions, after the fashion of the Greek gymnasiums, from morn until night, and to appoint special meetings for special subjects. The subject under discussion was pursued everywhere—at the table, during the sports, in the reception room, the garden, and the fields. The subjects were principally classical. Sometimes lectures were delivered in the presence of the king or queen, as in the instance of Bonafini, who visited the court in 1487. In order to get better acquainted with him and to present him to the court, the king, who subsequently appointed him his court historiographer, ordered him to deliver a lecture at his palace, in Vienna, where he then happened to hold his court. The whole court, together with the foreign ambassadors, appeared on this interesting occasion. At the conclusion of the lecture the writings of Bonafini were brought in and distributed amongst the chief prelates and the magnates.

The court dinners afforded favorable opportunities for scholarly discussions and conversations. A great number of guests had a permanent invitation to the king's table. Such were his near relatives, soldiers of high rank, dignitaries of Church and State, foreign ambassadors, and, especially, the scholars residing at his court. In an atmosphere like this it was quite natural that the discourse should take a lively turn, and include in its range both serious and amusing subjects. The king himself enjoyed a world-wide fame for his ready wit and attractive talk. He liked to propound riddles to his learned friends, and at times would give them a great deal of trouble by his cleverly-contrived oracular questions, particularly if he wished to confound some braggart. He delighted in disputes, in which he was seldom worsted, because he kept his temper to the last. But in most cases the discussion was begun by his guests—the king only joining in afterwards, and very frequently giving the decision. Some of his puns and anecdotes are remembered to this day. The theme of one of these was decidedly of a convivial nature. The discourse ran on eating, and the question was mooted as to which was the best dish. The king quoted the Hungarian proverb: "Nothing is worse than cheese" (*Habere nihil est pejus caseo*). This, of course, was denied by many, who maintained that cucumbers, apricots, and many varieties of fish were far worse than cheese. Every one was amused when the king explained the double meaning of the saying that "Nothing is worse than cheese" being equivalent to "Cheese is better than nothing." It happened, however, often enough that grave scientific propositions or Scriptural themes were under discussion, and, on such occasions, the king would send to his library for books calculated to support the soundness of his statements or argument.

This library was the king's chief glory and pride. It contained on his accession to the throne but a few volumes, but in the course of time it so increased in the number of books as well as their value, that it brought to the king even greater fame than his successes on the battle-field—not only in the age he lived in, but during the ages that followed. Over a hundred specimens of those books are still in existence, and from these we can form an adequate idea of its magnificence and richness. The library was in the castle of Buda, and the place assigned to it comprised two large halls, provided with windows of artistically stained glass, opening into each other. The entrance consisted of a semicircular hall commanding a magnificent view of the Danube. Both halls were provided with rich furniture. One of them contained the king's couch, covered with tapestry embroidered with pearls, upon which he spent his leisure hours reading. Tripod-shaped chairs covered with carpet were placed about, recalling the Delphian Apollo. Richly-carved shelves ran along the walls and were curtained with purple-velvet tapestry, interwoven with gold. It would be difficult to describe properly the magnificence of the books themselves. They were all written on white vellum and bound in colored skins, ornamented with rose-diamonds and precious stones and with the king's portrait or his arms. The pages are illuminated with miniature paintings and ornaments, vying with each other in excellence, and the work of some of the most famous illuminators of the age. At the time of the king's death there were over 10,000 such volumes in the library.

The king permanently employed at his court thirty transcribers and book-painters, and also gave occupation to Florentine and Venetian copyists and painters, who sent the volumes when finished to Buda. Although the art of printing had been already invented, yet its productions appeared so primitive when compared with these splendid works of art, that the collectors preferred having their books written and painted by hand. It was, to be sure, much more expensive. King Matthias spent over thirty thousand florins annually on his library, a sum equivalent in present currency to considerably over half a million of florins. He lavished larger sums even on architects, painters, sculptors, carvers, and goldsmiths. A whole army of artists were kept busy at his court, especially after his second marriage. During the first years of his reign he was content with the edifices and art memorials inherited from his ancestors, but the arrival of the new queen entirely changed the old modes of life. The habits of life which had been familiar in Italy long ago, with brilliancy, good taste, and wit in their train, were now domesticated on the banks of the Danube. The royal bride was a child of the sunny clime of Naples, a city which was one of the first to foster the new civilization. King Matthias had both the ambition and the ability to effect such changes in the royal residence, before the arrival of his bride, as would make her feel at home in Buda. Long before the new queen was to come, Buda presented a busy scene. The royal palace was enlarged and embellished. Its court-yards were beautified by bronze statues and sculptured marble fountains, and the ancient plastering gave way to porphyry and marble columns. The sides of the staircases were ornamented with frescoes, and from the niches statues of antique style peeped at the passer-by. Costly new tapestry covered the walls, and splendid carpets were spread on the floor of the wide vestibules, stately halls, and roomy chambers, which were filled with sumptuous furniture. The walls were hung with paintings representing heroic events or themes from ancient history or from the Scriptures. Modern carved furniture took the place of the old pieces, and every thing seemed to breathe a new life and to be rejuvenated.

The vaults gave up their old treasures, and new ones were added to the collections. Immense buffets were groaning under the weight of silver and gold, while antique gems, statuettes, and groups of vases were displayed on small tables and in sideboards with glass doors. The palace became a very museum of exquisite objects of art. We can picture to ourselves the vast main hall of the castle, with its peculiar mediæval splendor and brilliancy, in which the marriage took place in December, 1476. The walls of the hall were tapestried with silk interwoven with gold, and strewn with pearls and precious stones, and over the table of the bridal pair a tapestry of sheer gold came flowing down from the ceiling. In the centre of the hall, in front of the king's table, stood a buffet with four faces, each side containing eight shelves loaded down with enormous silver pitchers, cans, goblets, tankards, amphores, and glasses of every description. On this buffet, alone, there were over five hundred vessels, besides two unicorns, which ornamented the lowest shelf, and which weighed seven hundred marks of silver. A gigantic fountain of silver of artistic design, in the centre of the hall, spouted fiery wines. It was so high that a tall man could hardly reach its top. Near the fountain was a bread-basket of solid silver. Further on, silver casks were suspended from the ceiling dispensing various wines. The hall contained eight more tables, and by each stood a buffet weighed down by gold and silver vessels. Over nine hundred vessels and plate of all kinds were arrayed on the shelves of these buffets without being used. The vessels and plate on the table of the royal couple were all of pure and massive gold. Nor were the other palaces or summer residences, in which the court dwelt, inferior in splendor. The permanent seat of the court was the castle of Buda, but it was frequently shifted to Visegrád, Tata, Presburg, and Vienna, everywhere displaying the same pomp and sumptuousness. These royal residences appeared like real fairy castles, with their hanging gardens, fountains, fish-ponds, aviaries, game-parks, small pleasure-houses, arbors, and statues. Visegrád, became especially famous. One of the papal legates, a man of taste and education, and a great lord, used to sumptuous living, speaks of Visegrád, in a communication to the Pope, as an earthly paradise created anew by the hands of King Matthias.

Within this brilliant network of royal palaces pulsated the busy court life, with a frequent exhibition of exceptional gayeties and splendid feasts. The court was always thronged with the relatives of the king, with captains of the highest rank, and with hundreds of courtiers, from the chancellor down to the humble attendant, and great lords and high prelates, with their courtly trains, gathered around the king, hoping for advancement of one kind or other. The court was also a favorite resort for foreign diplomatists, who came for the purpose of settling questions relating to politics, church, or family concerns, and delivering messages of respect and homage to the king, whose strong arm was able to restrain and check the Turks, the Germans, and the roving bands of marauders. By degrees the Hungarian court took on a European, or cosmopolitan air, becoming more and more refined, gaining also the repute of being a seat of classical learning and culture. There was both compliment and truth in the remark made to King Matthias by his antagonist, Uladislaus, the Czech king, at one of the brilliant feasts given by the former: "Your Majesty, it is difficult to triumph over a king who is the possessor of so much treasure."

It was a great misfortune that Matthias died without leaving a son to succeed him, for all the accumulated splendor and culture vanished with the king who had introduced and developed them. It was at the zenith of his glorious career, while he was pondering on far-reaching plans for the future, that death surprised him. On Palm Sunday of the year 1490 he attended divine service, and, on returning from church, he was suddenly seized with extreme lassitude. He at once called for figs. They were brought, but on finding them mouldy, he angrily rejected them. Soon after he was overcome by dizziness, and a fit of an apoplectic character deprived him of the power of speech and memory. He expired on the 6th of April, after an illness prolonged for two days.

CHAPTER XI.

THE PERIOD OF NATIONAL DECLINE, AND THE DISASTROUS BATTLE OF MOHÁCS.

WE are now approaching one of the darkest pages in the history of Hungary. The nation which but thirty-five years before had occupied a commanding position in the world, had, within that short space of time, sunk so low as to become merely a bone of contention for foreign princes. The concluding act of that sad era was the calamitous battle fought on the field of Mohács, where were expiated the many national sins which had brought about this sorrowful state of things.

The period following the death of the great king was marked by feeble rulers; by hierarchical chiefs, unmindful of their duties; by an oligarchy acknowledging no restraints; by a military organization rotten to the core; and by discontented subjects. So rapidly did the fame of the nation decline that we find Erasmus of Rotterdam envying their king, Louis, the possession, not of his kingdom, but of an eminent teacher (Jacob Piso) then living there. The power of the king was even at a lower ebb than that of the nation. We find, for instance, John Szapolyai (or Zápolya), the head of the oligarchy, daring to attack King Uladislaus at the latter's own palace at Buda, in order to force from him the hand of Anna, his daughter. King Louis, the successor of Uladislaus, was told to his face by Thomas Bakacs, one of his councillors, at a meeting of the National Assembly, that, unless he acted according to the wishes of his councillors, and listened to their advice, they would drive him from the country, and elect another king in his place. These incidents clearly denote the character of the rulers, and of the leading men of the nation, whose province it was to defend the country against an enemy which the great Hunyadis themselves had hardly been able to withstand, namely, the Turkish power, and the ruinous effects of their misrule became evident soon enough. In rapid succession followed one loss of territory after another, coupled with loss of prestige abroad, and civil strife within, and shortly afterwards came the crowning disgrace of the Turkish yoke. It is but right to add that this melancholy period was not quite barren of good men, who both knew and strove to do their duty, and it will be a grateful task to make honorable mention of these noteworthy exceptions.

The partisans of four hostile candidates met on the 17th of May, 1490, on the field of Rákos, for the purpose of electing a king of Hungary. The National Assembly, at that period, greatly resembled the popular meetings held by the conquering Hungarians under the Árpáds. They gathered on horseback, numbering many thousands, on some extensive plain, taking counsel with each other, or, rather, listening to the utterances of their party leaders. These assemblies continued their so-called deliberations at times for many weeks, and their attendance entailed no little expense to those taking part. Many of them came with a large retinue of servants, and it frequently happened that the poorer members, the so-called middle, running short in provisions and money, were compelled to leave for their homes before the deliberations were concluded. This was precisely what happened on the present occasion. The powerful magnates purposely wasted time by delaying the deliberations, and thus compelled the smaller gentry to withdraw. Before leaving, however, these last elected sixty members from their number, who were to remain as representatives, but it was of no avail, for their party was defeated, owing to the withdrawal of such large numbers. This time the stratagem of the oligarchy proved more successful than at the former election, when, as we have seen, the impatient smaller gentry, who were greatly in the majority, succeeded in electing their candidate, Matthias Hunyadi.

Of the several candidates, John Corvinus, the son of King Matthias, had few adherents and many enemies. It was accounted a crime in him that he was not descended from a queenly mother. Beatrice, the widowed queen, was especially opposed to his election. She could not bear the idea of her husband's son ascending the throne. She flattered herself, besides, with the hope of being able to retain her regal position by the election of a prince who would make her his queen. With this view she became the partisan of Maximilian, the son of the emperor of Germany, and advanced his interests with the passionate vehemence characteristic of the Italian blood which ran in her veins. Her partiality for the imperial prince, however, soon gave way to feelings of disdain, upon being addressed by him, in one of his letters, as his "dear mother," and she transferred her affections to Ladislaus (styled by the Hungarians, Uladislaus), king of Bohemia. Her new favorite was descended, through the female line, from the Árpáds. The wealthy and influential magnates were also on his side, but with them the fact chiefly weighed in his favor that he was understood to be a kind-hearted, gentle, and feeble prince, whom it would be easy for them to govern. Both Báthory and the oligarchy wanted no king but a royal tool. Albert, the brother of Uladislaus, was the fourth aspirant for royal honors.

The States-General not being able to agree upon any one of the candidates, they at last resolved that he who should obtain the vote of Szapolyai, governor of Vienna, should become king. This decision greatly elated the party of John Corvinus, for as soon as they learned that the election of their candidate depended upon Szapolyai's decision, they felt assured of his triumph. They could expect no less of the man who, from having been twenty years ago a common trooper—at Visegrád—had been raised to his present exalted position by King Matthias. Szapolyai received in Vienna the deputation which had come to invite him to elect the king. In the consciousness of his power, the proud upstart lifted up his little boy, who afterwards became king of Hungary, and placing him upon his knee, said: "Wert thou, my boy, but that tall, I would make thee king of Hungary." This unscrupulous man was not inclined to obey a master, and, knowing that he himself had no chance of royalty, he preferred a weak king, such as he believed Uladislaus to be, and, in consideration of a large reward, he sold to him the throne.

The result of the election greatly disappointed and surprised the middle classes. John Corvinus himself was at first at a loss how to act, but finally determined to retire to the southern part of the country and to take with him the crown of St. Stephen, which was in his hands. Six thousand men ready to do battle for his cause accompanied him, and an occasion for the display of their zeal soon presented itself through the treachery of Stephen Báthory and Paul Kinizsy. These faithless favorites of the late King Matthias had promised him, on his deathbed, to stand by his son, and now, instead of redeeming their sacred obligation, they turned traitors to the cause they had vowed to defend. They were the first to assail the son they had promised to support. They came up with him in the county of Tolna, scattered his troops, and not only took from him the crown, but robbed him also of his personal treasures. John Corvinus himself became afterward reconciled to the new order of things, and, at the coronation, it was he who presented the crown to his more fortunate rival. A deputation was sent to Uladislaus, to invite him to the throne of Hungary. He received them most graciously, kissing each of them in turn, and crying with joy. In the month of August the newly elected king made his triumphal entry into Buda, accompanied by a gayly dressed cavalcade, and no one could have anticipated that the brilliant pageantry displayed on that occasion would be followed so soon by a series of humiliations terminating in a national tragedy.

The remaining rival candidates, however, were not disposed to consider their cause as lost. Each of them wanted his share of the kingdom, which was now become an easy prey to its neighbors, and the borders of Hungary on the east and west were simultaneously crossed by enemies. A few months had hardly elapsed since the death of Matthias, the great king, and Albert, Duke of Poland, brother to Uladislaus, was already laying waste the country to the east as far as Erlau (Eger), while the horsemen of Maximilian were tramping at Stuhlweissenburg over the grave of Matthias, and making booty of his treasures. Uladislaus remained inactive in the face of these outrages committed by Maximilian. He finally concluded a most humiliating peace (which to him seemed advantageous), by the terms of which all the former conquests of Matthias were to revert to Maximilian. The true patriots blushed at the news of the disgraceful treaty, and all the comfort they could obtain from the king was his favorite ejaculation, "Dobzse, dobzse." (It is all well, it is all well.)

Whilst the country was pursuing its downward course, the Czech attendants of the king were incessant in their clamors against poor Hungary. They complained that if they did not wish to starve they would soon have to leave the country. The king himself had not money enough at his disposal to provide for the ordinary expenses of the royal household. And yet the taxes were as high, and even higher, than during the reign of Matthias; nay, the chronicles of the time tell us that the people were better off under that Matthias who arbitrarily imposed taxes, than now under Uladislaus. In truth, the many burdens which were now weighing down the people were owing to the desire of many in high places to enrich themselves. The disorders of the time afforded a rare opportunity of doing so with impunity. It happened, though, at times, that the mismanagement of such greedy men would leak out, as in the case of Lukács, bishop of Csanád, and Sigismund Hampr, bishop of Fünfkirchen (Pécs), who were both treasurers of the realm, and whose fraudulent transactions were discovered. But the king was too weak to visit their crimes with condign punishment, and amongst the great of the land none were disposed to throw the first stone at the criminals. The impotence of the king caused the decline of the national strength, the ruin of the finances, and, as a natural consequence, the complete disorganization of the military institutions.

In this connection we have to record a strange encounter which took place in 1492 in the vicinity of Halas, in the county of Pesth. Paul Kinizsy, the terror of the Turks, the general who had grown gray on victorious battlefields, met there, in hostile array, the army he himself had formerly commanded, the famous "Black Guard" of Matthias. This very army, with their brave old leader, had a few months earlier repulsed the Turks near Szöreny. After this victory the soldiers demanded the pay which had long been in arrears. As usual on such occasions, tumults and disorders broke out in consequence of this failure to keep faith with the troops. The wisdom of the Hungarian National Assembly knew no better remedy than to instruct Kinizsy to march against the exasperated men. The old general obeyed orders. Seven thousand men were massacred, and the remainder, flying to Austria, dragged out their weary lives as robbers, constantly at war with the law. This cruel and impolitic measure deprived the nation, at a time when she was preparing for the life-and-death struggle against the formidable power of the Turks, of one of her main supports, in destroying that army which alone could have saved her. For Kinizsy, the former miller-boy, this was the last campaign, for very soon after he was stricken with paralysis and deprived of the power of speech. His contemporaries saw in this a punishment decreed by Providence for the part he had played on that bloody occasion.

The better part of the nation soon grew restless under this state of things, and a party arose which was hostile to the king. Stephen Verböczy was the leader of the new party. He was a thorough patriot and a skilled jurist, well versed in legislation. He was highly esteemed by the middle class, in whom he saw the only element which would restore to his country the universal respect she formerly enjoyed. This party aspired to the government of the land, and their choice of a ruler fell on Stephen Szapolyai, the son of John Szapolyai. If Stephen had not been, in 1490, still a child, his father would then have made him king. That he should become king was the highest ambition of his mother Anna, Duchess of Teschen, a woman more ambitious even than her son, and of whom it is said that she invariably concluded her daily devotions with a special prayer to God, asking that she might be permitted to live to see her son ascend the Hungarian throne. Szapolyai himself did not consider it an arduous task to accomplish this, for he argued that it was a precedent in his favor that Matthias, who was of no more exalted origin than himself, had become king. His partisans first tried to attain their end by marriage, and with this view Szapolyai asked of Uladislaus the hand of the young Duchess Anna. Uladislaus refused to accede to his request, and sought protection against the vaulting ambition of the national candidate in an alliance with the emperor Maximilian. The idea of a treaty of marriage between the two reigning dynasties was broached. The national party answered by convoking the National Assembly on the field of Rákos and passing the important law that, in case of the extinction of the male branch of the dynasty, they would elect a native king only. In the meanwhile Szapolyai renewed his wooing, and he was all the more confident of accomplishing his object, as Uladislaus was then seriously sick and still remained without any male issue. But Uladislaus could not be moved to reconsider his refusal. He told Szapolyai that he trusted to God that he would recover his health, and that a male child might yet be born to him. Nor was he disappointed in his hopes. He regained his health, and shortly afterwards his queen bore him a boy who reigned, at a subsequent date, under the title of Louis II.

Uladislaus now perceived the bearing of the Rákos resolution and, in consequence, entered into a new treaty with Maximilian. Under its terms Ferdinand, a grandson of Maximilian, was to marry Uladislaus' daughter Anna, whilst another grandchild of Maximilian, Mary, was betrothed to Louis, the boy just born. By virtue of this treaty Ferdinand, Archduke of Austria, took possession of the throne of Hungary after the fatal day of Mohács. This new alliance, however, did not deter Szapolyai from his bold purpose. Twice again he tried to gain Anna's hand, forcing his way into the presence of Uladislaus, but it was all in vain. His partisans now began to meditate the policy pursued by them later on, namely, to resort to Turkish friendship for assistance. The present state of things had become so intolerable, that the national party recoiled from no measures, however extreme, to bring about a change. One day a wicked hand sped two balls into the palace of Uladislaus; the king escaped, but to this day the suspicion of the foul deed rests on the adherents of Szapolyai.

The desperate contentions of the two parties gave frequent rise to lawlessness and stormy scenes. The nobility laid waste each other's estates and often even took unlawful possession of them. In this way many a castle which John Corvinus had inherited from his father passed at that time into the hands of Szapolyai. Duke Ujlaky ventured even to molest the royal domains, and upon being called to account for this by the king, Ujlaky disdainfully styled him an ox. The offended king, in order to avenge this affront, sent an army against him under the lead of Bertalan Drágfy, the vayvode of Transylvania, with the message that the king's second horn was now growing, and that henceforth the king would fight his unruly subjects with two horns. Szapolyai, the palatine of the kingdom, offered to intercede; the intercession, however, being nothing but a cloak to incite the people to rebellion against Uladislaus, the latter was compelled to yield, and to pardon Ujlaky. A most disgraceful brawl, such as is usually witnessed only amongst the drunken rabble, took place in the very presence of the king in the royal council-chamber. George Szalkán, the primate of Hungary, allowed himself to be carried away, during a heated discussion with Christopher Frangepán, to such an extent as to seize the latter by the beard, whereupon he was struck in the face by Frangepán. The king, by personally interfering, put an end to these most unparliamentary proceedings.

A dangerous movement was at this time gaining strength throughout Europe. The peasantry, weary of the servitude in which they were held, resorted to arms against their former oppressors. In Hungary, especially, this movement assumed ominous proportions. The rebellion broke out in 1514, and was commonly called either the Kurucz rebellion, from the fact that those who took part in it were originally intended to be soldiers of the cross (cruciferi), or, after the name of their leader, the Dózsa rebellion.

Julius II., one of the most distinguished popes, died at Rome in 1513. Amongst the aspirants to the papal see we find a Hungarian archbishop, Thomas Bakacs. He is said to have spent fabulous sums in the eternal city to further his object. In order to ingratiate himself with the populace he had his horses' feet shod with silver shoes, but so loosely that they were dropped on the road and picked up by the people. Being unsuccessful at the papal election, he begged of the new pope, Leo X., to be allowed, as a solace for his disappointment, to organize a crusade against the Turks on his return to Hungary. The arrival of Bakacs was the signal for a fierce struggle in the ranks of the Diet. A portion of the oligarchy, who hoped to derive some profit from this venture, warmly advocated his scheme, while by others, who were too much burdened already, it was violently opposed. Stephen Telegdy, the keeper of the treasure, stood at the head of the latter and threw the whole weight of his authority into the scale in order to prevent the passing of the law sanctioning the crusade. He vividly pictured the miserable condition of the peasantry, and resolutely objected to providing them with arms, saying that it would be equivalent to arming their own enemies. The law was passed in spite of this remonstrance, and the crusade was proclaimed on the 16th of July, 1514.

The condition of the Hungarian peasants at that period was a most wretched one. Those who inhabited the border were beggared by the incessant plundering expeditions of the Turks, while the remainder fared hardly better at the hands of their lords. Their masters were always in need of large sums of money to cover their enormous expenditures. A German contemporary, who lived for some time in Hungary, wrote of the landed gentry that they were in the habit of spending whole nights in riotous living, and passing the days with sleeping off the effects of their nocturnal orgies. The money required for this mode of life had to be wrung from the hard labor of the poor peasant, who was also weighed down by other burdens. The Hungarian nobility enjoyed privileges only; their shoulders knew no burdens. It was the peasantry who paid all the taxes, who had to pay out of their hard-earned farthings tithes to support the clergy; and over and beyond all this, they had to provide for their lords and masters. The peasant had to till the soil if he did not wish to starve, and in time of war he was compelled to ransom himself from military service. Against oppressions on the part of his lord he had no remedy, for his master was his judge. The lords' tribunal sat in judgment over the peasant, and it can be easily imagined what kind of justice was meted out to him.

Such was the sad condition of the peasantry when the crusade was proclaimed. No wonder that the oppressed peasants flocked in great numbers into the camps ready to exchange the abject drudgery of their daily life for the perils of crusading. A large portion of the nobility were from the first arrayed against this movement, all the more so as it happened during the season when there was most work to do in the field, and it was very difficult for them to get along without the laborers. The peasants looked with indifference upon the distress of their masters, and deserted them in daily increasing numbers to take up the holy cross. Bakacs had already provided a leader for them, singling out for that position a simple gentleman from Transylvania. His name was George Dózsa, a name which, coupled with a doubtful fame, will, nevertheless, continue to figure for all times in the history of his country. Hungarian historians of our days are fond of ascribing to him high and patriotic schemes, and love to portray him as a hero in the cause of liberty and one animated by a lofty spirit. Yet, if we attentively scan his actions, we are compelled to admit that he was little better than a brave and desperate peasant, whose whole conduct proves him to have bitterly hated the nobility. Nor was he indebted to any great qualities for the distinction he had won. His chief merit consisted in being a bold man, of a fine and martial appearance, in possessing a voice fit for command, and in having a few years before, in a skirmish, cleft in twain a Turkish pasha. The officers placed under him were for the most part poor nobles like himself, together with a few citizens from Pesth, and a certain Lawrence Mészáros, a priest from Czegléd. In a few days there were collected at the camp of Pesth no less than 40,000 men, who were to be marched against the Turks. But the army did not need to go so far to find an enemy—namely, their old oppressors, their Hungarian masters. The more hot-headed amongst the peasants were haranguing the others with vehemence, exciting their passions. Their chief, Dózsa, was himself swept into the new movement. Bakacs himself became terror-stricken at the direction things were taking. He called upon Dózsa to lead the army to their place of destination, and as the latter hesitated to obey, he was placed by this high church dignitary under the ecclesiastical ban. Dózsa, in answer to the archbishop's anathema, changed his programme, and led his men against the nobility. The struggle was short but bitter. It was fear rather than the badly armed troops of peasants that, at first, defeated the great nobles.

As soon as the first shock was over, every member of the nobility felt that to avoid the general ruin of all, they must stand together, in a well organized force. They gathered under the leadership of Stephen Báthory, the chief Comes (count) of Temes, and Nicholas Csáky, bishop of Csanád, but were destined to meet with yet another defeat. The cruelties then perpetrated by the blood-thirsty peasantry beggar all description. They overran the whole country, burning one castle after another, and massacred, by the light of the flames, all the noblemen with their families who were so unfortunate as to fall into their hands. Stephen Telegdy, who had so vehemently opposed the crusade, himself lost his life in this shocking manner, and Nicholas Csáky was captured on the battle-field, and was, to the delight of the whole camp, killed with torture.

Dózsa now proceeded to lay siege to Temesvár. He had singled out this fortified place as the point from which he would conquer the country for his peasants, but at this very spot he had to learn by painful experience that it was not an easy task to cope with the established power, no matter how demoralized for the time it be. The factions, admonished by the common peril, ceased for the time their party strife, and the chief Comes of Temes, a partisan of the king, did not hesitate to invoke the support of John Szapolyai, the vayvode of Transylvania, who was the leader of the national party. The vayvode, together with a strong force of the yeomanry of Transylvania, came to his assistance, and the struggle soon approached its termination. At the first engagement the army of Dózsa was utterly defeated, those who survived were scattered, and the leader with a few of his companions was taken captive. The savage work of retaliation now followed. The vayvode Szapolyai was the president of the tribunal. The victory he had achieved raised his authority with the nobility, who looked upon the late struggle as a war waged for their extermination, and he thought it would add to his glory if he presented to the excited nobles a harrowing spectacle. Mercy was shown only to Gregory, the brother of George Dózsa, inasmuch as he was merely beheaded. The remaining rebel leaders, including Dózsa, were thrown into prison, and were not permitted to taste any food for a fortnight. Nine of them still remained amongst the living. Dózsa was seated on a red hot iron throne, a red hot crown was placed on his forehead, and a red hot sceptre forced into his hand. Not a murmur of pain escaped him during this dreadful torture. Only when his famished companions in arms rushed upon him and tore the charred flesh from his body to appease their craving for food, he exclaimed: "These hounds are of my own training." This was the end of one of the episodes of this sanguinary domestic war. Four months of civil strife had cost the country the lives of 50,000 men. At a future period, not very distant, the nation might have made a much better use of these lives, but there seemed to be a fatality impelling the people to become their own destroyers. The Hungarian popular feeling has always sympathized with the peasantry in this bloody rebellion. Thus the story is, to this day, current amongst the people, that, as often as the Lord's body was raised, during mass, Szapolyai became maddened for a few minutes, because by his deeds he had rendered himself unworthy of beholding the sacred host. History, on the other hand, still cherishes the names of John Gosztonyi, bishop of Raab, and Gotthard Sükey, a captain from Pápa, of whom it is recorded that in order to scatter the peasantry with as little bloodshed as possible they loaded their guns with grass and rags instead of cannon balls. The 50,000 victims, however, did not suffice to appease the vindictive spirit of the victors, for in their opinion the crimes of the peasantry called for a sterner expiation. The crime of the fathers must be visited on all generations to come. The Diet, which met on the 18th of October, 1514, seemed to think that the peasants had been treated too mildly, and that all of them deserved death. The wise fathers of the land reflected, however, that if all were exterminated no one would be left to work for the nobles and to provide them with food and drink. They therefore let mercy prevail—but mercy as they understood it was the most refined cruelty. The peasants were to be allowed to live, but their life should become a calamity to them. The perpetual servitude of the peasantry was proclaimed, and it was ordained that they should be chained down to the soil.

This iniquitous law was passed and sanctioned by the king on the 19th of November, on the same day that he confirmed the celebrated *tripartite code* compiled by Stephen Verböczy, the Chief-Justice of the land. Truly a most remarkable contrast in legislation. On the one hand, a code which established law and order in the kingdom; on the other hand, the most inhuman measure in European history dictated by savage vindictiveness. Verböczy's tripartite code, or, as its title runs, "Decretum *tripartitum juris consuetudinarii*," is the most famous and the most important work of Hungarian jurisprudence, shedding also an interesting light on the social condition of the country at a remoter period. The *tripartitum* is a strong advocate of the privileges and immunities of the nobility. It establishes equal rights for all the members of the Hungarian nobility, acknowledging no difference between them except on grounds of personal merit. Every Hungarian noble accordingly was entitled to the privileges accorded to the whole body; he could not be deprived of his liberty without due conviction; above him there was but one lord and master, and that was the king, and he was exempt from taxation. It further limits the authority of the clergy over lay nobles, and denies the right of the Pope to the disposal of church benefices. After endeavoring in this manner to claim for the nobles independence as to those above them, the code at the same time tries to enlarge their rights as to those below them. The recent uprising of the peasantry offered a good opportunity for this tendency. It says: "The recent rebellion, aimed, under the pretext of a crusade, against the whole nobility, and led by a robber chief, has, for all days to come, put the stain of faithlessness on the peasants, and they have thereby forfeited their liberty and become subject to their landlords in unconditional and perpetual servitude. The peasant has no sort of right over his master's land save bare compensation for his labor and such other reward that he may obtain. Every species of property belongs to the landlords, and the peasant has no right to invoke justice and the law against a noble." This was the view taken by the nobility at that period, a view which they succeeded in forcing upon the feeble king.

The king, indeed was indifferent to the political and social changes which injured the best interests of the nation. His main purpose was to secure the throne to his family, and as long as he succeeded in this all the rest was "*dobzse*" to him. He had his sickly son crowned when he was but an infant of two years, and obtained for him the powerful protection of the imperial family. In 1506 his queen, Anna of Candal, an intelligent and energetic woman, the niece of Louis XI., King of France, died. The sorrow of the widowed king was boundless; for days he remained in his rooms weeping and moaning. Ten years later he followed the queen he had so much mourned, and his son, Louis II., succeeded him. Louis was a mere boy, but ten years old, when he ascended the throne, and his youth was another misfortune to the weakened and divided country. The events of his reign are usually summed up in one sentence: "He was prematurely born, married young, ascended the throne young, and died young." We shall, however, devote a larger space to this kind-hearted but unfortunate youth. Louis, as was stated, came prematurely into the world, and it required all the skill the medical science of the time afforded to keep alive the royal infant, who hardly breathed when he was ushered into the world. For weeks he was kept lying in the warm carcasses of animals slaughtered and cut open for that purpose, and in this manner was saved from death. But little attention was paid to his education during his father's life; it is reported that at a later period he blamed the latter for his neglect, and strove hard by redoubled exertions to make up for lost time. Although prematurely born he developed quite early in life, and was a tall and strong youth at the time his father died. Cardinal Thomas Bakacs, John Bornemisza, the castellan of Buda, and George of Brandenburg, Margrave of Anspach, were, by the king's last will, appointed his guardians. George became the ruin of the ambitious young king. The good lessons taught him by Jacob Piso, his excellent teacher, were set at naught by this guardian. He was not actuated by sinister motives in spoiling his ward; his conduct was the effect rather of a life-long habit of riotous living, of which he could not divest himself, and it was no wonder that the youthful king was quick to imitate the unworthy example. The more serious studies soon gave way to amusements of all kinds, and the boy-king spent his life in riding, hunting, and feasting, as long as his means would allow. Some of the frolicsome eccentricities recorded of him best illustrate his giddiness. He had among his courtiers a man named Peter Korogi, whose indestructible stomach was far-famed for its utter want of squeamishness. It was his great delight to summon before him Korogi, and see him devour living mice, cats' tails, carrion found in the streets, and inkstands with the ink in them. Poor Korogi lost his life afterwards at the battle of Mohács.

A glance at Louis' court and at his personal surroundings will suffice to give us a picture of the condition of the country. Uladislaus had already repeatedly complained that but a small portion of the revenues of the state ever reached his hands, and that his income during three years did not amount to as much as King Matthias used to spend on his clerks. Louis, who, besides, had to defray the expenses of his education, fared infinitely worse. He had to put off from day to day his journey to Prague, the capital of his Bohemian kingdom, because he was unable to procure the funds necessary for his travelling expenses. Things came to such a pass that the king could not provide decently for the royal table, which was all the more unfortunate for him, as he boasted of an excellent appetite; his contemporaries relating of him that when his resources permitted, seven meals were daily served at his court. His penury finally reached such a point that he lacked the means of paying the wages of his household servants, and then it was that a certain sum was set apart for royal expenses, to be paid into the hands of the treasurer and not of the king, a contrivance which was of little avail, the treasurers themselves being untrustworthy. King Louis remained as poor as he was before, and we read that at a reception given to the ambassadors of foreign powers, where the most brilliant display would have been in place, the young king sat on his throne in dilapidated boots. In spite of his poverty Louis found a way to indulge in pastimes and to squander money. At a time when they write of him that he could not call a sound pair of boots his own, he remitted to one of his courtiers a debt of 40,000 ducats in exchange for a trained falcon. George of Brandenburg wrote on one occasion that although the court was dreadfully poor, yet they managed to carouse all the time. These entertainments were marked by scenes and occurrences which but ill comport with the dignity of a court. The king was excessively fond of amusements, and on one occasion he wrote three months before the carnival: "Wherever we shall happen to be, even on a journey, we intend to make merry and to pass gayly our days." The carousing at the court, however, was not confined to the carnival season, for we read that on the very eve of the battle of Mohács, the king and queen were enjoying themselves right royally. The queen, too, was fond of gayeties. No one would have foretold of her that she should ever become so versed in matters of state. The difference between Mary the queen and Mary the widow might well elicit universal surprise. The eventful battle of Mohács sobered her. While her husband lived she so freely entered into the pastimes and frolics of the king that the partisans of the king himself were compelled to remind her more than once of the rules of decency and propriety.

A fierce struggle ensued between the oligarchical and the national party as to who should be selected for the royal council. This rivalry sprang by no means from patriotic motives, or from a desire to serve the country in the royal councils, but from the more sordid aim of making use of the royal authority to extend and increase their personal power and influence. The party leaders were still the same. Szapolyai and Verböczy stood at the head of the middle-class party, whilst the royal party, led by Báthory, made common cause with the Fuggers. The Fuggers were the Rothschilds of the sixteenth century; they had amassed immense wealth in Hungary by advancing at first an inconsiderable sum to the king, and obtaining for it the privilege of working the mines. They fraudulently exported from the land all the gold and silver obtained from the mines, while of the money advanced by them but very little got into the king's hands, as it had first to pass the hands of middle-men, who managed to keep large portions. In this way can it be accounted for that Thomas Bakacs' household was far more lavish and brilliant than that of the king himself, and that Count Alexius Thurzó, being in collusion with the Fuggers, was enabled at one time to advance to the king 32,000 florins. Emeric Szerencs' name figures most conspicuously amongst these money manipulators. He was a converted Jew, occupying a prominent position, and who subsequently became treasurer of the state. While he was never able to procure money for the treasury, he succeeded in constantly adding immense sums to his own fortune. The people at last rose against the unscrupulous treasurer, and attacked Szerencs in his own palace. He saved himself only with great difficulty from the fury of the populace by escaping through a window to which a rope ladder was attached.

The party of the nobility was at last victorious. At the Diet assembled at Hatvan 14,000 nobles assumed such a menacing attitude towards the government that all its members were compelled to give in their resignations, and Stephen Verböczy was elected by the triumphant party palatine of the kingdom. John Szapolyai became treasurer. To what extent the treasury was better managed under his direction it would be difficult to determine, for the sad fact remained that the treasury still remained empty, and that the new treasurer was constantly adding to the number of his estates and increasing his domain. The magnates as well as the burghers clearly saw that nothing had been gained by the change effected in the administration. They therefore combined to restore the former government, and were headed by the great nobles who had been deprived of their offices—Báthory, the late palatine, and Alexius Thurzó. The league is known in Hungarian history under the name of the "*Kalandos*" Society—the word "kalandos" having in the Magyar language the meaning of "adventurous," but in truth the word was derived from the "*Kalends*," the society being in the habit of meeting on the "Kalends," or first of each month. This patriotic band of would-be saviors of their country went on with their intrigues even after the news had arrived of another Turkish inroad threatening the country. The league at last succeeded. At the Diet convoked in Buda they reinstated their party in power. Verböczy himself was not slow in perceiving that he had been used by Szapolyai merely as a tool, and, refusing to be an instrument in his hands, he resigned the dignity of which he had been already deprived by the Diet. In order to save his life he fled to Transylvania, but he could not prevent the Diet from declaring him to be an enemy to his country.

Báthory occupied again his former position of a palatine, and announced his programme in these brief words: "We are not the cause of the ruin of the country"—a very strange assurance on the part of the councillors and leading statesmen of Louis II., coming too at a time when they were menaced on all sides by approaching perils. This conduct occasioned the papal nuncio's remark that "they were playing comedy with their mutual protests."

The Reformation added a new complication to the many dividing the nation, being a fresh source of discord amongst the people. This mighty religious movement spread as far as Hungary about the same time that it had won a large territory for itself in Germany. Here as there its adherents met with persecutions at the hand of the Roman Catholic Church. The new faith, although it had not gained large numbers, soon found its martyrs in the country. Both of the political factions were equally guilty of these persecutions, and we find a telling proof of this in the fact that Verböczy as well as Báthory, the respective palatines of the hostile parties, each had his share in the executions of the Protestants who laid down their lives for their faith. While Hungarian blood was thus shed by the Hungarians themselves, their proud neighbor, Sultan Selim, the mighty ruler of the Turkish empire, had registered a vow before Allah, in case he would vouchsafe victory to his armies over Persia, to build for his worship three magnificent mosques—one in Jerusalem, another in Buda, and a third in Rome. The sultan vanquished the Persians, but was prevented by death from fulfilling his vow. In Hungary they made merry, drinking death to the Turks, and little dreaming that the new sultan was destined to inflict upon them soon a most deadly blow.

Solyman the Magnificent succeeded the fierce Selim. He combined in his person the talents of a great warrior, a great legislator, and a great theologian. It was not long before the Hungarians themselves offered him an excuse for waging war against them. On his accession to the throne he had sent an ambassador to Louis II. for the purpose of prolonging the peace between them. The overbearing Hungarian nobles did not so much as enter into a parley with the envoy, but threw him into prison, dragged him with them all over the country, and finally, after cutting off his nose and ears, sent him back to his master. This dire offence against the law of nations, and the unprovoked insult to the sultan in the person of his representative, could not be left unpunished.

Solyman swore he would be avenged for this affront, and vowed he would get possession of that Belgrade which at one time had maintained its independence against the warlike genius of a Mohammed II. "He attacked simultaneously two of the strongest border fortresses—Shabatz and Belgrade. The king was just then too busy with his wedding with the Austrian princess Mary to allow himself to be disturbed by the hostile inroad, nor did his chief councillors take any heed of it. Báthory, the palatine of the kingdom, was also celebrating his nuptials, whilst Chancellor Szalkay's attention was entirely absorbed by the administration of the bishopric of Erlau that had been recently bestowed upon him.

Shabatz stood under the command of Simon Logody and Andrew Torma, both men of great heroism and rare courage. They shone out as conspicuous exceptions in this corrupt age. They preferred to face certain death rather than save themselves by deserting the fortress entrusted to their care, and solemnly swore to be true to the cause of the country unto death. They and their brave garrison kept their oaths faithfully; of five hundred men, but sixty were left on the 16th day of the siege. These sixty men were drawn up in soldierly array on the public square of the fort to receive the last assault of the Turkish army, and not one of them escaped with his life. Six weeks later Belgrade, the famous scene of Hungarian heroism, was taken by the Turks, and it is not often that an enemy achieved as easy a victory over such a stronghold as this border fortress as the Turks secured on the 29th of August, 1521. Francis Hedervári and young Valentine Török had been entrusted with the defence of Belgrade. These selfish nobles, unmindful of their sacred duties, left Belgrade and proceeded to Buda, in order to obtain from the government repayment for the expenses already incurred by them for the maintenance of the fortress. Failing in their errand, they did not return to their trust, but left the garrison, numbering seven thousand men, to themselves, under the command of their subordinate officers, the brave Blasius Oláh, and the treacherous Michael Moré. Their desertion sealed the fate of this fortress. Moré became a traitor to the cause of his country; he deserted to the enemy's camp, and, betraying to the Turks the weak points of the stronghold, he endeavored, at the same time, to prevail upon Oláh to aid him in his wicked designs. The patriotism of the latter, however, was proof against all the allurements of the tempter. The fall of the fortress was, nevertheless, unavoidable. The number of the garrison had dwindled down to seventy-two men, when a squabble ensued between those of them who were Hungarians and those who were Servians, which ended in their compelling Oláh to surrender the fortress. By the terms of the surrender the garrison was allowed to leave the fortress unmolested, but the Turks interpreted this clause in their own way. They were permitted to march into the Turkish camp, but on their wishing to leave the camp they were all of them massacred.

The fall of Belgrade spread terror all over the country—all the more as it was entirely unexpected, and certainly might have been prevented. Báthory, the palatine, and John Szapolyai stood, each with a great army, not very far from Belgrade; but these noblemen, obeying only the dictates of their mutual hatred, would not join their armies, and truly says the poet Charles Kisfaludy, that the deepest wounds inflicted upon the poor country were "no, not by her enemies, but by her own sons." Louis himself was roused from his lethargy upon hearing the sad news. He upbraided his councillors for neglecting to warn him of the dangers menacing the country, and for not having taken measures to avert them; nay, in his exasperation, as we are informed by his chaplain, he struck one of his councillors, Bishop Szalkay, in the face. Repentance was now too late, and the impending catastrophe seemed unavoidable. It is true that the Hungarians achieved one more victory in the Hungarian Lowlands. Paul Tömöry, the newly appointed archiepiscopal captain-in-chief of that section, defeated Ferhat Pasha on the field of

Nagy-Olasz, in Syrmia. But the passing glow of this success left no permanent effects; three years later the Turks were more formidable than ever to Hungary.

While the Hungarian Diet was the scene of fierce discussions, Francis I., King of the French, smarting under the defeat he had suffered at the hands of the Emperor Charles V., stirred up Solyman against Hungary and the Hapsburg crown-lands, in order to effect a division of the imperial army. In this scheme Francis I. succeeded so well that in the month of August, 1526, an army exceeding 300,000 men, with 300 cannon, under the lead of Solyman, was invading Hungary.

The news of Solyman's approach found the country unprepared. The treasury did not contain money enough to pay the messengers, still less to organize an army. A requisition of the gold and silver plate and vessels of the church was of little avail, for what little could be collected, owing to the resistance of the clergy, was appropriated again by the nobles, who were charged with the duty of coining them into money. Caspar Serédy owed his wealth to such transactions.

In soldiers they were even poorer than in money. The sultan was already crossing the southern frontier, and not a soldier was near King Louis. The cities bought their exemption from military service with money, and the great nobles were dilatory. The king finally marched alone against the enemy. The guilty were seized with shame at this noble example, and about the beginning of August four thousand men had already rallied round him. He was steadily proceeding southward and reached Mohács in the latter part of August. The army had swelled by this time to twenty-five thousand men, but it wanted a commander, and there was not in the whole country a single general capable of wielding large forces. The king, under these circumstances, had no other choice but to appoint, as commander-in-chief, Paul Tömöry, whose victory achieved over the Turks was still fresh in memory. Shortly afterwards the Turkish army, which had occupied Peterwardein (Pétervárad) a few days before, made its appearance. A serious discussion arose now whether the Hungarians should stand a battle, or, retreating first, join the army of Christopher Frangepán, coming from Slavonia, and that of John Szapolyai, marching from Transylvania. Tömöry was in favor of accepting battle at once, and was sustained by the king. Francis Perényi, the witty bishop of Grosswardein, on seeing that Tömöry's counsels had prevailed, is reported to have said: "The Hungarian nation will have twenty thousand martyrs on the day of battle, and it would be well to have them canonized by the pope." The battle took place on the 29th of August, on a fine summer's day. The Hungarians formed in battle array early in the morning. The king, surrounded by his lay and ecclesiastical magnates, occupied the centre. A thousand mailed horsemen were around the king, and in their midst John Drágfy, the Chief-Justice of the land, waving high up in the air the national banner. Seated on a white horse, he wore no spurs, according to the ancient custom, implying that flight to him was impossible.

Báthory, afflicted with the gout, rode with the king along the line of each troop, addressing words of encouragement to the men. The whole army impatiently looked forward to the moment when the battle should begin, and, finally, at five o'clock in the afternoon the Turks advanced. It was remarked that the king, on the silver helmet being placed on his head, became deathly pale, as if in anticipation of the near danger, but while it shocked the attendants, it by no means disheartened them.

The first onslaught came from the Hungarian horse, who rushed upon the enemy in front of them and drove them back. The Turkish troops thus attacked retreated without offering any resistance to the body of the army. The Hungarians, shouting victory, pressed on in hot pursuit, little dreaming that they were running into the jaws of sure destruction. The retreat was but a feint, for when the Hungarian army had been drawn on near enough to the Turkish centre, the retreating troops opened their ranks, and, through the gap left open, three hundred cannon and several thousand Janissaries poured a murderous fire on the advancing troops. The slaughter was dreadful; a large portion of the troops, including their commander and their standard bearer, fell at the first fire. The rest fled in every direction, but were greatly impeded in their retreat by a violent shower of rain which suddenly burst on the fugitives, among whom was also the youthful king. As he was trying to cross the Csele, a small brook, swollen by the rain, the horse, after reaching the opposite bank, stumbled backward into the waters below, and buried his rider under him.

The prophecy of Perényi was fulfilled. Twenty thousand martyrs strewed the field of Mohács, and among them was the witty prophet himself. The Hungarians paid the heavy penalty of thirty-six years' misrule and disorder, but the worst was yet to come. On the 10th of September there passed again a brilliant procession through the gates of Buda. This time it was not the crowned king of Hungary who made his entry into the fortress, but Solyman, who delivered it up for pillage to his soldiers. On this occasion was destroyed the famous library of Matthias.

CHAPTER XII.

THE TURKISH WORLD AND THE RISE OF PROTESTANTISM IN HUNGARY.

WHILE Islam was rapidly losing ground, and hurrying to irretrievable destruction on the peninsula south of the Pyrenees, it obtained a fresh foothold on another southern peninsula of Europe, in the regions of the Balkan washed by the Mediterranean Sea, and became there so powerful as to influence, for nearly five centuries, the political destinies of the Western world. At the same time that the power and culture of the Moorish state was declining in Spain, Europe found itself assailed by another Mohammedan nation, the Turks, who, taking up the standard of the crescent, attempted to force upon the Christian world their new ideas, religious, political, and social. On the first appearance of the Turks on the Balkan peninsula, they were met by the two states which opposed their further advance, and the struggle with these began at once. The first, the Byzantine empire, was, however, at this time already an effete and tottering organization, an ancient and venerable ruin, and it was able to make but a feeble resistance. It retreated step by step before the Asiatic conquerors, who got possession, first, of its entire outlying territory, and finally captured (in 1453) the seat of government, Byzantium, the renowned city of Constantine. The second opponent which withstood the advance of the Turks was Hungary, a state which, though still young, had shown a sturdy national vitality, and successively reduced to vassalage the countries of the Balkan, and was steadily engaged in extending its influence and authority towards the East. The Turks could not dispose of Hungary as easily and quickly as of the enfeebled Byzantine empire. More than a century of nearly constant conflict had to elapse before the Hungarian supremacy in the regions of the Balkan was put an end to, and the Turks were able to penetrate as far as Mohács, and there to inflict a mortal blow on the independence of Hungary. During this struggle of a century and a half the name and fame of Hungary were perpetuated by many a brilliant feat of war, and by many glorious victories, and when John Hunyadi, the most formidable foe of the Turks, died, all Europe mourned his death as the loss of the great champion of Christianity. His son, Matthias the Just, one of the greatest kings of Hungary, whose memory is held in pious reverence by the Hungarian people to this day, following in the footsteps of his illustrious father, through his many triumphs, made his own name, too, hardly less formidable to the Turks. But Hungary, as the offspring of the Western Church, the Church of Rome, turned her looks, at that time, to the West rather than to the East, and Hungarian statesmanship was far more intent upon humiliating the emperor of what was then known as the Roman empire, than upon breaking down the power of the Turks. King Matthias captured Vienna, and made large conquests at the expense of the German empire, but he chastised the Turks only now and then, and never seriously thought of endeavoring to thoroughly crush the Turkish power. Under his feeble successors, the Turks, who easily recuperated from the losses of single battles, grew into a formidable power, which soon brought Hungary to the verge of ruin. We have described, in the preceding pages, the fatal battle of Mohács, fought on the 29th of August, 1526, in which the youthful King Louis II. opposed an army of hardly 25,000 men to Solyman's 300,000, to be swept away by the torrent of overwhelming numbers. To give an adequate idea, however, of this awful catastrophe in the annals of Hungary, we will add here that seven bishops and archbishops, thirteen lords of the banner, five hundred magnates, and many thousand nobles laid down their lives on the bloody battle-field.

The nation was seized with indescribable terror on learning the details of this dreadful calamity; entire villages were deserted by their inhabitants, who scattered in every direction. The widowed queen, finding herself utterly deserted in Buda, fled to Presburg, and the capital of Hungary, one of the finest cities of Christendom, which but a little more than a generation before had been made one of the chief centres of European learning and culture, passed, in less than two weeks after the fatal day of Mohács, without any resistance, into the hands of the victorious Solyman. The Turks sacked and set fire to the beautiful city, and all its magnificent buildings, save the royal palace, were destroyed by the flames. The victorious enemy met with as little opposition in ravaging and massacring in the country as they had encountered at the capital. There was no one to stay their devastations. The miserable peasantry still made some feeble attempts at defence; here and there a few thousand men collected at some fortified position to protect themselves and their families. Thus some 20,000 men retreated into the Vértes mountains, and, under the leadership of Michael Dobozy, entrenched themselves near the village of Marót, in a camp fortified by a barricade constructed of wagons. But the Turks had their guns carried up to the nearest eminence, and opened a fire on the occupants of the improvised wall. The peasants were struck with terror, and the undisciplined boors, the wailing women and children, deserted their sheltering wagons in despair. Dobozy, seeing that all was lost, mounted his gallant steed, and placing his young wife on the saddle before him, he sought safety in flight. The elated Turks fell upon the flying Hungarians, frightfully massacring their ranks. Among the fugitives, Dobozy especially attracted the enemy's attention, owing to the superiority of his armor, indicative of gentle blood, and more particularly because of the young woman he carried in his arms. They pursued him like bloodhounds. The distance between the pursuers and pursued gradually diminished, and Dobozy's horse began to show signs of exhaustion under the double burden. Wife and husband saw the fierce forms, eager for prey, draw nearer and nearer. Still there was a gleam of hope for them if they could reach the near brook, cross the bridge, and destroy it before their pursuers came up with them. They succeeded in gaining the bridge, but, alas, the flying peasants had already broken it off, and there was no other thoroughfare to the opposite bank.

All was lost now. Dobozy told his wife to fly by herself, whilst he would remain and stay with his own breast the progress of their pursuers. But the young spouse would not part from her loving husband, not even in death, and besought him to kill her rather than to expose her to the chance of falling into the hands of the pagan enemy. The desperate husband, seeing the Turks quite near to them, stabbed his youthful wife with his own dagger, and then, turning upon his adversaries, dearly sold his life. The spot where Dobozy and his faithful wife lost their lives is, to this day, called Basaharcz (the Pasha struggle).

The immense Turkish army spread all over the country, everywhere plundering, ravaging, and destroying defenseless lives, and reducing, in a war of a few months' duration, the population of the country by nearly 200,000 souls. The capital in ruins, hundreds of other places deserted and laid waste, the country without a king, the church without any higher clergy, the greater part of the nobility, used to arms, killed—such was the condition in which Hungary was left by the Turks at the departure of Sultan Solyman. In October, 1526, he left the doomed country, having first laden his ships, sailing for Constantinople, with the treasures of the palace of King Matthias—its rare curiosities, its bronze statues, and a portion of the famous Corvinian library.

The fatal day of Mohács had entirely overturned the order in the state, and amongst the magnates who survived it party strife soon broke out. One party, acting upon the conviction that enfeebled Hungary was unable to resist, unsupported, the overwhelming power of the Turks, elected a Hapsburg archduke, Ferdinand of Austria, a brother of Charles V., the Roman emperor, king of Hungary, and since that time the royal crown has, in fact, remained in possession of the Hapsburgs. It was through this dynasty that the Hungarian people endeavored to secure the aid of the German empire against the Osmanlis. But another party amongst the great lords pursued an opposite course. In their opinion a native dynasty and peaceful relations with the invincible Turks were the means of rescuing the country from her pitiable plight. These patriots, therefore, elected as king of Hungary, John Szapolyai, the vayvode of Transylvania, and the most powerful lord in the country, and thus the nation had now two kings in the place of the one who had fallen at Mohács.

But neither of these parties nor their royal representatives could save the country from the Turks; on the contrary, the continual rivalries between the two kings not only demoralized public virtue and upset all law and authority within the kingdom, but they assisted not a little the foreign enemy in getting into their possession, by slow degrees, the larger part of Hungary, and enabled the Turks, within a brief period, to float their crescent on the towers of Buda, and there, to the ruin of the nation, and to the perpetual terror of the Christian world, it continued to wave for nearly one hundred and fifty years. The history of the Hungarian nation during this entire period is sad in the extreme—a tragedy, the scenes of which are supplied by an uninterrupted series of trials and sufferings. Owing to the incapacity of the leading statesmen and generals, the ruin of the country became more and more irretrievable. Yet, however dark and forlorn this period may seem, the national sufferings of those days are relieved and brightened by the glorious heroism and patriotism displayed by the people. The Hungarians, although menaced, in their very existence, by many enemies, by party strife, and religious dissensions, exhibited such rare moral courage, heroism, devotion, self-denial, and manliness, that the memory of the generations of that melancholy era will remain forever hallowed.

Heroes arose on every side, and the struggle, sustained by the nation for nearly a century and a half against the oppressive power of the Turks, reminds one, in many of its features, of the protracted contest between the Spaniards and the Moors, and, like it, abounds in poetry, romance, and those noble examples of patriotism and loftiness of soul which kindle the human heart, arouse the sympathies of the poet, and are treasured up by the piety of after-ages as glorious relics of the past.

Solyman's ambitious schemes looked for still wider fields of conquest, and in 1529 he marched towards Vienna, in order to attack King Ferdinand in his own capital. The city, however, was successfully defended. In 1532 Solyman advanced again upon Vienna. The sultan's progress was unopposed until he reached Köszeg (German, Güns), in the neighborhood of the Austrian frontier. The keys of sixteen fortresses and fortified cities lay at his feet; Köszeg alone refused to do homage, and arrested the sultan's triumphal march. Michael Juricsics was its commander; he was just about to remove his small garrison, consisting of twenty-eight hussars and ten cuirassiers, to Vienna, for whose defence all the available forces were being called in, when the Turks appeared beneath the walls of Köszeg. On beholding the approach of the immense Turkish army, Juricsics took a bold and noble resolution. He determined to hold the fortress, and to die rather than surrender it to the enemy. He immediately took measures to defend the place; he repaired the walls and bastions, armed seven hundred peasants who had sought refuge in the city, and purchased with his own money gunpowder and provisions. The Turkish army arrived under the walls of Köszeg on the 5th of August, 1532; a few days later the sultan himself joined them, and the siege was prosecuted at once with the utmost energy. The outer fortifications had already fallen into the hands of the enemy, the guns and mines had effected a breach sixteen yards wide in the main wall of the citadel, of its seven hundred defenders half had fallen, and on the 24th of August Juricsics had but one hundred weight of gunpowder left. Yet the plucky reply he gave to the sultan's summons to surrender was: "As long as I live I will not surrender." The Turks thereupon directed a fresh assault upon the citadel, and the garrison again lost many lives, while Juricsics himself was wounded. The Turks pressed into the city, but the inhabitants, at their approach, broke out into such dreadful howling and wailing that the frightened assailants retreated, and the city was once more miraculously spared. But Juricsics himself saw now the impossibility of further resistance; he had no more gunpowder, and most of the garrison were like himself wounded. For the purpose, therefore, of sparing the lives of the remaining inhabitants, he finally permitted the Turkish flag to be hoisted over the city. Solyman, seeing the Turkish flag floating over Kőszeg, thought he had captured the citadel, and retired from under the walls on the 31st of August. But it was not towards Vienna that he directed his steps, but homeward. He had been delayed nearly four weeks near Kőszeg, and during this time a powerful army had been collected in Vienna which the sultan had not the courage to face. Juricsics had thus, by his heroism, saved Vienna from a siege, the issue of which might have been calamitous to that renowned city of Christendom.

Many were still found in other parts of the country to follow the stirring example set by Juricsics, but unfortunately success but rarely attended their devotion. Most of them were fated only to be martyrs to the sacred cause, shedding their blood on the altar of their tottering country. The farther the Turkish conquests extended the more precarious and perilous became the position of the isolated commanders of the Hungarian border fortresses. The safety of a whole territory or country often depended upon the possession of one of these strongholds. Thus were the wealthy mining towns and the entire Hungarian mining region protected by the fortified place of Drégel, and it naturally attracted the attention of the Turks, always thirsting for plunder, who hastened to lay siege to it, hoping, by its possession, to open the road to the mines. Gallant George Szondi, the commandant of the fortress of Drégel, was a determined and magnanimous man who, fully conscious of the great importance of the place, was ready to defend it with his life. The fortress itself was not one of the first order, and was guarded only by a small garrison.

In July, 1552, a Turkish army numbering about 10,000 appeared under the walls. Ali, the Pasha of Buda, himself a chivalrous and noble-minded soldier, stood at the head of the besiegers, and, under the fire of his guns, the bastions crumbled to dust in the course of a few days. When the great tower too, was but a heap of ruins, and the walls were showing wide gaps everywhere, and all hope of being able to continue the defence seemed to have vanished, Ali sent a message to the commandant of Drégel. He employed a clergyman by the name of Márton, the parish priest of a neighboring village, to go to Szondi and to tell him that: "Ali reverently bowed before Szondi's bravery and determined spirit, the report of which had reached him long ago, and of which he had had good occasion to convince himself during the present siege, but as the position could be held no longer, Szondi ought to preserve his heroic life and to surrender the crumbling fortress, and if this were done free departure should be guaranteed for himself and his people." Szondi silently listened to the message of Ali, whom he knew to be a noble and chivalrous foe, but manfully declined to lay down his arms. He was resolved to defend the place to his last breath, and rather bury himself under its ruins than negotiate with the enemy. But he in turn asked now a favor of Ali Pasha, not for himself, but for two youthful troubadours, two young bards who were in the fortress, and for whom the Hungarian hero wished to provide before his death. He had the youths dressed in purple velvet and sending them, under the care of Father Márton, to Ali Pasha, he requested the latter to take these youths—some say they were his own sons—into his service, as he himself would not be able to bring them up, and to make brave men of them. Then summoning into his presence two Turkish captives remaining in the fortress, he bestowed upon them rich presents and allowed them to depart.

As soon as Márton had left with his youthful charges Szondi felt that the supreme moment, the moment of a glorious death, was near at hand. He ordered his money, his clothes, and all his valuables to be taken into the courtyard of the citadel, and, for fear they might fall into the hands of the enemy, he himself set fire to them and saw them reduced to ashes. Then he directed his steps to the stables, and thrust with his own hands his lance through his horses, his noble war steeds. Hastening now to his few remaining soldiers he addressed to them touching words of farewell. Outside, the approach of the Turks, preparing for the assault and shouting Allah, was already heard. Szondi, at the head of his two companies, rushed to the citadel gate and there laid down his life after heroically defending himself. A ball having penetrated his foot, the dying man sank on his knees and continued the fight to his last breath. He was finally cut down by the Turks, who surrounded him on all sides; his head was placed on a lance and carried in triumph to the victorious Ali. The generous Turk was deeply moved by this noble example of self-sacrifice, and, having given orders to seek out Szondi's body, he caused his remains to be buried with great military pomp, in a neighboring hill. For a long time the spot where Szondi was laid into the grave was marked by a pike and a flag. One of the greatest poets of modern Hungary, John Arany, has perpetuated Szondi's story in a beautiful ballad, and contemporary piety has just erected amidst the ruins of Drégel a chapel in memory of the departed hero.

Stephen Losonczy, another Hungarian hero, who shared Szondi's fate a few days later, had no such noble opponent as Ali to deal with. Temesvár, the largest fortress in the country, was entrusted to his care.

Fifty thousand Turks marched on Temesvár, and having quickly reduced all the smaller fortified places and cities near it, they reached the fortress in an over-confident mood. Losonczy immediately sallied out to meet the enemy, and so intimidated them that they soon gave up the siege and left the neighborhood. Yet only for a short time; they returned in greater numbers under the leadership of Ahmed Pasha. The latter at once called upon the Hungarian commandant to surrender the fortress. Losonczy collected in the public square the garrison which numbered altogether 2,200 soldiers, of whom 1,300 were Hungarians and the remainder Germans, Czechs, and Spaniards, and asked them if they were ready to defend to death the fortress in their charge. The enthusiastic shouts of the soldiers—that they were ready to die rather than yield up the place—was the answer he received. Losonczy at once swore in his men, and immediately answered the summons of the Turkish pasha by a sally from the fortress, driving the enemy from the vicinity of the trenches.

The Turks now proceeded to lay regular siege to the fortress—a branch of military science in which they were highly accomplished. They were masters in the art of reducing fortified places, in the mining works, and in the handling of the great battering guns. Thirty-six guns of heavy calibre soon poured their shots into the fortifications, which after a couple of days exhibited such breaches that the pasha thought the time for an assault had arrived. Thousands of brave Janissaries rushed at the tottering walls. There, however, they were met by the guard, who, themselves ready to die, made a frightful havoc amongst their assailants. The assault was repulsed in a few hours, the trenches were filled with the Turkish dead, and many a distinguished bey and officer of high rank was left lifeless on the scene of the sanguinary contest.

Losonczy, however, saw that all the heroism of his soldiers was thrown away if he did not receive aid from abroad. He therefore applied to the commanders of the royal and Transylvanian armies for soldiers, gunpowder, and other war requisites of which he had run short, but could obtain nothing from them. In this strait he resolved to devote his own fortune to the cause of his country, and wrote to his wife, the high-minded Anna Pekry, who was outside the fortress, to turn all he had into money, to mortgage his estates, and, with the funds thus obtained, to hire soldiers, purchase munitions, and send them into the besieged fortress. The generous woman was ready to bring any sacrifice to assist her husband in his extreme distress, and, taking into her pay five hundred volunteers (hayduks) whom she provided with the necessary military equipments, she bade them march to the relief of Temesvár. But the place was already completely invested, and the small troop was unable to penetrate the strong blockading cordon of the Turks. The five hundred hayduks were dispersed by the enemy, the gunpowder was taken away from them, and now Losonczy gave up all hope of aid from without.

Yet the gallant commander never for a moment wavered in his duty. He wrote, in one of his last letters: "We are patiently looking forward to the moment when we must die," and all he asked of the king was to take care of his little orphans. The hour was not far off, for the long siege had already exhausted their ammunition and provisions, and the Turks were constantly renewing their assaults. Although the enemy lost at times three thousand men in one assault, they returned each day in still greater numbers and repeated the attack. St. Anne's Day arrived, the day of the patron saint of Anna, Losonczy's wife, which in brighter days he used to celebrate, according to ancestral fashion, by merry carousing, but it was now a melancholy day for the brave commander. The provisions and ammunition were all exhausted, and the Turks, after immense losses, had finally succeeded in occupying the large entrenched tower lying between the inner citadel and the town.

Hungry, without gunpowder, and with no hope of relief from abroad, Losonczy's soldiers began at last to mutiny, and, wishing to save their lives, they insisted upon the surrender of the town. The Spanish soldiers—the foreigners—especially demanded the giving up of the place, while the Hungarians declared that they were still ready to follow their gallant leader to death. The inhabitants of the town, reflecting that by a capitulation they might save their lives and property, whereas if the Turks entered the city by force of arms they would be shown no mercy, finally sided with the Spanish party and were bent upon making terms with the enemy. At first Losonczy would not hear of yielding, but when Ahmed Pasha's messengers appeared at the fortress and promised every one safe departure, besides the right of taking with him all his movables, the Spaniards compelled him to sign the capitulation.

So the brave soldier at last gave up the struggle, and, troubled by sad forebodings, he withdrew from the ruined fortress at the head of his decimated troops, who were still fully armed. Outside the gate he was received with military honors by the Turkish commanders. Losonczy was proceeding on his good horse through the ranks of the enemy which were in a line drawn up on either side, when suddenly there came from the Hungarians in the rear shoutings and cries. He turned back and saw that the Turks, in shameful disregard of the terms of capitulation, had fallen upon his pages and were pillaging them. The old warrior could not witness this disgrace unmoved; he drew his sword, once more the war-trumpet sounded the attack, and he rushed to the rescue of his men. The engagement became general and the small band was almost entirely cut down. Losonczy fearlessly braved death, and, bleeding from numerous wounds, was finally taken by the perfidious enemy, who, cutting off the hero's head, sent it as a token of triumph to Stambul. Thus, in 1552, passed Temesvár, one of the most important fortified places in Hungary, into the possession of the Turks. It remained longer under the Turkish yoke than any other Hungarian stronghold of importance, for thirty years elapsed after the reconquest of Buda before it was again restored to the possession of the king of Hungary.

Szondi and Losonczy might have been spared martyrdom if the commander-in-chief of the royal army, who were all foreigners, had, in their vanity, had the courage to attempt their rescue. They witnessed, sunk in cowardly inactivity, the deadly throes of these heroes, and looked on with indifference while one fort after the other was falling into hostile hands. These foreign commanders, with their armies composed of foreigners, were never able to cope with the Turks. If they ventured to engage in a battle they were sure to lose it. In this way can it be accounted for that in spite of the superhuman efforts of the Hungarians who heroically battled for their country, the Turkish conquests grew apace, and the flat portions of the land, the rich and fertile lowlands, passed under the rule of the Osmanlis. Transylvania, the eastern portion of the country, had struggled into a sort of independence, and severing herself gradually from the mother-country, had a separate state organization of her own under her native rulers, so that Hungary may be said at this time to have been cut up into three parts. The largest portion accepted the Turkish supremacy, Transylvania asserted its independence, and the remaining and smallest division acknowledged the kings of the Hapsburg dynasty, whose residence was in Vienna. The German, Italian, and Spanish troops employed by the latter, together with those by whom they were led, so far from being instrumental in the liberation of the country, indulged in the same licentious and lawless behavior as the Turks themselves. They were utterly ignorant of the language, customs, and institutions of the Hungarian people, and were entirely indifferent to the interests of the country. These irresponsible military bodies harassed and plundered the native population to such an extent that it was not long before the Hungarians came to hate the foreign soldiery, and the Germans in general, as much as they did the Turks.

But even during the most depressing days, and under circumstances of a most desperate and hopeless character, the spirit of heroism did not die out amongst the Hungarian people. Shortly after the reduction of Temesvár the immense Turkish army marched against Erlau. Stephen Dobó was the commandant of the latter place. He knew by the sad examples of Losonczy and Szondi what was in store for him, and, although the royal troops were near, he also knew, from experience, that he could not depend upon any help from that quarter, and must needs look to his own resources to stay the progress of the overwhelming forces of the Osmanlis. "We expect aid from God only, and not from men," he wrote at the approach of the enemy. He immediately took measures to defend the place; he laid in large supplies of ammunition, sulphur, saltpetre, and provisions, sent his lieutenant, Mecsey, a soldier worthy of his chief, into the adjoining counties to fire the hearts of the young men, and to invite them to enroll themselves amongst the defenders of the fortress. He made up his garrison of Hungarians only, knowing, from experience, that the foreign hirelings could not be trusted. He had altogether only nine guns and nine gunners, but he hurriedly drilled the students and the more intelligent amongst the peasants in artillery practice, and formed them into a separate corps of cannoniers. Having provided every thing in time, and placing his trust in God and his own strength, he calmly awaited the enemy.

No sooner had the immense Turkish army arrived, when Ahmed Pasha summoned Dobó to surrender the fortress. Dobó collected about him his men and publicly read to them the pasha's letter. The gallant Hungarian garrison shouted, as with one heart, that they would never surrender the place. Dobó, his fellow-officers, and all the men, then took a solemn oath to fight to the bitter end, and that, if any one but breathed about the surrender, he should be hanged on the pillar of the town well. As an answer to Ahmed's missive, Dobó caused to be placed upon one of the lofty towers of the bastion a large iron coffin with two lances, one of them floating the Hungarian flag, and the other the Turkish. This was to convey to the enemy that on this place either the Turks or the Hungarians must perish, and in order to give weight to his answer he sallied forth with part of his garrison that very night, and brought away from the besiegers a great deal of booty.

Ahmed retorted by opening a fire on the town and citadel from 120 guns, some of which sped balls of fifty pounds as far as the bastion, but eighteen days elapsed before the enemy could summon up sufficient courage to try an assault. It proved ineffectual, the assailants being gallantly repulsed by the Hungarians. A few days later a great calamity befell the denizens of the citadel. The powder magazine, struck by a hostile ball, exploded, and a portion of the wall of the citadel was thrown down by the explosion. Taking advantage of the wild confusion the explosion had created amongst the garrison, the enemy directed another assault against their works, but quite as ineffectually as before. They were driven back; Dobó had the wall repaired, and in the cellar vaults he established a gunpowder factory, which proved sufficient to furnish the necessary supply.

After several unsuccessful minor attacks, the Turks prepared for the great final assault. They came against the fortress in overwhelming numbers on every side, and already the garrison began to show symptoms of exhaustion and wavering. At that moment of supreme danger, however, the gallant defenders of the citadel obtained help from quite an unlooked-for quarter. Wives, mothers, and daughters armed themselves, and rushed to the walls to fight by the side of their dear ones. Some of these amazons robbed the dead of their swords, and rushed, thus armed, where the enemy was thickest; others brought boiling water and oil, and poured it upon the heads of those who attempted to scale the walls; and, with the help of these brave women, the assault was beaten back at the most dangerous points. The women of Erlau had a large share in the saving of the city, and the fame of their heroic devotion still survives in Hungary. The Turks were quite panic-struck; in one day alone they lost 8,000 men: and the soldiers loudly declared that God was fighting on the side of the Hungarians, and who could struggle against God? After a siege of thirty-eight days, the Turkish army at length withdrew, and Dobó and his brave men were left in possession of the now ruinous citadel, thus preserving it for their country. The glory of their daring deeds has passed into a common saying. Of any one accomplishing a great deed, the people say: "He has won the fame of Erlau." The place, nevertheless, passed under Turkish rule in 1596, its Hungarian commandant having been compelled by the foreign garrison to capitulate.

In 1566 Sultan Solyman, who, though old, was still full of vigor, placed himself at the head of a formidable army, and invaded Hungary for the sixth time, his object being to take Erlau and, eventually, to march against Vienna. On reaching, with his 200,000 men and 300 guns, Hungarian territory, he was met by the news that Mohammed Pasha, his favorite, together with his army, had been massacred by the Hungarians at Szigetvár. The aged sultan desired to avenge this affront at once. Szigetvár and its brave commander, Nicholas Zrinyi, had long since been troublesome to the Turks. Zrinyi, the scion of a most ancient family, had been engaged for years in constant fighting against the Moslem power, during those periods even when peace was officially established. His possessions and castles lay in the border territory, and the fearless man was ever at war with the Osmanlis, making them feel the weight of his irresistible sword. The storming of Szigetvár had been attempted once before, but the enemy had been beaten back with great slaughter. And now the great sultan determined himself to bring him to terms, and to invest in person the small fortress. Zrinyi was prepared for the worst, and calmly got ready to face the formidable foe. Szigetvár was not a fortress of the first rank, but only one of the minor strong places. The main feature of its strength was that it lay almost entirely surrounded by lake and marsh, the only road leading to the place being over the bridge communicating with the gate. In front of the citadel, on an island, was the old town, and south of it, on another island, the so-called new town. Szigetvár, therefore, consisted, in point of fact, of three places, each fortified, but differing from each other in the strength of their works of defence. The two towns were, in reality, advanced fortifications of the fortress itself. Without much aid from any quarter, Zrinyi undertook the defence of this small place. His own money purchased the necessary ammunition and military supplies; he filled the granaries with provisions, produced on his own estates, and from his cellar came the necessary wine. There was an abundance of provisions in the place, but there were not soldiers enough. When it became quite certain that the sultan was marching his whole army against Szigetvár, all Zrinyi could obtain from the king, after repeatedly urging his want of soldiers, was the permission to hire one thousand foot-soldiers. German soldiers, it is true, were offered to him, but those he did not want, preferring to select his troops from amongst the garrisons of his own castles, so as to have only tried men by his side. All the force he could muster to oppose to the hundreds of thousands of Solyman numbered, at the highest, 2,500 men. He had 54 guns and 800 hundredweights of gunpowder, and, what was worth more than all that, he and his men were inspired by the sublime resolve, rather to die on the field of honor than to submit to the cruel enemy, who had turned into a desert a large portion of their beautiful country. His soldiers worshipped their heroic leader, and enthusiastically pledged their devotion by oaths of fidelity and obedience.

On the 31st of July, 1566, the advance guard of the enemy showed itself. During the first few days several minor engagements took place, but the siege began in real earnest on the 7th of August. On that day the first assault was attempted; it was directed against the weakest point, the new town, but it met with no success. A few days later, however, Zrinyi himself deemed it expedient to give up the defence of this advanced position, and, after having set fire to the new town and reduced it to ashes, he abandoned it to the enemy. The besiegers immediately occupied it and erected their batteries, protected by bags and baskets filled with earth, and sacks of wool. The batteries were hardly ready when the Hungarians surprised them one night and destroyed them all. Chance, however, now favored the Turks. A drought had prevailed during two months, and the terrain surrounding the old town had become so dry, as considerably to facilitate the approach of the enemy. The besiegers attempted also to drain the lake surrounding the fortress, and planned to accomplish this by cutting through the great dam around it, so as to provide an outlet for the waters. The neighborhood of the dam became the scene of fierce struggles. The position was heroically defended by the Hungarians, while the Turks quite as heroically again and again returned to the attack. After a sanguinary contest lasting the whole day, the Turks finally took the old town on the 19th of August, and Zrinyi with his shrunken garrison entirely withdrew to the citadel, after having demolished the bridge leading to the old town.

Sultan Solyman, however, now thought that lives enough had been lost, and he therefore tried to get possession of the fortress by peaceable means. He tried Zrinyi with fair promises; he sent him messages that he would make him prince of Dalmatia, Croatia, and Slavonia, and tempted him with treasures and estates. Then he tried him with threats. The enemy had captured one of the trumpeters of Zrinyi's son, George. The trumpet found in the prisoner's possession had the arms of the Zrinyi family painted on it, and Solyman sent this trumpet to Szigetvár as a token that Zrinyi's son had been taken captive, and threatened that the prisoner would be cruelly executed unless the place was surrendered. Neither promises nor threats were of any avail. Zrinyi did not for a moment waver, but was steadfast in his determination to follow the dictates of duty and patriotism alone.

The wrath of Solyman at the wearisomeness of the siege knew no bounds. He had been patiently expecting day after day the reduction of the place, and finally, tired of further delay, gave the order for a general assault on the 29th of August. The superstitious sultan thought this a particularly lucky day, for it was the anniversary of the day on which he had taken Belgrade and of the battle at Mohács.

The aged ruler, who now, but rarely showed himself to his soldiers, mounted his favorite charger and appeared amongst the Janissaries, in order to rouse and encourage them. His troops rushed enthusiastically into the fight, for which the artillery and the engineers conducting the siege had made every preparation many days before. But Zrinyi was ready and wide-awake, and drove the assailants back with great slaughter. Aliportug, a Portuguese renegade, who was the enemy's most distinguished artillery officer and military engineer, and had conducted the siege of Sziget, lost his life during this engagement. The Hungarians, although they too had suffered severe losses, celebrated their triumph with bonfires and feasting. They now fondly hoped that their heroic resistance would at last induce the royal troops to come to the relief of Sziget, and to attack the exhausted troops of the sultan. Some negotiations to that effect had been carried on, but the result was as usual; the German commanders allowed the scanty garrison to perish.

The besiegers, after their last repulse, passed an entire week without renewing the attack. They employed this pause to lay unobserved a powerful mine under the walls of the bastion, which was fired by them on the 5th of September. The explosion shattered the walls, the bastion fell down, and a terrible gale carried the flames into the citadel in every direction. All the buildings were soon on fire, and the Turks too began a general assault. Hemmed in by the dreadful conflagration and the storming enemy, the Hungarians finally yielded. They retired from the outer fortification, and Zrinyi with his men—who had dwindled down to a few hundred—withdrew into the inner or smaller fort. Further resistance seemed now hopeless, yet Zrinyi did not think of capitulating. The cannon-balls of the enemy set on fire the smaller fort on the 7th of September. Zrinyi, in this extremity, had all his valuables, his thousands of gold and silver, his precious vessels and plate, brought into the public square of the citadel and cast into the flames. He then divested himself of his armor and helmet, donned a dolmány (a short jacket braided in front), and threw over it a dark-blue velvet cloak, placing in each of his pockets a hundred ducats as a reward to the man who should discover his dead body. He wound a costly chain of gold around his neck, in place of his helmet he put on his head a kalpag (a Hungarian fur cap), ornamented with a heron's feather and diamond rosettes, and, arming himself with a curved sabre and a light shield, he took with him the keys of the citadel, to make sure that they should pass into the enemy's hands only upon his death. In this attire he appeared before his men, who were assembled in the courtyard. He addressed them in a speech full of his generous spirit, "lauding them for their gallant conduct, which would earn for them the respect of the Christian world and of generations to come. The conclusion of their heroic career," he added, "ought to be worthy of their brilliant feats of the past. There is but one road before us," he continued, "that of honor; all the other courses are those of shame. You must either meet with death here amid the flames, or must sally forth, and, dearly selling your lives, die the deaths of heroes. Choose between the two." The kindling words of their leader did not fail of their effect. At this supreme moment the people of Szigetvár, in their exalted enthusiasm, thought only of their honor. The very women wished to follow the men on this their last journey. Zrinyi had the bridge lowered and was the first to advance upon it. Lawrence Juranics was at his side carrying the large banner, and the other officers promptly followed. About six hundred people joined the sally of their heroic leader, who, after a fierce struggle, laid down his devoted life. Of his companions-in-arms but few escaped.

Thus, after a glorious resistance of over six weeks, did Szigetvár fall into the hands of the Turks. Sultan Solyman did not see the victorious end of the siege; he had expired a few days before in his camp. The Turkish army returned home, and thus through Zrinyi's noble self-sacrifice was the entire campaign of the enemy rendered barren of results. The formidable army which had menaced the whole country wasted its strength at Szigetvár, and the capture of this fortress alone cost the enemy 30,000 lives. Zrinyi's heroic death roused the admiration and sympathy of the whole European world, and his name became famous as one of the martyrs of Christianity.

Nor were the muses silent, in the midst of the heroic combats which marked this sad period. With so many inspiring themes presenting themselves, the poet, the successor of the mediæval troubadour, soon appeared on the scene to perpetuate in song the memory of the glorious deeds. Among others was Sebastian Tinódy, who described in verse some of the most glorious of the episodes in the sad chronicle of the sixteenth century. He visited the scenes of the battles and engagements, sought out the survivors or those who had taken a conspicuous part, the captains and their brave followers, collecting the incidents presented in his ballads. Tinódy did not confine himself, however, to his lyre, but was also an adept in the use of arms, and often took part in the contests of his time, and had more than once been wounded. Another and even more interesting figure was that of Valentine Balassa, who was as gallant a soldier as he was eminent as a poet. His works, consisting in part of religious poems and partly of lyric songs, have been, for three centuries, the favorite reading of the Hungarian people. Some of his writings have, however, come down to us in manuscript only, and present a most valuable example of the poetic genius of the Hungarians of his time. Balassa lived a stirring, eventful and dangerous life, which came to a glorious end on the field of honor. At the storming of Gran, in 1597, he was among the Hungarian besiegers, and the gallant poet received a wound during the engagement, which soon proved fatal.

In the midst of these perpetual struggles and successive calamities closed the sixteenth century, and began the seventeenth quite as inauspiciously for the Hungarians. Until now they had cherished the hope that the Hapsburg kings would rescue them from the cruel rule of the Osmanlis. But after a lapse of seventy years they not only saw their hopes of liberation from the hated yoke destroyed, but had the mortification of witnessing the continual spread of the Turkish power. Besides, a sharp antagonism of another kind gradually arose between the nation and their king. The national spirit, in spite of the sad condition of the people, asserted itself more and more, and frequently came into collision with the foreign royal dynasty, whose seat of government was without the frontiers of the country. This antagonism was not only of a national, but also of a religious character, for, while the largest part of Hungary was overwhelmingly Protestant, the kings of this period were among the staunchest supporters of the Church of Rome. In addition to this, the kings, who were at the same time emperors of Germany, had brought themselves, by their autocratic actions, into direct opposition to the constitution of the country and to the rights and privileges guaranteed by law. As a consequence a fierce constitutional contest was raging, during the whole of the seventeenth century, between the nation and their kings, which quite overshadowed the struggle against the Turks. In these contests the Hungarian people leaned for support chiefly on the principality of Transylvania, whose rulers, Stephen Bocskay, Gabriel Bethlen, George Rákóczy I., not only made their comparatively small country the bulwark of Hungarian nationality and of the Protestant Church, but raised her to a position of exceptional influence in European politics.

Before continuing to sketch the period of the Turkish rule in Hungary, we will take a rapid glance at the rise of Protestantism amongst the Hungarians.

The fall of Luther's hammer upon the door of the castle-church of Wittenberg, as he nailed to it his famous theses, reverberated even in Hungary, and produced an intense commotion in that distant country. The period of the *renaissance*, the revival of art and literature, had prepared all active and inquiring minds for changes in church and religion. The country had maintained an active intercourse, political, commercial, and cultural, with the western nations, and when Luther began the great work in Germany, which was to mark a new era in the history of the world, his ideas spread like wildfire all over Hungary, and, especially, found favor amongst the German inhabitants, who formed at that time an important element of her population. The cities of Buda, Oedenburg (Soprony), Presburg, the wealthy mining regions in the north, the Királyföld in Transylvania, were settled by Germans. Many of their clergy, attracted by ties of national kinship had finished their studies in Germany, and their merchants were closely connected in business with those of the old fatherland. Owing to the intimate relations thus established between the Germans of Hungary and their brethren abroad, the teachings of Luther gained almost as rapidly ground among them as among their countrymen in Germany, where the new doctrines had first been promulgated. In the course of a few years the new movement had assumed such formidable proportions that it attracted the attention of the whole nation.

The Catholic clergy, threatened in their supremacy, were the first to take the field in defence of the Church thus assailed. Round them very soon rallied that class of the nation which, alone, enjoyed political rights in the land, the entire nobility. In siding with the Catholic clergy, in this conflict against the Reformation and its followers, the Lutherans, the nobility were by no means actuated by religious motives only. Their hostile attitude was rather owing to important political considerations. The throne was then occupied by Louis II., who was of Polish extraction, the same youthful king who, noted for his frivolous character, expiated the errors of his reign upon the battle-field of Mohács. This unfortunate ruler was personally as indifferent to religion as to every thing else involving a serious turn of mind. But his wife, Queen Mary, the sister of the German emperor, Charles V., was all the more enthusiastic in the defence of Luther's teachings. The queen and her German courtiers, by exerting a baneful influence over the affairs of Hungary, had incurred the ill-will of the nobility, which was identical with the national party. This party, with a view to striking a blow at the German and Lutheran sympathizers surrounding the king, enacted from the outset most rigorous laws against the Lutherans. Thus, as early as 1523, a law was promulgated declaring Lutherans and their protectors (clearly indicating by the latter term the German courtiers of the king) foes to the Holy Virgin Mary, the patroness of Hungary, and as such, punishable with death and confiscation of their property. The persecutions against the adherents of the new faith began immediately. Luther's works and writings, which had been largely imported into Hungary, were seized and consigned to the flames. The Reformation, nevertheless, steadily gained ground.

In the diets which, owing to the attacks threatening the country from abroad and troubles at home, were then held three or four times annually, the national party, headed by John Szapolyai, one of the most powerful lords of the land, was constantly urging the cause of the Catholic Church. But there were other political reasons, besides their antipathy to the German courtiers, which determined the national party to persist in their antagonism to the new faith. The Osmanlis were continually harassing the southern frontiers, and the country was always on the brink of a war with them. The nobility, representing the nation, felt instinctively that a catastrophe was near at hand, which

Hungary, by her unaided strength alone, would be unable to avert. They had to look for foreign aid, and effective help from abroad could be expected only from the two most powerful rulers in Christendom, the pope and the emperor of Germany, both of whom were Luther's most determined opponents. They succeeded in securing the good-will of the pope, who, having no armies at his disposal to aid Hungary, assisted the country by abundant supplies of money. In return the nobility deemed it their sacred duty to keep a faithful watch and ward over the interests of the Catholic Church, and, in order to do so effectively, they inaugurated relentless measures against the Lutheran heretics. In 1525 another law was passed against the votaries of the new creed, ordering their extermination throughout the country, and declaring that Lutherans, wherever they were found, should suffer death by fire. This cruel law began its abominable work, and the funeral stakes soon sent forth their lurid flames. The religious persecutions thus inaugurated hastened the downfall of the Hungarian kingdom.

The dreadful catastrophe at Mohács, in 1526, forced Hungary into untrodden roads, not only politically, but also in the matter of religion. The death of her king, and the slaughter of so many prelates and of thousands of nobles, on the fated battle-field, gave a violent shock to the organization of both state and church, and rendered easy the further extension of the Reformation. Many of the great lords and nobles, who hitherto had been the most ardent supporters of the Catholic Church, speedily became, from political motives or private interest, zealous apostles of the new faith, so that the doctrines of Luther, before principally confined to the inhabitants of the cities, now found many adherents among the magnates. The bondmen, too, who, even in matters of religion, were compelled to obey the behests of their masters, embraced the religion of their lords. As a consequence, the victory of the Reformation became, a few decades only after the battle of Mohács, complete through the larger part of Hungary. The doctrines of Luther had paved the way for the teachings of Calvin. The latter, owing to their puritanic spirit and democratic tendencies, which suited the rooted predilection of the Magyar race for self-government, spread mostly over the Hungarian section of the country. The religion of Calvin, or the Helvetic confession, had such a hold upon the Hungarian-speaking population that it was soon designated by the special name of the Hungarian faith, while the Lutheran tenets were held chiefly by the German denizens of the cities and the Slavic inhabitants of the upper country. The ancient Roman Church was confined to a comparatively small territory, and during the seventeenth century hardly numbered one seventh of the population.

One of the most shining pages in the law records of Hungary—an enactment granting to the two Protestant churches equal rights with the Catholic Church—is connected with the name of Stephen Bocskay.

Although the Catholic Church had, during the sixteenth century, lost most of its followers, yet legally, and owing to the circumstance that the Hapsburg kings were the most zealous propagators of the Roman faith, it continued to be the only recognized church, and to exercise an unduly preponderating influence in public life, which, at that time, bore an exclusively religious impress. The Hungarian magnates and noblemen, then almost all Protestants, under the leadership of Prince Stephen Bocskay, took up arms against this privileged position of the Catholic Church, as well as in defence of the laws of the land, and succeeded in obtaining, in 1606, at the peace of Vienna, a law whereby perfect equality between the Protestant churches and the Catholic Church was established. This great victory, achieved by the Protestants, had the effect of rousing the Catholic Church to energetic action. The anti-reformation movement began in Hungary, as it had already all over Europe, and produced, under the direction of Cardinal Peter Pázmány, the archbishop of Gran, in a comparatively short time, the most surprising results. In the course of a few decades, the most influential and leading families of the aristocracy returned to the fold of the Catholic Church.

The mass of the people, however, the nobility, the inhabitants of the cities, and the peasantry, still remained Protestants, and when the Transylvanian princes, Gabriel Bethlen and George Rákóczy I., were about to engage in war against the Hapsburgs, they readily rallied around these bearers of the standard of the national faith. The peace of Linz, a confirmation of the treaty of Vienna, was concluded under Rákóczy, again solemnly proclaiming the perfect equality of the Protestant churches with the Roman Catholic Church, an equality, however, which, in point of fact, was never put into practice. The written law and their good right was of no use to the Protestants, for the power was gradually slipping from their hands. Under the patronage of the royal court, the anti-reformation movement had made great conquests amongst the lower classes of the people, and sometimes by the use of violence, sometimes by other means, whole districts and large territories again became Catholic. Elated by these successes, the court of Vienna for a long time ignored its promise of freeing the Hungarian people from the Turkish yoke, and about sixty years elapsed without any hostilities against the sultans. The chief endeavor of the court was forcibly to deprive the Hungarian nation of her constitutional institutions which were based upon her nationality, and to subject to imperial absolutism the people, jealous of their liberties and accustomed to freedom. These unconstitutional proceedings on the part of the government produced popular risings and party strife, and were, in their sad consequences, fatal to thousands of fanatics, spreading misery and poverty even to those parts of the land which, from their geographical positions, had been exempt from the ravages of the Turks.

The cessation of hostilities did not interrupt the continued ravages and devastations. Officially, it is true, there was, for about sixty years, peace between the royal court and the sultans, but this did not prevent the latter from constantly indulging in minor military operations. In 1663, however, when Leopold I., who was of an eminently peaceful disposition, held the throne, the Turks officially declared war. Although it had already then become apparent that the Turkish empire was impaired in strength, and, more particularly, that her military organization had degenerated, yet the Turks were eager for new battles, and war was determined upon in Constantinople. Hostilities soon commenced, and at St. Gotthard, in 1664, the Turks got their first repulse, for Christian arms there dealt them a heavy blow. Not once during the two centuries that had gone by were the Turks so overwhelmingly defeated on the continent as on this occasion. Enslaved Hungary breathed more freely, and already thought that the long-hoped-for hour of shaking off Moslem thraldom had arrived. But she was doomed to disappointment. The brilliant triumph was not turned to Hungary's advantage in Vienna. A hasty peace was concluded with the terrified Turks, and thus was prolonged for many decades the Turkish rule, which, though enfeebled, was still ruinous to Hungary.

It was at this period, too, that a man of great genius, and a true patriot, preached, with genuine apostolic zeal, a crusade against the Turks. His name was Nicholas Zrinyi. The namesake and great-grandson of the hero of Szigetvár, he was himself a gallant soldier and famous poet, and has immortalized, in a grand Hungarian epic, the martyrdom of his heroic ancestor. By his writings he fired the hearts of his countrymen, and his life was passed on bloody fields, in perpetual warfare against the Turks. From his youth he had been inspired by one thought only, to live and die for his country, and, although a devout Catholic, he nobly proclaimed religious toleration, at a time when the country was torn by religious dissensions. His educated mind led him to cultivate poetry, and to study the works of classical authors on history and philosophy, but his chief interest always remained the battle-field and the struggle against the Turks. On one of his estates he had a small fortress erected, called Zerinvár, from which the Hungarians were in the habit of sallying forth into the neighboring Turkish territory. This little place was a thorn in the side of the Turk, and the main cause of the declaration of war of 1663. Zrinyi, however, defended it gallantly, and beat back the assault of the enemy. In the course of the war he took several Turkish fortresses, and burned down and destroyed the bridge across the Drave, 4,000 paces in length, near Eszék, which had been built under Solyman, and which, being the main road leading into the western part of the country, was defended by trenches and other fortifications. The repute made by Zrinyi's extraordinary feats of war resounded in all Europe, and he was loaded down with distinctions by the pope, Louis XIV. of France, and by the princes of Germany and Italy, as the hero of Christendom. In the zenith of his glory, he lost his life by a cruel accident. While engaged in the chase, a wild boar rushed upon him, and wounded him mortally. He was found by his servants, lying on the ground, bathed in his own blood, and expired shortly afterward. All Hungary and Christian Europe lamented the loss of the distinguished soldier and poet.

His devout wish, to see the Hungarian nation freed from the oppressive rule of the Turks, did not approach its fulfilment until twenty years after his death. But even then it was not the royal court which accomplished the work of liberation, for, instead of making preparations in that direction, the government initiated the most cruel persecutions against the Protestants, compelling them to resort to armed resistance. The struggle between the Kuruczes, or the armed Hungarians, and the imperial troops was at its height, when Kara Mustapha Pasha, the ambitious grand-vizier of Sultan Mohammed IV., saw in this intestine war a favorable opportunity to conquer the remaining territory of Hungary, and even to menace in his own residence, Vienna, the emperor of the Romans. Leopold I., the emperor of Germany and king of Hungary, did all in his power to conciliate the

Turks and to delay the war. But Kara Mustapha remained inexorable, and boldly ventured on an enterprise which was destined to be fatal to him, and which, after a long and sanguinary contest, finally led to the overthrow of the Turkish power in Europe and the liberation of Hungary.

In the spring of 1683 the sultan and his grand-vizier commenced their march at the head of a force numbering 250,000 men, carrying with them 300 cannon. In Hungary they were joined by the so-called Kurucz king, Count Emeric Tökölyi, and his adherents. This tremendous army was already under the walls of Vienna in July, but two months of a severe siege had already elapsed and the city could not be taken. The Christian forces, led by John Sobieski, King of Poland, and Charles, Duke of Lorraine, were meanwhile hastening to the relief of the city, and on the 12th of September they succeeded in completely routing the Turkish army, which lost 60,000 men, the remainder scattering in wild flight in every direction. This was the last great campaign undertaken by the Osmanlis against the Western world. They could never recuperate from the effects of the defeat then suffered, and the great calamity which befell the Turkish power rendered it, at length, possible for Hungary, the bulwark of Christianity, which had been the scene of continual wars during a century and a half, to regain her liberty.

Leopold I., who had seen his capital menaced by the Turks, now took energetic measures to continue the war, and very soon his forces recaptured Gran, the ancient seat of the primate of Hungary, which for a long time had owned the Turkish rule. The whole line of the Danube fell into the hands of the Christians, and in 1684 an attempt was made to capture Buda, the once famous capital of Hungary. The siege, however, failed on this occasion, in spite of the heroic efforts made by the Hungarians. But they were more fortunate in the case of another powerful Turkish stronghold, Neuhäusel (Érsekujvár), the recapture of which, a brilliant military feat, was made the occasion for feasting and merriment in many European cities. At length, in 1686, Buda, too, was restored to Hungary. Volunteers flocked into Hungary, from every part of Europe, when the news spread that Duke Charles of Lorraine, the commander-in-chief, was making preparations for the recapture of the ancient and famous seat of the Hungarian kings. A powerful army gathered around his banners, and in the middle of June the duke arrived under the walls of Buda, which was defended by Abdi Pasha, then seventy years old, and a garrison of 16,000 determined soldiers. The siege lasted seventy-seven days, during which time the Turks made two sallies, and the grand-vizier made three attempts to come to the relief of the garrison, but the enemy was each time driven back by the Christian forces. The strongly fortified city, which had been heroically defended, fell, at length, after five unsuccessful assaults, on the 2d of September, 1686, into the hands of Duke Charles. On the afternoon of that day, at four o'clock, began the sixth assault; 9,000 Christian heroes resolutely stormed with fixed bayonets (an arm at that time still new and here employed for the first time) the walls which had been reduced to ruins by the guns of the besiegers. After a sanguinary contest lasting about one hour, a gallant Hungarian, David Petneházy, succeeded in penetrating, first, with his 800 hayduks, into Buda, whose garrison and inhabitants were almost entirely put to the sword. Thus after a lapse of 145 years was Buda freed from the Turkish yoke, and the whole Christian world was jubilant over the glorious news.

Many bloody battles, however, occupying a considerable period of time, had to be fought before the Moslem oppressors were entirely swept away from Hungarian territory. Duke Charles marched to the southern parts of Hungary and destroyed the Turkish army near Mohács, there, where 161 years before the Hungarian army had been annihilated by the Moslems. Soon after, Transylvania, too, passed under the supremacy of the king of Hungary. All the principal fortresses and towns were successively occupied by the royal troops, and when, in 1691, a Turkish army numbering 100,000 men was sent again to Hungary by the Sublime Porte, they were completely routed near Szalánkemén. It was one of the most sanguinary battles of that century; the grand-vizier himself, the aga of the Janissaries, seventeen pashas, and 20,000 Turkish soldiers lost their lives during the engagement. During a few years succeeding this great battle, lesser engagements only were fought, but hostilities never ceased. In 1697, however, Duke Eugene of Savoy, the "noble knight" and illustrious general, assumed the commandership of the royal forces. In the battle near Zenta he utterly annihilated, after a contest of two hours, a Turkish army led by Sultan Mustapha II., inflicting frightful losses upon the enemy; 10,000 Turks met their death in the waters of the Theiss, 20,000 were killed, and among the dead were the grand-vizier, 4 pashas, and 13 begler beys. These successive disasters and the frightful loss of men, amounting to many hundreds of thousands in the course of the fifteen years of warfare, finally prevailed upon the sultan to accept the terms of peace proposed by Leopold I. The treaty of peace was signed at Carlowitz in 1699, and under its terms Transylvania and the greater part of the Hungarian territory was restored to the king of Hungary by the sultan, but a smaller portion, lying between Transylvania and the Theiss, the ancient county of Temes, was still permitted to remain in Turkish hands. The court of Vienna, instead of attempting to regain the remaining territory, elated by the recent military successes, again renewed its attacks upon the nationality of the Hungarians and their ancient liberties, which it had always looked upon with decided dislike, and the complete subversion of which it now attempted. The nobility, weary of the absolutism of the court, combined at last with the peasantry, who had suffered severely under the lawlessness and illegal exactions of the soldiery, to raise the standard of rebellion, under the lead of Francis Rákóczy II. The great national struggle for liberty was initiated by electing Rákóczy king of Hungary and Transylvania, and, very soon, the Kurucz troops roamed as far as Austria. Later on, however, the fortunes of war changed, and Rákóczy retired to Poland hoping to obtain aid from the Russian Czar Peter the Great. During his absence he entrusted one of his generals, Alexander Károlyi, with the command of his army, who, however, instead of continuing the struggle, made his peace with the king. The peace of Szatmár, in 1711, finally put an end to the period of constitutional struggles between the nation and the king.

Now, at last, came the time for the still enslaved Hungarian territory to be freed from Turkish rule. The new war began in 1716. The imperial troops were again commanded by Prince Eugene, who, once more defeating the Turks near Peterwardein wrested, at last, Temesvár and the county of Temes from the Turks, in whose possession they had remained one hundred and sixty-four years. At the peace, concluded in 1718, the Sultan relinquished also his claim to that part of the country, and thus the entire territory belonging at the present day to the crown of Hungary was at last freed from Turkish thraldom.

There was now an end to the Islam rule in Hungary, as there had been to the same rule in Spain. But whilst the Moors had immortalized their name by memorials of a grand civilization, leaving behind them flourishing and wealthy cities, numerous works of art, and marvels of architecture, the Turks left Hungary ruined and devastated. Throughout the whole territory of the reconquered country, only a few miserable villages could be met with here and there, population had sunk to the lowest ebb, endless swamps covered the fertile soil of the once flourishing Alföld (Lowland), and the genius of the Hungarian nation had now to engage in the arduous labor of subduing, by the arts of peace and civilization, the sterile waste they had regained at last by their bravery and endurance. The work, hard as it was, was done. For a century and a half the severe task of colonizing and civilizing has been going on bravely, until finally that tract of land, which they recovered from the Turks an uninhabited desert, has grown to be populous, flourishing, and one of the richest granaries of Europe.

CHAPTER XIII.

THE AUSTRIAN RULE, 1526-1780.

THE preceding chapter gave an account of the varying fortunes of that part of Hungary which, although geographically appertaining to the domains of the crown of St. Stephen, was virtually occupied and ruled by the Turks, and this account was brought down to the time when the country succeeded in shaking off the foreign yoke. The thrilling episodes of that sad era deserved a place by themselves. Yet in describing these tragic events but little was said of the kings of the ruling dynasty and the destinies of that portion of the country which remained subject to their rule, or so much only was touched upon in a general way as was absolutely necessary for a proper understanding of the occurrences related there. This hiatus will now be supplied, by resuming, in a succinct form, the historical narrative of the events following the disastrous battle of Mohács.

We have already seen that at no time was the Turkish power so strong as during the first half of the sixteenth century, and that Hungary was never so weak as after the death of Matthias Hunyadi. The innovations of Matthias had broken down the ancient military organization, which recruited its armies from the ranks of the nobility and the armed bands in their train, and established in its place a standing army. But on the death of the genius which had called it into existence, the standing army also disappeared. We have described elsewhere the sad fate of his valiant "black guard." The disastrous reverses at Belgrade and Mohács were the consequence, and it became evident that Hungary, single-handed, could not withstand the power of the Osmanlis.

Under these circumstances the nation was compelled to look for assistance from abroad, and, in searching for a powerful alliance, it was quite natural that public attention should be drawn to the house of Hapsburg, the great authority and influence of which gave the fairest promise of effectual support to the prostrate country. This dynasty occupied at that time a front rank amongst the reigning families; its rule extended over Austria, Germany, the wealthy Netherlands, Spain, with her American colonies and dependencies, Naples, Sicily, and Sardinia—an immense domain, of which it might have been then truly said that "the sun never set in it." No dynasty, since the Cæsars, had controlled the destinies of so many nations and of so vast a territory. Ferdinand, a scion of that influential dynasty, who at this time was also elected king of Bohemia, owed his elevation to the throne of Hungary to hopes and arguments of this kind. He gave the people assurances of support on the part of his family; he vowed to respect the rights and liberties of the nation, and promised to live in the country and to confide the conduct of her affairs to Hungarians only.

Every thing turned out quite differently from what the royal electors had hoped and expected. The Turks were decidedly averse to any augmentation of the power of the Hapsburgs by the acquisition of the Hungarian throne. They desired to see Hungary under a separate king of her own, and to accomplish this the Turks shrank from no sacrifices, and succeeded in embroiling the unfortunate country in continual wars. Unhappy Hungary was placed between the hammer and the anvil. The Turks were unwilling to yield, and the Hapsburgs, quite as reluctant to give up the country, were, nevertheless, unable to defend it. The result of the cruel war, waged for over thirty years, was, in the end, that Hungary was torn into three parts. The heart of the land, the Alföld, was seized by the Turks; the hilly plateau of Transylvania was ruled by native princes, acknowledging the suzerainty of the sultan; and the remaining portion only, the northern and western part, owned the supremacy of the Hapsburgs in their capacity of kings of Hungary. Thus the new dynasty, so far from proving a protection to the country, rather led to its dismemberment.

The condition of Transylvania was, comparatively speaking, more favorable than that of either of the two other sections of the country. She had to pay her tribute to the Turks, but beyond that she experienced no interference on the part of her paramount lord. She was allowed to elect her own rulers, to convene her national assemblies, to keep up an army of her own, and to live as before under the ancient laws of Hungary. The Alföld, in the hands of the Turks, was governed in Turkish fashion. The Turks never settled down in the country they conquered; they only garrisoned it, as it were. The government and the spahis were the new landlords, and their chief care was, not to watch over the welfare of the people, but to fleece them and to extort from them heavy taxes and all sorts of vexatious imposts. The effects of such an administration became soon visible. The ancient culture perished, the population gradually decreased, and the once fertile soil relapsed into barrenness.

Nor were the complaints fewer and less bitter in the western and northern parts, ruled by the Hapsburg kings of Hungary. The hope of obtaining, through these kings, aid from the West gradually vanished. The nation, besides, was quick to perceive that Hungary was looked upon by the Hapsburgs as an unimportant province, rather than an independent country. The king did not reside in Hungary, but in Vienna, which was the permanent seat of his government, and all the remonstrances coming from the various diets against this state of things led only to bare promises. There were numerous grievances besides. After the first vacancy in the dignity of a palatine no other palatine had been appointed, German advisers alone were listened to in affairs concerning Hungary, the country was flooded with German officials and soldiers, and distinguished Hungarian magnates were thrown into prison without due form of law. These evils were already felt under Ferdinand, the first Hapsburg king, but they still increased under his successor, King Maximilian (1564-1576). The latter proceeded quite openly in his anti-national policy. He promised Germany for himself and his successors, in return for her aid, to use every endeavor to bring about the annexation of Hungary to that country. The Diet of 1567, in enumerating the many abuses of the government, bitterly inveighed against the foreign soldiery, charging them with arbitrarily raising tolls, taking the thirtieth part, imposing unlawful taxes on the communes, wasting the substance of the peasantry and robbing them of their last penny, and, finally, selling their children into slavery to the Turks. The Diet declared that, "There is no salvation, no hope for us; we have no other alternative but to leave our native land and emigrate to foreign parts."

These complaints remained unheeded by Maximilian, nor was his son and successor, Rudolph (1576-1608), more disposed to remedy the ills complained of. The office of the palatine still remained vacant; the affairs of Hungary were administered, without consulting the Hungarians, by a court cabinet and a military council. Rudolph's reply to the remonstrances of the Estates of the realm, that "these things have been in practice long since," was certainly a cynical apology for the continuance of abuses. Thus was the continual infringement of the law claimed to have become a law in itself, and independent Hungary became virtually subject to the authority of foreigners. The temper of the diets which met during the first years of Rudolph's reign clearly indicated the state of irritation produced by the king's presumptuous treatment of the liberties of the nation; the exasperated Estates spoke of refusing to vote subsidies, and some of them, although in the minority, threatened even to join either Poland or Turkey. Rudolph, wearied with these boisterous scenes, turned his back upon the country, and the nation did not see her king for twenty-five years.

The country was compelled patiently to suffer the encroachments on her ancient rights, for to no quarter could she look for help. Alone she was too weak to right herself, and the only alliances that offered themselves were either the German or Turkish. A sad alternative, indeed, for the Turks on the one hand never ceased to harass and devastate the country, threatening even to absorb the territory yet free, and the Germans on the other utterly ignored the constitution and liberties of Hungary, although the kings on their election and coronation always swore to respect and to defend both. The Turks were extirpating the nation, whilst the Germans were trying to rob her of her Hungarian nationality. The Germans, being considered the lesser evil, carried the day, and hopes were besides entertained that, after all, Germany would finally rid the country of the Turks. These hopes were further encouraged after the death of Solyman (1566), when it became apparent that the Turkish power was declining from day to day. But the country was doomed to disappointment, for the Viennese government, instead of arraying itself against Turkey, was on the eve of trying the patience of her people again with measures and acts hostile to their nationality.

The great obstacle to the Germanizing schemes had always been the Hungarian Diet and the stiff-necked independence of the nobles composing it. It was impossible for the government to do away with the diet, as it had done away with the dignity of palatine and the other exalted Hungarian offices, as the grant of taxes and soldiers required in an emergency depended upon the good will of the diet. If there was no diet in session, no supplies of money and soldiers could be voted. The government therefore determined to resort to measures which would bend the majority of the diet to its will. The royal free cities had at that time the privilege of sending members to the diet of Hungary to represent them. But the influence at the diet of these municipalities, of whom there were but few, and most of these with German inhabitants, was very slight. A great number of private boroughs were made by the government royal free cities, and an attempt was made to use the new members sent by these constituencies as a counterpoise to the hostile nobles in the diet. But the nobility loudly protested against this innovation. Some of those who protested were charged with treason, but, unable to obtain their conviction before a Hungarian tribunal, the government had them brought to Vienna before a military council, which pronounced them guilty of the charge against them. One of the victims of these illegal proceedings, a certain Illesházy, a wealthy magnate, saved his life by flight only. His immense estates were confiscated, and an inquiry into his case fully proved that the cruel sentence passed upon him was not meant so much to punish his supposed crime, as it was intended to be a means of getting possession of his vast property. But the persecutions of the government did not stop there; the turn of the Protestants soon came. Thus was one of the captains ordered to take away by violence from the Protestants the cathedral at Kassa, and to hand it over to the Catholics. The city authorities of Kassa recaptured the church, but it was taken from them again by force, and the city was mulcted by the government in a heavy fine of money. This outrage might well excite indignation at a time when three fourths of the population of Hungary were Protestants. It became evident that the German influence was bent upon attacking the people in their liberties as well as their religion, and whilst the government was yet inclined to show some indulgence to the Catholics, it was determined to show no kind of mercy to the Protestants of the country.

The excitement and indignation of the people, throughout the whole land, at these lawless proceedings, were reflected in the temper of the Diet which met in 1604. They protested against the illegal persecutions, stood up for the freedom of worship, and warned the government not to stir up dissensions amongst the followers of the antagonistic churches. A fresh injury, however, was added to those complained of, by Rudolph's arbitrarily supplementing the 21st article enacted by the Diet with a 22d article, in which the Diet was enjoined from discussing religious topics; intimations were thrown out at the same time that heresy was to be persecuted.

This 22d article was the spark which set ablaze all the inflammable material that had accumulated in the country since the time that the Hapsburgs had occupied the throne of Hungary. The North of Hungary, allied with Transylvania, rose in arms, and the entire Upper Country was soon gathering in the camp of Stephen Bocskay, the prince of Transylvania. The Turks favored the insurrection and proclaimed Bocskay king of Hungary, bestowing upon him, at the same time, a crown of gold. The insurgents aimed at the entire overthrow of the Hapsburgs, but the politic Bocskay opposed this, being disinclined to deliver up the whole of Hungary to the tender mercies of the Osmanlis. Bocskay saw in the Germans a counterpoise to the overweaning power of the Turks and counselled a policy of conciliation. The result of his counsels was the peace of Vienna, concluded in 1606, in which the abuses complained of were remedied, and constitutional government and freedom of worship were guaranteed for all time to come.

Remarkable as were the results of Bocskay's rising, they were quite eclipsed by the effects of the astute policy inaugurated by him as the ruler of Transylvania, a policy which he bequeathed to his princely successors, enjoining upon them in his last will always to adhere to it. It consisted in maintaining, at all hazards, the independence of Transylvania, in order to enable her, according to the necessities of the moment, either to combine with the Turks in defence of the Hungarian nationality against the encroachments of Germanism, or joining the Germans to keep, with their aid, the Turks out of the remaining Hungarian territory. This course, marked by rare political acumen and inspired by the purest patriotism, was effectively aided by the mutual jealousies of the Turks and Germans, and enabled the Transylvanian princes ultimately to achieve their noble aim of saving the liberties of Hungary, their common country.

The terms of the peace of Vienna were soon forgotten by the Viennese government, and its proselyting Catholicism brought it again into collision with the Hungarian Protestants. The successor of Rudolph, Matthias (1608-1619), succeeded in restraining to some extent the outbreaks of hatred by which the various sectaries were animated, but hardly had the succession to the throne of Bohemia been secured to his cousin Ferdinand (II.), who had been brought up by the Jesuits, and was their zealous pupil, than the Czech Protestants took up arms, severed their connection with the Hapsburgs, and inaugurated the religious war which raged in Germany for thirty years, and which stands in history unexampled for its horrors (1618).

This movement could not leave Hungary indifferent. In Hungary, too, Romanizing was being strenuously carried on. The Jesuits gained a foothold in the country, and bringing with them their schools, books, and well-organized machinery they soon succeeded, under the patronage of the government of Vienna, in supplanting the Protestants. Peter Pázmány, who, from a simple Jesuit, had risen to the primacy of Hungary, was the life and soul of the proselyting movement. He brought to the work of Romanizing the country an irresistible eloquence, invincible arguments in his writings, and unsurpassed religious zeal. All the great powers of his mastermind, and the resources of his enormous wealth were employed by him to add to the Catholic fold. By his own personal influence alone, thirty of the most conspicuous Hungarian families returned to the Catholic faith of their ancestors, families among whom some owned domains larger than a dozen of the smaller principalities of Germany. Protestantism gradually lost ground, its followers became a minority in the Diet, and the Catholics became daily more arrogant. Under these circumstances the Protestants of Hungary (where in 1618 Ferdinand was elected king, to succeed on the death of Matthias) could not look on with unconcern when their Czech brethren rose in arms nor could they permit their defeat by the Catholic court, for such an event was sure to hasten the moment when they, in their turn, would have to resist the violent measures of coercion practiced now against the Czechs.

They therefore joined the Czechs and took up arms for the defence of their liberties, for freedom of worship was with the nation closely interwoven with the cause of constitutional liberty. Gabriel Bethlen, who had become prince of Transylvania in 1613, stood at the head of the movement. On his first appearance on the scene of action, Bethlen is thus spoken of by a Frenchman in a report to his own government: "Bethlen is a distinguished soldier who has taken part, in person, in forty-three engagements; he is a man of wise judgment and great eloquence * * * in short, the great Henry IV. excepted, there is no king like him in the world." The high expectations entertained of his abilities were not disappointed. The whole Upper Country as far as Presburg passed into his hands during the first year of the rebellion, and in 1620 he obtained possession of the greatest part of the territory beyond the Danube. But while he was carrying on hostilities with such signal success, the Czechs were completely routed by Tilly near Prague, and this defeat cost Bohemia her independence. Bethlen, being left without allies, hastened to make terms with the Viennese government, and the result was the Treaty of Nikolsburg, concluded in the beginning of 1622, based upon the peace of Vienna.

Bethlen, perceiving, with his wonted judgment, that the dissensions among the Protestants of Germany augured nothing favorable for the future, endeavored to enter into amicable relations with the court of Vienna. He used every means to prevail upon it to abandon the persecution of the Protestants, and to unite with him in a common war against the Turks, in order to drive them from Hungary. But the court was not disposed to listen to his overtures, and seemed to consider it a matter of greater importance to accomplish the destruction of Protestantism than to free the country from the Turks. Bethlen, seeing that all attempts in this direction were doomed to failure, returned to the old policy of the Transylvania princes. His political connections reached as far as France, England, and Sweden, and, upon the breaking out of the Danish war (1625), he again began armed hostilities, which, however, although crowned with victory, gave way to a new treaty of peace, owing to the defeat of Bethlen's allies in Germany. When Gustavus Adolphus made his appearance in the West, achieving victories for Protestantism, the great Transylvanian prince was no more amongst the living; he died in 1629. Bethlen was, no doubt, one of the most conspicuous figures in the history of Hungary. Through his exertions little Transylvania moved, in politics, abreast of the most powerful European nations, and under him she became rich, powerful, and greatly advanced in culture, and a strong prop to the rest of the Hungarian nation. His premature death deprived the country of the advantages which he certainly would have drawn from the triumphs of Gustavus Adolphus.

Toward the close of the Thirty Years' War, the prince of Transylvania, George Rákóczy I., took advantage of the distressed position of Ferdinand III. of Hapsburg (who had succeeded his father, Ferdinand II., on his thrones in 1637) to strike a successful blow for the liberties of Hungary. The beginning of the reign of the successor of Ferdinand III., Leopold I. (1657-1705), witnessed the downfall of Transylvania's power.

This event disturbed the balance of power between the Turks and Germans, and alone was sufficient to bring about the great changes which soon took place in the affairs of Hungary. In order to account for the overthrow of the power of Transylvania, it must be remembered that both the Turks and Germans had for a long time back looked askance at the strength and influence of this little principality. They were filled with apprehensions of having their Hungarian territories gradually absorbed by Transylvania, and there was an agreement between these two powers, to the effect that she should not be allowed to add to her territory. It is impossible to suppose that the then ruler of Transylvania, George Rákóczy II., had no information of this secret treaty, but he apparently paid no heed to it, or entertained no fears as to its effects. He quietly continued to extend his power, and for that purpose entered into an alliance with the Swedish king for the partition of Poland. In vain did the Viennese court oppose this aggressive course, in vain did the Turks command him to desist from it; the Transylvanian prince crossed the Carpathians, with a gallant army, in 1657. The allied forces of Sweden and Transylvania were everywhere victorious, and the power of Transylvania stood higher than ever. It was at this conjuncture that Leopold I., who had succeeded Ferdinand III., inaugurated, at once, a warlike policy, parting with the peaceable traditions of his predecessors. Leopold divided the attention of Rákóczy's Swedish ally by setting on him his ancient enemies, the Danes, and sent his own armies into those Hungarian domains belonging to Rákóczy, which the Transylvanian princes had extorted from the Hapsburgs, in the treaties of Vienna and Nikolsburg, and on other similar occasions. Nor were the Turks behindhand in co-operating with the Hapsburgs. A Tartar army was sent into Poland against Rákóczy, and he himself was deposed from his princely office as a punishment for his disobedience. Rákóczy, thus left to fight his own battles, without an ally, and hemmed in by Turks, Germans, and Tartars, suffered defeat on every side, the flower of his army fell into the hands of the Tartars, and it was only by paying a large sum that he obtained peace from Poland. When he returned to Transylvania in August, 1657, with the wreck of his army, the principality was involved in utter financial and military ruin.

The Turks, however, did not pause here; they wished to get the whole of Transylvania into their possession. Twice the unhappy country was devastated by Tartar hordes, and the inhabitants repeatedly carried away into slavery by thousands; a prince was given to her at the dictation of the Turks, and part of her territory actually passed under direct Turkish rule (1662). The hearts of the patriotic Hungarians bled at this cruel sight, and they appealed to and incessantly urged their king to interfere, and not to allow the principality to perish. Leopold I. turned a deaf ear to these appeals; he was not inclined to venture on a war with Turkey, on behalf of Transylvania, and was, at best, careful to get his share of the common plunder. It was a gloomy outlook for the Hungarian nation; the Turks, on the one hand, oppressing her with their formidable forces, and their own king languidly looking on.

The Turkish successes in Transylvania only served to whet the Moslem appetite for further conquests. In 1663 the Turks attacked Leopold without any warning, and obtained possession of the region of the Upper Danube, and of the lower valley of the Vág. This was a great blow to Hungary, for the conquered territory was thrust like a wedge into the semicircular national territory, dividing it again into two new parts. Although an imperial army was sent to meet the Turkish forces, no efforts were made to stay the continual advances of the latter as long as they were on Hungarian territory, but as soon as they neared the Austrian frontier they were opposed by the imperial forces. This imperial army achieved at St. Gotthard, near the Raab, a brilliant victory over the Turks.

This victory gave fresh courage to the despondent Hungarians. They now hoped that the war would be successfully pushed forward, and would end only with the liberation of their country, and the less sanguine expected at least a peace which would restore to the possession of the king of Hungary, Transylvania, and all the other territories obtained by the Turks since 1657. A sad disappointment, however, fell upon the country. The peace concluded by the victorious government left in the possession of the Turks all the territory they had previously taken, thus virtually leaving the country in her former maimed condition.

This disgraceful peace which had been concluded by the court of Vienna without consulting the Hungarians, at last shook even the faith of those Catholic Hungarians who, until now, had been the unconditional adherents of the Hapsburgs. They had, heretofore, acquiesced in the forlorn condition of their country, being persuaded that the Viennese government lacked the ability of rescuing her, but recent events showed them that it was lack of good will on the part of the government which was precipitating the ruin of the country. It became the universal conviction that the Hapsburgs would gladly see the country in the hands of the foreign invader, in order to enable them, by reconquering her anew, to do away with the uncomfortable trammels of the national constitution. Leopold did not heed the general discontent; he pursued the great aim he had proposed to himself, of uniting, after the illustrious example of Louis XIV., all the dependencies of his dynasty into one homogeneous empire. Things had come to such a pass in Hungary that the most inveterate enemies of Turkey openly counselled amity with the Turks, declaring that they preferred paying a tribute to the latter rather than to see the country go to ruin by the Germanizing machinations of the Viennese court.

The general discontent soon budded into a conspiracy in which, this time, not only the Protestants, but chiefly the Catholic population took part, who were now quite as eager to rid themselves of the Germans. The heads of the conspiracy were all Catholics. Their leader was Wesselényi, the palatine of the realm and the king's representative, and affiliated with him in the leadership were the largest landlords in the country: Peter Zrinyi, Nádasdy, Francis Rákóczy, and Frangepán. Their aim was to rid the country of the Germans by the aid of the Turks, or, if possible, of the French. The conspiracy, however, failed. Wesselényi died, and the plot was betrayed to the government before it had ripened into the intended rising. Leopold, without loss of time, swooped down upon the principal conspirators. Zrinyi, Nádasdy, and Frangepán were seized, and without being given the benefit of the laws of their country, were decapitated. Their immense estates were confiscated, and Rákóczy himself could only save his life and obtain mercy by paying a ruinous ransom (1671). The government, however, was not satisfied with the cruel punishment of the ringleaders alone; it deemed this a propitious time for the introduction of various oppressive measures. Without convoking the Diet, a land and corn tax was imposed upon the country, excise duties were introduced, and a poll tax levied on every inhabitant, including the nobles. The land was swarming with a foreign soldiery brought there to restrain the rebellious Hungarians. The government added injury to insult; not satisfied with insulting the nation by entirely ignoring its constitution, and keeping down the national aspirations by quartering foreign garrisons in national territory, it raised illegal taxes wherewith to pay the armed oppressors. The government at Vienna threw off its mask at last; the Hungarian constitution was abolished, and Hungary reduced to the condition of a province of Austria (1673).

Whilst the government thus succeeded in subverting the constitution of the country, it showed no less activity and success in the prosecution of its other aim, the Romanizing of the people. There was no law to protect those professing the new faith; they could be oppressed with impunity; their churches were taken away from them; hundreds of their ministers and teachers were sentenced by the tribunal to slavery on the galleys, or were sent adrift by private persecutions. It was an open secret that the king himself was eager to exterminate the last heretic, and just as the oath of the king to protect the constitution had been forgotten, so were the various treaties of peace, guaranteeing the freedom of worship, doomed to oblivion, as soon as there was no Transylvanian prince to recall them to royal memory by force of arms.

And yet it was Transylvania, in her weakened condition, that now came to the assistance of Hungary, which had become a prey to Austrian rapacity. Many of those who were compelled to fly from the persecutions of the sanguinary policy of the government sought and found a refuge in Transylvania, and they were continually urging Apaffy, the prince of Transylvania, and the Turks to intercede with arms in behalf of the Hungarian cause. The Viennese government assailed Stambul with letters requesting the sultan not to allow Transylvania to be the place of refuge of certain "thieves," but to no purpose. The Porte, indeed, so far from favorably receiving these epistles, secretly promised aid against the Austrians. A fresh insurrection broke out in 1672. The refugees flocked into the Upper Country and inaugurated a warfare which, for cruelty and mercilessness, stands alone in the history of Hungary. The era of this contest, commencing in 1672, and covering a period of nearly ten years, is called the Kurucz-Labancz era. This aimless and purposeless struggle was kept up between the Kuruczes (insurgents) and Labanczes (Austrians), within the limits of the territory lying between Komárom and Transylvania, and there was no end of the horrors the contestants were guilty of in the course of their hostilities against each other. To cut tobacco on the enemy's bare back, or to cut strips from his quivering skin, to drive thorns or iron spikes under the finger-nails, to bury him in the ground up to his head and then fire at him, to skin him alive, to put a stake through him,—in a word, to perpetrate tortures at which humanity shudders, these were the every-day courtesies exchanged between the two belligerents. The combatants of that day respected neither God nor man; they acknowledged only one guide for their actions: a bitter and undying hatred of all that called itself Labancz. They were the misguided creatures of a period during which the insane policy of the government had robbed the people both of their religion and their teachers.

The ruling powers had thus conjured up days of terror, but were utterly inadequate to the task of terminating them. Indeed after several years of this schemeless struggle, the rebellion became at last organized and conscious of a fixed object. The rebels received aid from the French and from the Porte, and Transylvania, as a state, was ready to make common cause with her countrymen. Tökölyi, a magnate of the Upper Country, a youth only twenty-one years old, but of eminent abilities, placed himself at the head of the rebels, and, now in 1678, began the war in good earnest. The rebels soon became masters of the Upper Country, and the government which had been unable to cope with the headless Kuruczes, proved quite helpless against the organized rebellion, led by an able chief. Austria was, besides, continually harassed by Louis XIV. in the west, and, to add to her difficulties, it was rumored that the Turks were preparing to invade Hungary with an immense army, which, uniting with the forces of Tökölyi, should drive the Austrians from the country.

The government, thus driven to the wall, surrendered. Negotiations soon began, the Diet was convoked in 1681, and constitutional government and freedom of worship were restored with a show of great alacrity. The concessions came too late. The rebels had no faith in the government after the cruel deceptions of which it had been guilty, and placed no trust in promises wrung from its necessitous condition. They refused to submit, and Tökölyi was proclaimed by the Porte king of Hungary. The threatened Turkish invasion became also in 1683 a fact. At this moment Hungary seemed to be lost forever to the Hapsburgs; the whole country sided with the Turks, the territory beyond the Danube also acknowledging the authority of Tökölyi.

The destinies of Hungary, nay of all Eastern Europe, hung upon the fate of besieged Vienna. The siege of Vienna was raised through the victory of Sobieski the Polish king; and the rapidly succeeding victories of the Christian armies, already referred to in the preceding chapter, awakened the hopes of the Hungarian nation, and showed that, at last, the emperor-king concerned himself in the liberation from Turkish rule of Hungarian territory. The decisive victories of Prince Eugene of Savoy finally accomplished this, and the Turks henceforth gave up all hopes of reconquering Hungary.

The liberation of the Hungarian soil, however important in itself, proved no immediate panacea for the ills of which the country had to complain. Even while the struggle was going on, many things happened which pointed to troubles in the future. The Hungarian inhabitants along the course of the Danube were rudely interrogated by the soldiers of the imperial army of liberation as to what faith they professed, and if they were found to adhere to the new tenets they were mercilessly set adrift. In the Upper Country a certain Caraffa, the military commandant of that district, committed acts of the most cruel atrocity. This bloody monster pretended to have discovered a conspiracy, and obtained from the government, which was disposed to suspect the loyalty of the Hungarians, full powers to deal with it and to put it down. Caraffa made a terrible use of his commission. He made wholesale arrests of the suspected and loyal alike, threw into prison men of high standing against whom he had a personal grudge, and rich people whose property he coveted, and extorted from them by dreadful tortures the confession of crimes they had never committed. These unfortunates were then executed upon the strength of their confessions. This *bloody tribunal of Eperjes*, of ill-fame, which inspired horror all over the land, continued its malevolent functions until the first months of 1687, when it was abolished, through the intercession of the Diet which had just been convoked. This Diet, however, was in most of its work not at all anxious to hamper the government. On the contrary, it displayed a pliability which made it forget the true interests of the country. Thus it substituted for the ancient right of the nation to elect their kings, the hereditary right of succession in the male branch of the Hapsburg dynasty, and it was this Diet that relinquished the time-honored right of the people, guaranteed by the Golden Bull, to resist with arms any illegal acts of the king, without incurring the penalty of treason for so doing. There were some malicious critics who pretended that this unpatriotic legislation was due to the pressure of imperial guns pointed at the place in which the Diet met. At all events the servile spirit exhibited by the Diet gave color to the apprehensions of those Hungarians who were of one mind with Tökölyi, that Hungary must be irretrievably ruined if she passed under the authority of the Austrians.

As the Turkish wars were drawing to an end, more melancholy portents began to darken the horizon. Hungary was reorganized by the government at Vienna without the Hungarians being consulted. Transylvania remained a separate "grand duchy," and the district beyond the Drave was formed into a separate province, and all this was done from the fear lest united Hungary might become too strong to suit Austria's schemes. A large portion of the recovered territory was distributed amongst German landowners, the southern portion of the Alföld was colonized by Servians, and in other parts of the land, especially in the cities, the settlement of German-speaking people was encouraged, for the purpose of tempering the hot blood of the rebellious Hungarians. The fortified castles scattered throughout the whole country, the property of private owners, were blown up by the hundred, without the consent of their proprietors, lest in case of a fresh rising these strongholds should be used as centres of a factious spirit.

The Protestants were not allowed to settle in the reconquered districts. In other places the freedom of their worship was interfered with, the churches were taken from them, their ministers driven away, and if any one, appealing to his constitutional rights, had the courage to resist these illegalities, he was thrown into prison. In a word, regular dragonnades, as they flourished in France under Louis XIV., now became the order of the day.

The government imposed upon the people such oppressive and burdensome taxes that it almost seemed as if it dreaded the prosperity of the country. If the people complained of the heavy burdens, they were instigated against the nobles, whose exemption from taxation was pointed out as the only cause of the heavy burdens. The country was again flooded by a foreign soldiery, whose chief business consisted in robbing and plundering, the common soldiers oppressing the common people, and the officers the nobility. The honor and the property of the people were at the mercy of these brutal troops, and those who complained of such outrages found themselves always in the wrong. This forlorn condition is reflected in many of the plaintive popular songs of that period, but there was no means of remedying these evils crying throughout the land, for no Diet had been convoked since 1687. The aim of the Viennese government became daily more evident, to put the Austrian rule in the place of the Turkish, and to ignore altogether the Hungarian national aspirations. The nation herself seemed to the government too much enfeebled and trodden down to give any ground for apprehending any resistance in defence of her rights, but to make assurance doubly sure every effort was made to crush the national spirit.

Yet the nation could not brook oppression, she could not be kept quiet, deprived of constitutional government, and as soon as she had found again a leader in Francis Rákóczy II., she rose in arms. The new leader was the bearer of a great name. His ancestors had been princes of Transylvania. He himself was the grandson of that George Rákóczy II., who in 1657 invaded Poland, and subsequently lost his life fighting against the Turks in defence of his country and his throne. His father Francis had taken part in the Wesselényi conspiracy, and escaped the scaffold only at the cost of an immense ransom. His maternal grandfather, Peter Zrinyi, met with his death on the scaffold, and his only great uncle perished in prison in spite of his innocence. His stepfather, Tökölyi, together with his own mother, Ilona Zrinyi, ate the bitter bread of exile in Turkey. He and his sister were, in their early youth, torn from their parents, and their education entrusted to Germans. In Vienna he was subjected to many humiliations, and as he grew up he left that city and retired to one of his estates, intending to pass his life peacefully near his wife. He was averse to action, and the bloody shades of his family seemed vainly to beckon to him, who alone bore yet the famous name and was the master of immense possessions, to follow in their footsteps.

But all this was changed as soon as he came to Hungary. He could not bear to witness the wrongs perpetrated about him, and he could not move a step without becoming aware that the nation expected from him, the descendant of a line of heroes, their salvation. Meanwhile the Spanish war of succession had broken out in 1701, and very soon all Europe was involved in it. This appeared to Rákóczy to be a propitious time for the reconquering of the liberties of the people, and, aided by the French king, he hoisted in 1703 the flag of the rebellion, bearing the inscription "pro patria et libertate," for the fatherland and liberty.

The sages at Vienna would not at first credit the news of the rising of the people; they had long ago made up their minds that such an event was impossible. But when the movement spread like wildfire throughout the Upper Country, Transylvania, and ultimately all Hungary, and the great majority of the nation unsheathed the sword, they became frightened, and resorted to—negotiations and fresh promises. The rebels were inclined to cease hostilities provided their liberties were secured. But mere words did not satisfy them now, having been taught by sad experience the futility of royal words, oaths, and solemn treaties of peace, and they therefore endeavored to obtain more substantial guaranties from the government. They exacted the independence of Transylvania, under a Hungarian prince and the guaranty of the European powers. To these propositions the government neither would nor could accede, while the rebels insisted upon their first proposals, declaring that it was impossible for them to have any faith in Austrian or—as it was popularly termed—in German promises. This universal sentiment of distrust, pervading the nation, is admirably reflected in a popular song, to which that period gave birth, and of which we subjoin a translation:

> "Magyar, trust not the Germans,
> No matter how or what they protest;
> Naught is the parchment they give thee,
> 'Though it be as large as thy round cloak,
> And though they set a seal on it
> As big as the brim of the moon,
> Spite of all, it lacks all virtus (trustworthiness).
> Confound them, Jesus Christus!"

These overtures failed to lead to peace, and the struggle continued throughout the land, giving up to ruin what had been left intact by the Turkish slavery of a century and a half and the sixteen years' war of liberation. The government was unable either to quell or to crush the rebellion, standing in need of all its strength for the struggle in the west. At this conjuncture Leopold I. descended into his grave in 1705, and his well-intentioned son, Joseph I., succeeded to the throne (1705-1711).

Joseph sincerely wished for peace, and, convinced of the mistakes of the policy of his father, he did all in his power to allay the apprehensions of the rebels, but his constitutional sentiment failed to efface the baneful effects of his predecessor's misgovernment and duplicity. Nor was it possible for him, either, to accept the terms of the rebels, and thus it came to pass that the dynasty of Hapsburg was dethroned in Hungary, during the reign of this upright monarch, in 1707. This was a great mistake on the part of the rebels, but Joseph had now the advantage of being able to show his respect for the liberties of the nation, under the most adverse circumstances, and he thus, by slow degrees, won the confidence of the people. The French had, meanwhile, been thoroughly defeated, and Joseph was thus enabled to oppose larger forces to the rebels, while the latter could not secure aid from any quarter. The rebels, exhausted with the protracted struggle, met with repeated defeats, and, to add to their distress, the black plague made its appearance and fearfully thinned the ranks of their troops. The king, however, did not abuse his increasing power. He granted an amnesty to all, without exception, who were willing to return to their allegiance; he governed constitutionally, remedied the ills inflicted upon the country by his predecessors, and finally placed a Hungarian commander-in-chief at the head of the army. His earnest and sincere endeavors were at last rewarded by peace. The issue of the various negotiations was the compact of Szatmár, concluded in 1711, by the terms of which a general amnesty was granted, and constitutional and religious liberty secured.

This peace was a grateful conclusion to the sad days which had been weighing down Hungary for two hundred years, a period during which both Turks and Austrians were compassing the ruin of the country. The former were perpetually threatening her territorial integrity; the latter, her political liberties, and the nationality to which those liberties were closely wedded. By dint of rare courage, an undying love of liberty, and acute statesmanship, they succeeded in preserving both their territory and their liberties. The sad events of those two centuries had put the endurance and energies of the nation to the severest test, but, in the end, she triumphantly passed through the cruel ordeal.

A new era now dawned in the history of Hungary. Wars no more threatened the territory of the country, and her liberties and nationality were no longer exposed to stubborn violence. Yet the dangers to her national life were not yet quite removed, for what the sword and brute force had been unable to accomplish during the preceding centuries, the eighteenth century attempted to achieve peaceably by means of the Western civilization.

Charles III. (Charles VI. as Emperor of Germany), the brother and successor of Joseph, inaugurated this new policy, and his daughter, Maria Theresa (1740-1780), continued to pursue, during her long reign, with great success, the course traced by her royal father. The protracted wars, whilst laying waste the country and reducing her population, had also retarded her culture, and it became now necessary to find means to remedy both evils. Attempts were made to supply the lack of population by colonizing. The Alföld, the special home of the Hungarian race, was particularly depopulated, and there we see the work of establishing new settlements most zealously carried on during the whole century. The Slavs from the Upper Country, the Servians from the South, and multitudes of German-speaking peoples from the West, soon spread over the great plain, and the numerous villages of the last could be met with at every step. The government was especially solicitous in promoting German colonization, partly because these settlers were industrious, and partly because this course favored the Germanization of the country. But soon the Hungarians, who had been crowded back into the hilly regions of the country, returned to their beloved Alföld, and for a while a regular hand-to-hand fight ensued between them and the strangers for the possession of the broad acres of the fertile plain. Hardly one generation passed and all those motley populations became Magyarized, and proudly proclaimed themselves to be members of the Hungarian community. Only there where the foreign element had settled in compact masses, they remained strangers still, but the national encroachment on their borders went constantly on. In connection with the colonization was also carried on the work of draining the swamps and improving the soil, and we see the population day by day increasing in numbers and wealth.

Great changes, too, were effected in the country by means of legislation. Successive Diets endeavored to remedy the many palpable defects, and it may be said that the tribunals existing up to 1848 originated in the time of Charles III. At this period, also, was introduced the system of a standing army and with it that of permanent taxation. Both soldiers and taxes are still granted by the Diet, yet, not for special emergencies only, as they arise, but until the next Diet is convoked. About this time the relations between Hungary and the Austrian provinces were more clearly defined by the Pragmatic Sanction of 1723. By it Hungary and the Austrian provinces were declared inseparable, and the ruler of both was always to be one and the same person from the Hapsburg dynasty, in the regular order of succession in the male and female lines; but, otherwise, Hungary was to remain perfectly independent, and was to be governed by her own laws.

The nation was offered an opportunity to prove by her alacrity in complying with the wishes of Charles in regard to a change in the order of the dynastic succession, that his kind feelings towards the country were fully reciprocated by the trustfulness of the people. The right of succession was thus extended to the female line too of those very Hapsburgs, whose dynasty the nation, not many years before, had declared to have altogether forfeited their right to the throne. The country was soon called upon at Maria Theresa's accession to the throne to prove by deeds its attachment and gratitude. The young queen was attacked by all Europe, the enemy being eager to rob her of the fairest portions of her Austrian possessions. In this extreme danger she appealed to chivalrous Hungary for protection, and the nation, forgetting the old quarrels, exclaimed with one voice: "*Vitam et sanguinem! moriamur pro rege nostro Maria Theresia!*" Eighty thousand soldiers went into the war to meet the queen's enemies, who were anxious to divide the spoils of the empire, and during a combat of eight years the Hungarians, whilst defending their Pragmatic Sanction, upheld, at the same time, the integrity of the Austrian possessions. The dynasty had thus won in Hungary, by a spirit of conciliation, a country upon which it could count as a trusty support in case of danger from without.

Maria Theresa showed herself grateful for the sacrifices and devotion of the nation. The district of Temes, which had been retaken from the Turks by her father, was re-annexed to the kingdom of Hungary, and it was Maria Theresa who gave Hungary the city of Fiume, in order that the country might have a seaport town to promote her commerce and industry. A great deal, too, was done by her, in many ways, to improve the material condition of the country, and still more for the advancement of higher culture through the erection of churches and the foundation and organization of schools. In a word, she always remained, to her end, the "gracious queen" of the nation.

A great social revolution had also taken place during the reigns of Charles and Maria Theresa. The magnates of the country deserted in the piping times of peace their eagle's nests on the rocky crests of the hills and descended into the smiling valleys below, building there palaces for themselves after foreign patterns. Life in those rural abodes, owing to the lack of pastimes and refinement, soon became dull to the great lords, and, as there was no national capital to offer distraction, they went abroad, and soon came to like the foreign mode of life better than the lawlessness of their country homes. The Viennese court bade them welcome, overwhelmed them with distinctions, and Maria Theresa, especially, understood the art of fascinating them. Gradually they became foreigners in their dress and manners, and all the Hungarian that was still preserved by these absentees was their names and the estates they possessed in Hungary, the revenues of which they spent abroad. The atmosphere and the graces of court life succeeded in doing what the sword and violence had failed to accomplish. The great lords became estranged from their country and thoroughly Germanized.

If the great noblemen alone had still the exclusive charge of defending the independence and nationality of Hungary as they had done in days of old, then indeed these blessed days of peace would have brought ruin on both. It was fortunate, however, for the country that there was still left the gentry, numbering hundreds of thousands, who, after the peace of 1711, went on in their lives as before, and concerned themselves, in their old way, with the national affairs; the counties, where self-government reigned supreme, being the scene of their action. This class of nobles did not go abroad, nor was it possible to subject any large numbers of them to the fascinations of Viennese court life. They remained at home, retained their Hungarian customs and manners, their national language and dress, and with these it was impossible to make them part. Their counties were so many bulwarks of their nationality and the independence of Hungary, and these numerous seats of self-government furnished the counterpoise to the Germanizing influences of the court, which were thus destined, as far as the nation as a whole was concerned, to come to naught in times of peace, as they had failed before when coercion was employed.

CHAPTER XIV.

THE EMPEROR JOSEPH II. THE NATIONAL REACTION AND THE NAPOLEONIC WARS.

THE royal crown of Hungary has ever been, from the time it encircled the brow of St. Stephen, an object of jealous solicitude and almost superstitious veneration with the nation. It continued to loom up as a luminous and rallying point in the midst of the vicissitudes and stirring events of the history of the country, during all the centuries that followed the coronation of the first king. The people looked upon it as a hallowed relic, the glorious bequest of a long line of generations past and gone, and as the symbol and embodiment of the unity of the state. The different countries composing Hungary were known under the collective name of the *Lands of the Sacred Crown*, and, at the period when the privileged nobility was still enjoying exceptional immunities, each noble styled himself *membrum sacræ coronæ*, a member of the sacred crown. In the estimation of the people it had ceased to be a religious symbol, and had become a cherished national and political memorial, to which the followers of every creed and all the classes without distinction might equally do homage. Nor was the crown an every-day ornament to be displayed by royalty on solemn occasions of pageant. The king wore it only once in his life, on the day of his coronation, when he was bound solemnly to swear fidelity to the constitution, before the high dignitaries of the state, first in church, and to repeat afterwards in the open air his vow to govern the country within the limits of the law. Thus in Hungary it has ever been the ancient custom, prevailing to this day, that, on the king's accession to the throne, it is he who, on his coronation, takes the oath of fidelity to his people, instead of the latter swearing fealty to the king. The right of succession to the throne is hereditary, but the lawful rule of the king begins with the ceremony of coronation only. It requires this ceremonial, which to this day is characterized by the attributes of mediæval pomp and splendor, to render the acts of the ruler valid and binding upon the people; without it every public act of such ruler is a usurpation.

During eight centuries all the kings and queens, without exception, had been eager to place the crown on their heads, in order to come into the full possession of their regal privileges. Joseph II., Maria Theresa's son, who succeeded his mother in 1780, was the first king who refused to be crowned. He felt a reluctance to swear fidelity to the constitution, and to promise, by a solemn oath, to govern the country in accordance with its ancient usages and laws. The people, therefore, never called him their crowned king; he was either styled emperor by them, or nicknamed the "*kalapos*" (hatted) king. His reign was but a series of illegal and unconstitutional acts, and a succession of bitter and envenomed struggles between the nation and her ruler. The contest finally ended with Joseph's defeat. He retracted on his deathbed all his arbitrary measures, and conceded to the people the tardy restoration of their ancient constitution. The conflict, however, had left deep traces in the minds of his Hungarian subjects. It roused them from the dormant state into which they had been lulled by the gentle and maternal absolutism of Maria Theresa. Thus Joseph's schemes not only failed, but, in their effects, they were destined to bring about the triumph of ideas, fraught with important consequences, such as he had hardly anticipated. The nation, waking from her lethargy, gave more prominence than ever to the idea of nationality, an idea which, as time advanced, increased in potency and intensity.

Yet this ruler, who on ascending the throne disregarded all constitutional obligations and waged a relentless war against the Hungarian nationality, must be, nevertheless, ranked amongst the noblest characters of his century. Thoroughly imbued with the enlightened views of the eighteenth century, and those new ideas which had triumphed in the war of independence across the ocean, he was ever in pursuit of generous and exalted aims. He sincerely desired the welfare of the people, and in engaging in this fruitless conflict he was by no means actuated by sinister intentions or by a despotic disposition. To introduce reforms, called for by the spirit of the age, into the Church, the schools, and every department of his government, was the lofty task he had imposed upon himself. A champion of the oppressed, he freed the human conscience from its mediæval fetters, granted equal rights to the persecuted creeds, protected the enslaved peasantry against their arbitrary masters, and enlarged the liberty of the press. He endeavored to establish order and honesty in every branch of the public service, being mindful, at the same time, of all the agencies affecting the prosperity of the people. In a word, his remarkable genius embraced every province of human action where progress, reforms, and ameliorations were desirable.

Unhappily for his own peace of mind and for the destinies of the nation he was called upon to rule, he committed a fatal error in the selection of the methods for accomplishing his humane and philanthropic objects. He desired to render Hungary happy, yet he excluded the nation from the direction of her own affairs. He wished to enact salutary laws, yet he reigned as an absolute monarch, unwilling to call the Diet to his aid in the great work of reformation, ignoring and disdaining the constitution and laws of the country. He was impolitic enough to attack a constitution which, thanks to the devotion of the people, had withstood the shock of seven centuries. He was unwise enough to suppose that the people, in whose hearts the love of their ancient constitution had taken deep root, for the defence of which rivers of blood had been shed, could be prevailed upon to relinquish it to satisfy a theory of royalty. The old political organization was eminently an outgrowth of the Hungarian nationality, and all classes of the people, including the very peasantry to whom the ancient constitution meant only oppression, clung to it with devoted fervor. The people were as anxious for reforms as Joseph himself, but they wanted them by lawful methods, and with the co-operation of the nation and their Diet. Joseph might have become the regenerator and benefactor of Hungary if he had availed himself, for the realization of his grand objects, of the national and lawful channels which lay ready to his hand. But he, unfortunately, preferred attempting to achieve his purpose out of the plenitude of his own power, by imperial edicts and arbitrary measures, thus conjuring up a storm against himself which well-nigh shook his throne, and plunging the nation into a wild ferment of passion bordering on revolution.

The people presented a solid phalanx against Joseph's attacks upon their nationality and language, which to them were objects dearer than every thing else. They little cared for the emperor's well-intentioned endeavors to make them prosperous and happy as long as he asked, in exchange, for the relinquishment of their nationality. And this, above all, was his most ardent wish. He wanted Hungary to be Hungarian no more, and wished its people to cast off the distinctive marks of their individuality, and to adopt the German language, instead of their own, in the schools, the public administration, and in judicial proceedings. In a word, he made German the official language of the country, and was bent on forcing it upon the people.

Henceforth every reform coming from Joseph became hateful to the people. The oppressed classes themselves spurned relief which involved the sacrifice of their sweet mother-tongue. By proclaiming equal rights and equal subjection to the burdens of the state, he arrayed the privileged classes against his person. The Protestants and the peasantry, who had hailed him in the beginning as their new Messiah, and fondly saw in his innovations the dawn of brighter days, also turned from him as soon as he attacked them in what they prized even more than liberty and justice. It was not long before the whole country, without distinction of class, social standing, or creed, combined to set at naught the Germanizing efforts of Joseph. The hard-fought struggle roused the people, hitherto divided by antagonisms of class and creed, to a sense of national solidarity. It was during the critical days of these constitutional conflicts that the foundations of the modern homogeneousness of the Hungarian nation and society were laid down.

The privileged classes looked upon Joseph, on his advent to the throne, with distrust. They foresaw that he would not allow himself to be crowned, in order to avoid taking the oath of fidelity to the constitution of Hungary. The first measures of his reign concerned the organization of the various churches of the country. He extended the religious freedom of the Protestant Church. By virtue of the apostolic rights of the Hungarian kings, he introduced signal reforms into the Catholic Church, especially regarding the education of the clergy, which proved, in part, exceedingly salutary. He abolished numerous religious orders, especially those which were not engaged either in teaching or nursing the sick. One hundred and forty monasteries and nunneries were closed by him in Hungary. The ample property of these convents he employed for ecclesiastical and public purposes and for the advancement of instruction. He exerted himself strenuously and successfully in the establishment of public schools and in the interest of popular education. He removed the only university of which the country could then boast from Buda to Pesth, a city which was rapidly increasing, and added a theological department to that seat of learning. All these innovations met with the approval of the enlightened elements of the nation, whilst the privileged classes and the clergy opposed them with sullen discontent. The opposition was all the more successful, as the emperor had contrived to insult the moral susceptibilities of the common people by some of his measures. Thus, with a view to economizing the boards required for coffins, he ordered the dead to be sewed up in sacks, and to be buried in this apparel. This uncalled-for meddling with the prejudices of the lower classes had the effect of creating a great indignation among them, and of driving them into the camp of the opposition. Trifling and thoughtless measures of a similar nature impaired the credit of the most salutary innovations. The people looked with suspicion at every change, and, heedless of the lofty endeavors of the emperor, everybody, including the officials themselves, rejected the entire governmental system of Joseph.

The emperor also wounded the national feeling of piety by his action concerning the crown he had spurned. According to ancient custom and law the sacred crown was kept in safety in Presburg, in a building provided for that purpose. In 1784 the emperor ordered the crown to be removed to Vienna, in order to be placed there in the royal treasury side by side with the crowns of his other lands. The nation revolted at this profanation of their hallowed relic, and the highest official authorities, throughout the land, protested against a measure which, while it created such widespread ill feeling, was not justified by any necessity. A dreadful storm, accompanied by thunder and lightning, was raging when the crown was removed to Vienna, and the people saw in this a sign that nature herself rebelled against the sacrilege committed by the emperor. The counties continued to urge the return of the crown in addresses which were sometimes humbly suppliant in their tone and sometimes threatening, but Joseph did not yield either to supplications or menaces.

When the edict, which made German the official language of the country, was published, the minds of men all over the country were already greatly disturbed. It is true, that hitherto the Latin and not the Hungarian language had been the medium of communication employed by the state. But the national spirit and the native tongue, which during the first seventy years of the eighteenth century had sadly degenerated, were awakening to new life during Joseph's reign. The literature of the country began to be assiduously cultivated in different spheres. Royal body-guards belonging to distinguished families, gentlemen of refinement, clergymen of modest position, and other sons of the native soil labored with equal zeal and enthusiasm to foster their cherished mother-tongue. It would, therefore, have been an easy matter for Joseph to replace the Latin language, which had become an anachronism, by the Hungarian, and thus to restore the latter to its natural and legal position in the state. He was perfectly right in ridding the country of the mastery of a dead tongue, but he committed a most fatal error in trying to substitute for it the German, an error which avenged itself most bitterly. Joseph entertained a special antipathy to the Hungarian tongue, a dislike which betrayed him into omitting the teaching of the native language from the course of public instruction, and refusing to allow an academy of sciences to be established which had its cultivation for its object.

The emperor's attack upon the language of the nation irremediably broke the last tie between him and the country, and, henceforth, the relations between them could be only hostile. The counties assumed a threatening attitude, some of them refusing obedience altogether. Thus most of them declined to give their official co-operation to the army officers who had been delegated by the emperor to take the census. The count, nevertheless, proceeded, but in many places the inhabitants escaped to the woods, and in some there were serious riots in consequence of the opposition to the commissioners of the census. A rising of a different character took place amongst the Wallachs. The Wallachs, smarting under abuses of long standing, buoyed up by exaggerated expectations consequent upon the emperor's innovations, and stirred up by evil-minded agitators, took to arms and perpetrated the most outrageous atrocities against their Hungarian landlords. The ignorant common people were assured by their leaders, Hora and

Kloska, that the emperor himself sided with them. The Wallach insurgents assassinated the government's commissioners sent to them, destroyed 60 villages and 182 gentlemen's mansions, and killed 4,000 Hungarians, before they could be checked in their bloody work. Although they were finally crushed and punished, a strong belief prevailed in the country that the court of Vienna had been privy to the Wallach rising.

Joseph subsequently laid down most humane rules regulating the relations between the bondmen and their landlords. But the country could not be appeased by any boon, especially as the high protective tariff, just then established for the benefit of the Austrian provinces, was seriously damaging the prosperity of the people. Joseph's foreign policy tended to increase the domestic disaffection. In 1788 he declared war against Turkey, but the campaign turned out unsuccessful, and nearly terminated with the emperor's capture. The nation, emboldened by his defeat, urged now more emphatically her demands, and requested the emperor to annul his illegal edicts, to submit to be crowned, and to restore the ancient constitution. Joseph continuing to resist her demands, most of the counties refused to contribute in aid of the war either money or produce. In addition to their recalcitrant attitude, they most energetically pressed the emperor to convoke the Diet at Buda, a few counties going even so far as to insist upon the Chief Justice's convoking it, if the emperor failed to do so before May, 1790.

The courage of the nation rose still higher when the news of the revolution in France and the revolt in Belgium reached the country. The people refused to furnish recruits and military aid, and the emperor was compelled to use violence in order to obtain either. The counties remained firm and continued to remonstrate in addresses characterized by sharp and energetic language. Joseph yielded at last. He was prostrated by a grave illness, and feeling his end approaching he wished to die in peace with the exasperated nation he had so deeply wounded. On the 28th of January, 1790, he retracted all his illegal edicts, excepting those that had reference to religious toleration, the peasantry, and the clergy, and re-established the ancient constitution of the country. Soon after he sent back the crown to Buda, where its return was celebrated with great pomp, amidst the enthusiastic shouts of the people. Before he could yet convoke the Diet death terminated the emperor's career on the 20th of February. The world lost in him a great and noble-minded man and a friend to humanity, who, however, had been unable to realize all his lofty intentions. The effect of his reign was to rouse Hungary from the apathy into which it had sunk, and at the time of Joseph's death, the minds of the people were a prey to an excitement no less feverish than that which had seized revolutionary France at the same period.

But while in Paris democracy was victorious over royalty, the latter had to yield in Hungary to the privileged nobility. The restored constitution was a charter of political privileges for the nobles only, and as such was most jealously guarded by them. This class kept a strict watch over the liberal tendencies of the age, preventing the importation of democratic ideas from France from fear of harm to their exclusive immunities.

Joseph was succeeded by his brother, Leopold II., who until now had been Grand Duke of Tuscany. The new ruler was as enlightened as his predecessor, and had as much the welfare of the people at heart; but he respected, at the same time, the laws and the constitution. He immediately convoked the Diet in order to be crowned, and by this act he solemnly sealed the peace with the nation. The people hailed with joy this first step of their new king, and there was nothing in the way of their now obtaining lawfully from the good-will of the king the salutary legislation which Joseph had attempted to force arbitrarily upon them. But the fond hopes in this direction were doomed to disappointment.

The national movement had not helped to power those who were in favor of progress, equality of rights, and democracy. No doubt there were people in the country who differed from the men in authority, who were sincerely attached to the doctrines of the French Revolution and eager to supplant the privileges of the nobles by the broader rights belonging to all humanity. The national literature was in the hands of men of this class. They combated the reactionary spirit of the nobility, and contended for the recognition of the civil and political rights of by far the largest portion of the people, the non-nobles. They boldly and with generous enthusiasm wielded the pen in defence of those noble ideas, and indoctrinated the people with them as much as the restraints placed upon the press allowed it at that period. They succeeded in obtaining recruits for their ideas from the very ranks of the privileged classes, and many an enlightened magnate admitted that the time had arrived for modernizing the constitution of Hungary by an extension of political rights. Their number was swelled also by the more intelligent portion of the inhabitants of the cities, and those educated patriotic people who, although no gentle blood flowed in their veins, had either obtained office under Joseph's reign or had imbibed the political views of that monarch. But all of these men combined formed but an insignificant fraction of the people compared to the numerous nobility, who, after their enforced submission during ten years, were eager to turn to the advantage of their own class the victory they had achieved over Joseph. During the initial preparations for the elections to the Diet, and in the course of the elections, sentiments were publicly uttered and obtained a majority in the county assemblies, which caused a feverish commotion amongst the common people and the peasantry. The latter especially now eagerly clung to innovations introduced by the Emperor Joseph, so beneficial as regarded their own class, and were reluctant to submit to the restoration of the former arbitrary landlord system. Their remonstrances were answered by the counties to the effect that Providence had willed it so that some men should be kings, others nobles, and others again bondmen. Such cruel reasoning failed to satisfy the aggrieved peasantry. Symptoms of a dangerous revolutionary spirit showed themselves throughout a large portion of the country, and an outbreak could be prevented only by the timely assurance, on the part of the counties, that the matter would be submitted to the Diet about to assemble.

The Diet, which had not been convened for twenty-five years, opened in Buda in the beginning of June, 1790. The coronation soon took place. Fifty years had elapsed since the last similar pageant had been enacted in Hungary. After a lengthy and vehement contest extending over ten months, in the course of which the Diet was removed from Buda to Presburg, the laws of 1790-1791, which form part of the fundamental articles of the Hungarian constitution, were finally passed. By them the independence of Hungary as a state obtained the fullest recognition. The laws, which were the result of the co-operation of the crown and the Estates, declared that Hungary was an independent country, subject to no other country, possessing her own constitution by which alone she was to be governed. Important concessions were also made to the rights of the citizens of the country. The privileges of the nobility were left intact, but the extreme wing of the reactionary nobles had to rest satisfied with this acquiescence in the former state of things, and were not allowed to push the narrow-minded measures advocated by them. The majority of the Diet was influenced in their wise moderation, partly by the exalted views of the king, and to a greater extent yet by the disaffected spirit rife amongst the people, and especially threatening amongst the Serb population of the country. The laws secured the liberties of the Protestant and the Greek united churches, remedied the most urgent griefs of the peasantry, and declared those who were not noble capable of holding minor offices. Although the most important measures of reform were put off to a future time by the diet of 1790-

1791, several preparatory royal commissions having been appointed for their consideration, yet the work it accomplished was the salutary beginning of a liberal legislation which culminated, not quite sixty years later, in the declaration of the equal rights of the people as the basis of the Hungarian commonwealth.

After the meeting of this Diet, however, very little was done in the direction of reforms. The good work was interrupted, partly by the premature death of Leopold II. (March 1, 1792), and partly by the warlike period, extending over twenty-five years, which, in Hungary as throughout all Europe, claimed public attention, and diverted the minds of the leaders of the nation from domestic topics. Francis I., the son and successor of Leopold II., caused himself to be crowned in due form, and much was at first hoped from his reign. But the Jacobin rule of terror in Paris, and the dread of seeing the revolutionary scenes repeated in his own realm, wrought a complete change in his character and policy. He soon stubbornly rejected every innovation, and gradually became a pillar of strength for the European reaction, that extravagant conservatism which expected to efface the effects of the French Revolution by an unquestioning adherence to the old and traditional order of things. This illiberal spirit of the monarch rendered impossible for the time any further reform-movement in Hungary. Every question of desirable change met with the most obstinate opposition on the part of the king, and the reforms submitted by the royal commissions were considered by every successive Diet without ever becoming law. The period which now followed was gloomy in the extreme, as well for Hungary as for the Austrian provinces of Francis I. The inhabitants of these countries were constantly called upon by the king in the course of the wars to make sacrifices in treasure and blood, by furnishing recruits and by paying high taxes. At the same time the government resorted to the most absolute and arbitrary measures to prevent the people from being contaminated with French ideas. The press was crushed by severe penalties. Every enlightened idea was banished from the schools and expunged from the school-books. Only men, for whose extreme reactionary spirit the police could vouch, were appointed to the professorships or to other offices. A system of universal spying and secret information caused everybody to be suspected and to suffer from private vindictiveness, whilst those who dared to avow liberal views were the objects of cruel persecution.

The numerically few but staunch adherents of democracy, being thus debarred from openly laboring for their views, endeavored to accomplish their purposes by secret combinations. A secret society was formed in Pesth, the centre of the political life of the country. This league of Hungarian Jacobins had but a confused idea of its own aims, and of the means of achieving them. They produce, at this distance of time, the impression of an organization, indulging in crude, exaggerated, and even thoughtless visions, but theirs, nevertheless, is the credit of having been the first society of the kind in the country, and of thus furnishing a link in the political development of the public spirit in Hungary. Although the members of the league were unable to secure any tangible results, yet they deserve a place in the national history as the first martyrs of universal freedom and human rights in Hungary, for they forfeited their lives or suffered long imprisonments for the holy cause. The movement was originally planned by Ignatius Martinovics, a learned abbot who entered into relations with the Jacobins abroad, first with those of Paris, and afterwards with their sympathizers in Germany and Austria. With the assistance of these he intended to bring about a republic of Hungary, and to establish there the doctrines of equality and liberty. He organized for that purpose a secret society in Pesth, after the pattern of the masonic societies, which were then flourishing throughout the country. There were in point of fact two distinct associations, one called the reformers, the other styled the friends of liberty and equality. The former knew nothing of the designs of the latter, whilst these, occupying a higher rank, were fully initiated into the secrets of the reformers. The aim of both alike was to insure the triumph of the principles of the French Revolution. The members recognized each other by secret signs, and used in their correspondence a cipher devised for the purpose. Martinovics' scheme was to hoist the revolutionary flag as soon as the increased number of members in both societies might render such a step advisable. Meanwhile the sole business of the members consisted in spreading among the people a catechism conceived in a revolutionary spirit.

Martinovics commenced the organization of the secret society in the spring of 1794. He was assisted in his work by John Laczkovics, formerly a captain in the army, Joseph Hajnóczi, an ex-alispán (vicecomes or deputy sheriff of a county), and Francis Szentmarjay, a young man of distinction, who were all zealously engaged in recruiting members for the new association. Among the latter, however, but few knew of Martinovics' ultimate object, or of his French connections. Most of them thought that it was his intention to secure the introduction of reforms by lawful means. As to the secret character of the society, they looked upon it as a concession to the fashion of the period, introduced by the freemasons. During the eighteenth century a real mania for secrecy of this kind prevailed all over Europe, and secret societies sprang up in every quarter for purposes which, if publicly proclaimed, would have met with no opposition whatever. The society of the Hungarian Jacobins did not owe its existence to subversionary tendencies, but to that eagerness for reforms which never ceased to agitate the nation. With the exception of a dozen unreflecting men who dreamt of overthrowing the Hungarian monarchy with the aid of the French, the rank and file were entirely composed of men who believed in reforms achieved by lawful methods. The leaders themselves, Martinovics, Hajnóczi, and Laczkovics, had filled important offices under the Emperor Joseph, and had subsequently supported King Leopold in his efforts at reform. If

Leopold had lived, every one of them would have borne a conspicuous part in public affairs. But the triumph of the reactionary spirit under the reign of King Francis made them conspirators. Those of their friends who joined them were all honest and enthusiastic patriots, who saw in the success of democratic ideas the welfare of Hungary. But they did not look to a revolution for the realization of their fond hopes. They entered the society for the sole purpose of preparing the minds of their countrymen for reforms to be obtained by constitutional means. Almost every Hungarian writer, who was not in some dependent position, belonged to the society. Amongst these was Francis Kazinczy, the regenerator of Hungarian literature, and one of the most respectable members of the literary guild. The French ideas found a grateful echo among the intelligent elements of the country. The reports of French victories were hailed with joy in the capital, by the professors at the university, and the students, as well as by people in the country, especially in the county of Zemplén, the home of Kazinczy. Liberty poles were erected in several places, many hoping that the victories of the French would establish in Hungary the reign of liberty and equality. These demonstrations, however, were entirely independent, and were not inspired by Martinovics. Such occurrences reflected only the effect of foreign events on the public mind of Hungary, which had at all times been open to influences from abroad, and which did not fail, in this instance, to respond to the voice of humanity which then rang out through a large portion of the Western world.

The secret society confined its work to procuring fresh members and to a wide distribution of their political catechisms. The number of the members amounted altogether to seventy-five, of whom twenty-seven lived in Pesth, and the remainder belonged to every part of the country. Only three months had elapsed after the organization of the society when Martinovics was arrested in Vienna, and Laczkovics, Szentmarjay, and Hajnóczy in Pesth. The Viennese police had discovered the Austrian fraternity, and, finding Martinovics amongst its leaders, detained him at once. Martinovics while in prison made a full confession of every thing, and the arrests in Hungary were the consequence. About fifty men were thrown into prison. At the time of their arrest, the distribution of a few revolutionary pamphlets excepted, no deed, subversive of the public order, could be traced to the secret society of which they were members. It was therefore hoped that the government, in punishing them, would act with moderation and humanity. King Francis disappointed such hopes. He ordered them to be prosecuted without mercy, being determined to set a terrifying example, and, by inaugurating a reactionary reign of terror, to discourage his subjects from sympathizing with French ideas. Eighteen prisoners were sentenced to death, but Martinovics and six of his companions only were executed. They lost their heads by the executioner's sword on the meadow in Buda, a spot called to this day the field of blood. The remaining prisoners, with few exceptions, were sentenced to longer and shorter terms of imprisonment, and two of the suspected escaped arrest by suicide. Francis Kazinczy suffered severe imprisonment in an Austrian dungeon during eight long years, and numerous other Hungarian writers were similarly deprived of their liberty.

These bloody executions created widespread dismay in the country. No one felt safe, for everybody was ignorant of the nature of the crimes with which the unhappy victims had been charged. The counties remonstrated, in addresses sent to the king, against these cruel proceedings, but without any effect. Francis pensioned off five liberal professors at the university, interdicted the teaching of Kant's philosophy at that seat of learning, began to persecute every enlightened man in the country, and especially delighted in vexing in every possible way the intelligent element of Zemplén County. The friends of liberty, the men of progress, were thoroughly frightened. The press, too, was fettered by the government, and thus, by degrees, public life in Hungary became torpid and stagnant, the adherents of reform were reduced to silence, and innovations had to bide their time. The reactionary government achieved a complete victory. It banished from the high offices even the most moderate men, and filled every place of importance with persons who delighted in relentlessly repressing every democratic impulse in Hungary.

The Diets which met during this period paid no attention whatever to reforms. Their main function consisted in voting considerable supplies in money and soldiers for the war against the French. The Hungarian nation sacrificed a great deal for her king during the Napoleonic wars, and, when the hostile armies were approaching the border of the country, every noble personally took up arms to defend the throne of his crowned king with his life and blood. The gentry distinguished themselves by their devotion, especially in 1809. Napoleon made the Hungarians the most enticing offers in order to seduce them from their allegiance to King Francis. He called upon them by proclamation to abandon Francis, to elect, under the French protectorate, a king of their own, and to restore Hungary to complete independence. But the Hungarian nation remained unshaken in their devotion to the king, and rallied round him and the ancient dynasty. The French, failing in their scheme, entered Hungary. The Hungarians gallantly defended their native soil, but were defeated near Raab, owing to the incapacity of their Austrian generals. During the whole Napoleonic contest, to its termination, in 1815, Hungary made immense sacrifices for the royal throne, and thousands of her sons shed their blood in its defence, on the most distant battle-fields of Europe.

Francis but scantily rewarded the fidelity of the nation. He always had words of praise for the Hungarians, but constantly put off remedying the evils they complained of. The long wars, paralyzing commerce and trade, had fatally affected the prosperity of the country.

The government, in order to meet the expenses of the continuous wars, had issued paper money to such an enormous extent that the paper currency became completely depreciated. The depreciation of one florin to one fifth of its face value was subsequently officially promulgated by the government, causing thereby immense losses to the people. To these miseries were added the numerous illegal acts and arbitrary and unconstitutional proceedings of the government, which continued even after Napoleon had been safely chained to the rock of St. Helena and peace began anew to dawn upon the world. The reign of reaction and absolutism which set in in Europe in 1815 extended its baneful influence also over Hungary. The constitution was completely ignored by the king and no Diet was convened. These were sad days for Hungary. There was no one to promote her national interests, and her advancement in culture was hampered by the meddling rule of the Austrian police. And, indeed, had not, about this time, the national literature infused a fresh and hopeful spirit into the body politic, Hungary would have presented a most deplorable picture of apathy and despair. Literature, science, and poetry, the cultivation of which was sadly interrupted by the imprisonment of most of their votaries in 1795, in consequence of the Martinovics conspiracy, became powerful agencies in rousing the nation to renewed political activity. Numerous distinguished writers sprang up, exerting themselves to inculcate lessons of patriotism and national self-respect into the minds of the people who had been arbitrarily debarred from the most telling influences of legitimate culture by the Viennese government. The latter at last thought that the time had arrived when the absolute government prevailing in her Austrian dominions might be established with safety also in Hungary. The first attempt made by King Francis in this direction was to levy, arbitrarily, solely by his own authority and without the consent of the Diet (which was necessary under the law), 35,000 recruits for the army. This illegal exaction of the king created a tremendous commotion amongst the people, and resulted in a most desperate conflict between the Hungarian nation and the Viennese government. The political contest which lasted five years newly inflamed the national enthusiasm. King Francis finally saw the error of his ways, acknowledged the illegality of his action, and returned to constitutional government. He summoned the Diet, in 1825, which, continuing the work of reform checked in 1791, gave the impulse to a new era of modern progress in Hungary.

CHAPTER XV.

SZÉCHENYI, KOSSUTH, AND THE STRUGGLE FOR LIBERTY IN 1848-1849.

ON one of the most picturesque positions in Buda-Pesth, on the left bank of the majestic Danube, stands the bronze statue of Stephen Széchenyi, the greatest Hungarian of this century. The piety of the nation has placed it in the midst of her most conspicuous creations. At its feet rolls the mighty river whose regulation was commenced by Széchenyi, who made it a line of communication in the commercial system of Europe; in front is seen the grand suspension bridge, and beyond it is visible the mouth of the tunnel which, piercing the castled mountain of Buda, connects the dispersed parts of the city. In the rear rise the palatial edifices of the Hungarian Academy of Sciences, which owes its existence to Széchenyi's munificence, and round about stretches noisy, surging Buda-Pesth, to whose embellishment and enlightenment no one ever devoted himself so zealously as Stephen Széchenyi. Every thing surrounding the statue reminds us of the transcendent genius of Széchenyi, who raised for himself by his indefatigable labors, which form a link between old and modern Hungary, a monument more lasting and grander than the one cast in bronze.

Stephen Széchenyi was born on the 21st of September, 1791. He was the scion of a family which had given many distinguished men to their country, and with whom patriotism was traditional. His father, Count Francis, was the founder of the greatest institute of Hungary, having public culture for its aim, the National Museum of Buda-Pesth, which is now reckoned one of the finest and richest of the kind in Europe. Count Francis clung with passionate devotion to the cause of his country. The tender mind of his son Stephen was often puzzled to see his father melancholy and lost in thought, and later only, when grown to manhood, did he learn that his father had been grieving over the backwardness of his country. Count Stephen inherited the patriotic sentiments of his father, and never for a moment lost sight of the one great object of his life, to revive the now decaying nation, which had acted so proud a part in the past, and to secure for her a better future by promoting her material and cultural interests. Stephen Széchenyi became the apostle of this patriotic mission; he devoted his whole life to this one lofty thought, studying for many years, reflecting, travelling, gathering knowledge, and when the hour arrived to enter upon the scene of action, he took the lead of the nation, aptly equipped for the severe task.

He finished his studies under the roof of his father, who was a man of high culture. The turmoils of the Napoleonic wars, shaking all Europe and with it Hungary, allowed but scant opportunity for peaceful avocations when Count Stephen had reached his sixteenth year. He accordingly entered the army and gallantly took part, as a young officer, in the wars of the period, being present at the famous battle of Leipsic. The Congress of Vienna put an end to the wars which had raged in Europe for twenty-five years, and during the protracted period of peace following it, Széchenyi bestowed his attention upon the affairs of his country. Before taking an active part, however, he travelled for a considerable time through Italy, France, and England, and only after having become familiar with the advanced civilization of foreign countries did he return to his own, filled with grand ideas, with lofty, patriotic feelings, his brain seething, and his soul thirsting for action, in order to conquer for himself a sphere of public activity.

The Diet of 1825 afforded him a fitting opportunity in this direction. During the thirteen years preceding the convoking of this Diet the country had been ruled in the most absolute manner. The government ignored, during that period, the constitution, collected by force of arms and arbitrarily illegal taxes, filled, in the same despotic way, the ranks of the army, fettered the liberty of the press, and deprived the nation of her ancient rights. These acts of violence stirred up the indignation of the country, and the natural reaction was still more roused and fostered by the dawning Hungarian literature which proclaimed a brighter future to the nation. Csokonai, Francis Kazinczy, Alexander and Charles Kisfaludy, Michael Vörösmarty, Francis Kölcsey, and other eminent writers were the fathers of a new era in Hungarian literature, and by their works they kindled the national feeling and roused the public spirit. The nation awoke and was eager to march in the footsteps of the civilization of Europe. She only lacked a leader, but in the course of the deliberations of the Diet of 1825, that leader was found.

Stephen Széchenyi, being a member of the Upper House by right of birth, took his seat there among the aristocracy of the land. His first act was destined to be the precursor of a new epoch in the history of the nation. On the 25th of October he made a short speech; his manner was embarrassed and confused; but he spoke in Hungarian, a proceeding which was looked upon at that time as a revolutionary act, full of boldness, and which excited the utmost indignation of the highest circles. The Latin language had until then remained, in keeping with the traditions of the past, the official language of the House of Magnates, Széchenyi was the first magnate who dared to cut loose from the ancient tradition, and, although a great portion of his fellow-magnates, especially the older ones, were shocked at the innovation, yet the number of Hungarian-speaking great lords continually increased after this, and the bold stand he took on that occasion had much to do with the restoration of the national language to its rightful place.

Shortly after the Lower House witnessed the triumph achieved by him in the cause of Hungarian culture. During the preliminary sessions preceding the plenary ones, the question had been deliberated upon for several days as to the best means of fostering the national language.

Széchenyi, with several of his noble friends, was present at one of these conferences, listening and looking on. Each deputy in turn stated his views on the subject. One of them, Paul Nagy, a distinguished orator of the opposition, declared, with an air of deep conviction, that to cultivate the Hungarian language with a view to make it successfully compete with the Germanizing tendencies of the government, and with the Latin language, it was necessary to establish a Hungarian academy of sciences. To accomplish this, he added, money was needed, and this could not be obtained from the government, which was hostile to the scheme. Let the nation furnish the money, the great lords, the owners of the vast fortunes and landed estates, setting first a good example to the rest. The effect of these kindling words was a thrilling one. Széchenyi immediately stepped forward, and, addressing the presiding officer, asked leave to say a few words. Amidst the general attention of those present he briefly stated that he was ready to contribute one year's entire income from his estates to a fund wherewith to found an institute whose object would be the fostering of the Hungarian language. These simple words were received with a storm of applause. A remarkable spectacle now ensued. One man after another arose eager to contribute to the fund of the future Hungarian Academy of Sciences, and the sum was soon swelled to 154,000 florins, Széchenyi's contribution alone amounting to 60,000 florins. The institute was soon established, and, thanks to the patriotic support of the nation, the funds of the Academy exceed at present 2,000,000 florins. The activity of this institute has proved, for the last fifty years, most beneficial to the development of the Hungarian language and the advancement of science in the country.

This munificent act placed Széchenyi at once in the front ranks of the nation, and the very enthusiasm roused by his generous patriotism was the means of exciting his best energies, and of spurring him on to further action. Széchenyi, although acting, on the whole, with the exceedingly moderate opposition, which was conservative and not unfrequently quite reactionary, influenced as it was by the famous policy of Prince Metternich, never became a member of either of the political parties. His leading idea was that the first thing to be done was to improve the material and intellectual condition of the people, and to increase the prosperity and culture of the country. He had founded in the interest of civilization the Hungarian Academy, and now he labored enthusiastically to improve the commercial, industrial, and economical condition of the country. In this work he had to contend with all sorts of obstacles and prejudices on the part not only of the higher circles, but of the very class that was to be benefited by his reforms. But Széchenyi did not lose heart, and, undisturbed by many a bitter experience, he undeviatingly pursued his own course, and carried through with an iron will every measure deemed beneficial by him. His busy brain never ceased to devise new patriotic schemes, and to make them acceptable to the people. He won back the estranged aristocracy of the country, and assigned to them a leading position in national politics; he strove to raise the capital to a European level, and advanced the national prosperity by the discovery of new resources, the opening of new roads of communication, and by the creation of many useful public institutions. He had equal regard for the interests of all classes, from the lord to the peasant, and thus strove, while yet surrounded by the antiquated order of things, to awaken the people to a sense of national consciousness, and to promote the recognition of the solidarity of interests between all the classes of the nation. His busy brain embraced every public interest, and he exerted every social and economical agency to ripen in the nation the notions of modern European civilization. He was a powerful agitator, in equal degrees master of the sword and the pen, and although his whole individuality, his character, and his habits bore the stamp of the aristocratic circle in which he was born and educated, yet, by dint of his conspicuous and many-sided labors, he in reality was the most indefatigable champion and pioneer of democratic ideas in his own country.

His first great literary work (a smaller one had preceded it), entitled "Credit," was published in 1830, and in it he treated of economical questions of the most immediate importance to the country. It was a work of great power, marked by scholarly thoroughness, practical statesmanship, and poetic elevation, and produced an extraordinary sensation throughout the country. It was read everywhere, in the palaces of the magnates, in the mansions of the provincial gentry, and in the homes and offices of merchants and tradesmen. The book was spoken of in the most exalted terms by some, while others declared its author to be a communist and revolutionary agitator. The foes to progress, the defenders of the decaying privileges of the nobility, burned the book, while the friends of the new ideas, and especially the rising generation, saw in it the gospel of a new era. It was in this work that Széchenyi, addressing the generation that vainly clung to the reminiscences of the past, said: "Do not constantly trouble yourselves with the vanished glories of the past, but rather let your determined patriotism bring about the prosperity of the beloved fatherland. Many there are who think that *Hungary has been*, but for my part I like to think that *Hungary shall be.*"

Under the influence of these exalted ideas Széchenyi persevered in his practical efforts for the common weal. He wrote a great deal up to the time of his death, and some of his works are justly ranked among the gems of Hungarian literature. But more precious than these are his practical creations, which still, for the most part, survive, and which are destined to perpetuate his fame for many centuries to come. His busy mind attended to every variety of matters of public concern. Thus it was he who introduced horse-racing into the country, not for the purpose of affording a mere gentlemanly pastime, but with the object of developing horse-breeding in Hungary, an object which has been very successfully accomplished by the new sport. In furtherance of this object he formed a society which subsequently became the National Breeding Association, which flourishes to this day. In order to afford to the gentry permanently a rallying and central point in the country, he established the Buda-Pesth National Casino, a social club of high distinction, still in existence and enjoying an enviable reputation in the best European circles. He took quite an active part in the management of the new Academy of Sciences; zealously supported the efforts made to found a permanent national theatre, efforts which subsequently proved successful; started and realized the scheme for building a permanent bridge across the Danube, connecting Pesth and Buda, and for the construction of a tunnel under the castled mountain of Buda; conducted for years the work of regulating the Danube, especially in the vicinity of the Vaskapu (Iron Gate); and also aided in the establishment of the Danube Steam Navigation Company, which at this day has hundreds of ships engaged in the local and export trade. His most glorious work, however, was the regulation of the Theiss, resulting, in the course of time, in the reclaiming of a marshy territory containing one hundred and fifty square miles, and turning it into a rich and fertile soil. His mind was teeming, besides, with various schemes looking to the building of railways, and to the promotion of commerce and industry; but all these various undertakings were marked by the same steady spirit of patriotic endeavor.

For fifteen years, up to 1840, the popularity of Széchenyi had gone on increasing throughout the country, and his name was cherished by every good patriot in the land. About this time, however, the great statesman was destined to come into collision with a man who was his peer in genius and abilities. The two patriots were representatives of different methods, and in the contest produced by the shock of antagonistic tendencies Széchenyi was compelled to yield to Louis Kossuth, his younger rival. Although there was no material difference between their aims, for both wished to see their country great, free, constitutionally governed, prosperous, and advanced in civilization, yet in the ways and means employed by them to attain that aim they were diametrically opposed to each other. Széchenyi, who descended from a family of ancient and aristocratic lineage, and presented himself to the nation with connections reaching up into the highest circles of the court, with the lustre of his ancient name, and with his immense fortune, wished to secure the happiness of his country by quite different methods from those adopted by Louis Kossuth, a child of the people, who, although he was a nobleman by birth, yet belonged to that poorer class of gentry who support themselves by their own exertions, and who, in Hungary, are destined to fulfil the mission of the citizen-classes of other countries. It is from these classes of the gentry that are, for the most part, recruited the tradespeople, the smaller landowners, professional men, writers, subordinate officials, lawyers, physicians, clergymen, teachers, and professors. By virtue of their nobility, it is true, they belonged to the privileged class of the country, and were not subjected to the humiliations of the oppressed peasantry, yet they had to earn a living by their own work, and were therefore not only accessible to, but were ready enthusiastically to receive, the lofty message of liberty and equality which the French Revolution of 1830 began to proclaim anew throughout all Europe. These doctrines formed a sharp contrast to the views of Count Stephen Széchenyi, views which, owing to the social position of the man who held them, were not devoid of a certain aristocratic tinge, and according to which the most important part in the regeneration of the Hungarian nation was assigned to the aristocracy. It was a part, however, which the Hungarian aristocracy was itself by no means disposed to assume. Among its younger members, indeed, could be found, here and there, enthusiastic men who were devotedly attached to the person of the lordly reformer, but the great majority of his class were hostilely arrayed against Széchenyi's aims, and, obstructing the granting of even the most inoffensive demands of the nation, supported the Viennese government, which was rigidly opposed to political reforms and to any changes in the public institutions of the country. This attitude of the aristocracy compelled Széchenyi to avoid as much as possible all questions concerning constitutionality and liberty, and to confine the work of reform chiefly to the sphere of internal improvements. The only way in which he could hope to obtain the support of the court of Vienna and of the majority of the Upper House for his politico-economical measures, was to remain as neutral as possible in politics. The idea which chiefly governed his actions was that the country should be first strengthened internally, and that afterwards it would be easy for the nation to bring about the triumph of her national and political aspirations.

After 1840, however, the bulk of the nation, and especially the small gentry whose preponderating influence was making itself continually felt, were unwilling to follow Széchenyi in his one-sided policy. The reformatory work of Széchenyi during the preceding fifteen years had educated public opinion up to new and great ideas, but the leaders of that public opinion were now to be found in the House of Representatives in the persons of Francis Deák and Louis Kossuth. They wished to obtain for their country both political liberty and material prosperity. They knew the effect of political institutions upon the material well-being and civilization of a nation, and they no longer deemed it possible to attain these objects without a modern constitutional government. Louis Kossuth, who was born in 1802, was the very incarnation of the great democratic ideas of his age. He was entirely a man of work and entered the legal profession, after having completed his studies with great distinction, for the purpose of supporting himself by it. Kossuth was present at the Diet of 1832, when the government, which conducted itself most brutally and arbitrarily towards the press, refused to allow the newspapers to print reports of the deliberations of the Diet in spite of the repeated urgings by the deputies for such an authorization, and it was owing to his ingenuity that this prohibition was evaded. The censorship was exercised on printed matter only and did not extend to manuscripts. Kossuth wrote out the reports of the Diet himself, had numerous copies made of them in writing, and circulated them, for a slight fee, in every part of the country, where they were looked for with feverish expectation, and, owing to the spirit of opposition with which they were colored, were read with the greatest eagerness. This manuscript newspaper produced quite a revolutionary movement amongst the people, frightening even the Austrian government. The latter now attempted to silence Kossuth by gentle means, promising him high offices and a pension, but he refused the enticing offers and continued his work for the benefit of the nation. Foiled in the attempt to lure Kossuth from his duty, the government resorted to violence, seized the lithographic apparatus by means of which Kossuth planned to multiply his manuscript newspaper, and gave directions to the postmasters to detain and open all those sealed packages which were supposed to contain the reports. But these arbitrary proceedings of the government could not put an end to the circulation of the newspaper; the country gentlemen, by their own servants, continued to send each other single copies, and the matter was given up only when the Diet ceased to be in session. Then Kossuth, at the urgent request of his friends and, one might say, of the whole country, started a new manuscript newspaper at Buda-Pesth, which reported the deliberations of the county assemblies. The effect produced by this new paper was fraught with even greater consequences than the first had created, for it was instrumental in bringing the counties into contact with each other, thus affording them an opportunity to combine against the government. The latter, however, soon prohibited its publication, but the prohibition gave rise to a storm of indignation throughout the whole country. The counties in solid array addressed protests to the government against the illegal act and on behalf of Kossuth, who continued to publish the paper in spite of the inhibition. The government at last resorted to the most barefaced brutality. Kossuth, the brave champion of liberty, its eloquent pen and herald, was dragged to a damp and dark subterranean prison-cell in the castle of Buda, and detained there, whilst his father and mother and his family, who were looking to him solely for their support, were robbed of the aid of their natural protector.

Although at that period lawlessness was the order of the day, yet this last cruel and illegal act of the government greatly exasperated the public mind, which was already in a ferment of excitement. But while the excited passions raged throughout the country, the government, nothing loth, caused Kossuth to be prosecuted for high treason, and, having obtained his conviction, had him sentenced to an imprisonment of three years. Kossuth applied himself during his detention to serious studies, and acquired also, while in prison, the English language to such an extent that he was enabled to address in that language, during his exile, with great effect and impressiveness, large audiences both in England and in the United States of America. His imprisonment lasted two long years, after the lapse of which he obtained, in 1840, a pardon in consequence of the repeated and urgent representations of the Diet.

Kossuth returned to the scene of his former activity as the martyr of free speech, and the victim to the cause of the nation. He very soon found a new field in which to labor. The government perceived at last that violence was of little avail, and that those questions which were occupying the minds to such a degree could no longer be kept from being publicly discussed by the press. Kossuth now obtained permission to edit a political daily paper. Its publication was commenced under the title of *Pesti Hirlap* (Pesth Newspaper) in 1841, and may be said to have created the political daily press of Hungary. It disseminated new ideas among the masses, stirred up the indifferent to feel an interest in the affairs of the country and gave a purpose to the national aspirations. It proclaimed democratic reforms in every department; the abolition of the privileges of the nobility and of their exemption from taxation, equal rights and equal burdens for all the citizens of the state, and the extension of public instruction, and it endeavored to restore the Hungarian nationality to the place it was entitled to claim in the organism of the state.

The wealth of ideas thus daily communicated to the country appeared in the most attractive garb, for Kossuth possessed a masterly style, and his leaders and shorter articles showed off to advantage so many unexpected beauties of the Hungarian language, that his readers were fairly enchanted and carried away by them. His articles were a happy compound of poetical elevation and oratorical power, gratifying common-sense and the imagination at the same time, appealing by their lucid exposition to the reader's intelligence, and exciting and warming this fancy by their fervor. Kossuth always rightly guessed what questions most interested the nation, and the daily press became, in his hands, a power in Hungary, electrifying the masses, who were always ready to give their unconditional support to his bold and far-reaching schemes.

The extraordinary influence obtained by Kossuth through his paper frightened Széchenyi, and, to even a greater degree, those whose prejudices were shocked or ancient privileges and interests were endangered by the democratic agitations for reform. Kossuth was attacked in books, pamphlets, and newspapers, but he came out victorious from all contests. In vain did Széchenyi himself, backed by his great authority in the land, assail him, declaring that he did not object to Kossuth's ideas, but that his manner and his tactics were reprehensible, and that the latter were sure to lead to a revolution. The great mass of the people felt instinctively that revolution had become a necessity and was unavoidable, if Hungary was to pass from the old mediæval order to the establishment of modern institutions, and was to become a state where equality before the law should be the ruling standard. The masses were strengthened in this conviction by the unreasonable, short-sighted, and violent policy pursued by the government of Vienna, which obstructed the slightest reforms in the ancient institutions and opposed every national aspiration, and under whose protecting wing the reactionary elements of the Upper House were constantly paralyzing the noblest and best efforts made by the Lower House for the public weal, while the same government arbitrarily supported claims of the Catholic clergy, in flat contradiction to the rights and liberties of the various denominations inhabiting the country. The government, in its antipathy to the national movement, went even further. It secretly incited the other nationalities, especially the Croats, against the Hungarians, and thus planted the seeds from which sprang the subsequent great civil war. In observing the dangerous symptoms preceding the last-mentioned movement, and the bloody scenes and fights provoked at every election by the hirelings of the government, in order to intimidate the adherents of reform, the friends of progress became more and more convinced that the period of moderation, such as preached by Széchenyi, had passed by, and must give way to that resolute policy, advocated by Kossuth, which recoiled from no consequences. Numerous magnates, all the chief leaders of the gentry, boasting of enlightenment and patriotism, and imbued with European culture, rallied around Kossuth, until finally the public opinion of the country and the enthusiasm of which he was the centre caused him to be returned, in 1847, together with Count Louis Batthyányi, as deputy from the foremost county of the country, the county of Pesth.

During the first months the Diet of 1847—'8, which was to raise Hungary to the rank of those countries that proclaimed equal rights and possessed a responsible parliamentary government, differed very little from the one preceding it. The opposition initiated, as before, great reforms, but there was no one who believed that their realization was near at hand. Kossuth repeatedly addressed the House, and soon convinced his audience that he was as irresistible an orator as he had proved powerful as a writer. But there was nothing to indicate that the country was on the eve of a great transformation.

The revolution of February, 1848, which broke out in Paris, changed, as if by magic, the relative positions of Austria and Hungary. Metternich's system of government, which was opposed to granting liberty to the people, collapsed at once. The storm of popular indignation swept it away like a house built of cards. At the first news of the occurrences in Paris Kossuth asked in the Lower House for the creation of a responsible ministry. Kossuth's motion was favorably received by the Lower House, but in the Upper House it was rejected, the government not being yet alive to the real state of affairs, and still hoping by a system of negation to frustrate the wishes of the people. But very soon the revolution reared its head in Vienna itself, and the wishes of the Hungarian people, uttered at Buda-Pesth, received thereby a new and powerful advocate.

At that time the Hungarian Diet still met at Presburg, but the two sister cities of Buda and Pesth formed the real capital of the country, and were the centre of commerce, industry, science, and literature. Michael Vörösmarty, the poet laureate of the nation, lived in Pesth, and there the twin stars of literature, Alexander Petöfi and Maurus Jókai, shone on the national horizon. Jókai, who is still living and enjoys a world-wide fame as a novelist, and Petöfi, the eminent poet, who was destined to become the Tyrtæus of his nation, were then both young men, full of enthusiasm and intrepid energy, and teeming with great ideas. About these two gathered the other writers and youth of the university, and all of them, helping each other, contrived, upon hearing the news of the sudden revolutions in Paris and Vienna, to enact in Buda-Pesth the bloodless revolution of the 15th of March, 1848, which obtained the liberty of the press for the nation, and at the same time, in a solemn manifesto, gave expression to the wishes of the Hungarians in the matter of reform. The only act of violence these revolutionary heroes were guilty of was the entering of a printing establishment, whose proprietor, afraid of the government, had refused to print the admirable poem of Petöfi, entitled *Talpra Magyar* (Up Magyar), and doing the printing there themselves. The first verse of this poem, which subsequently became the war song of the national movement, runs in a literal translation thus:

> Arise, oh Magyar! thy country calls.
> Here is the time, now or never.
> Shall we be slaves or free?
> That is the question—choose!
> We swear by the God of the Magyars,
> We swear, to be slaves no longer!

This soul-stirring poem was improvised by Petöfi under the inspiration of the moment, and at the same establishment where it was first printed was also printed a proclamation which contained twelve articles setting forth the wishes of the people.

While the capital was resounding with the rejoicings and triumphant shouts of her exulting inhabitants, the proper department of the government for the carrying through of these movements, the Diet, assembled at Presburg, lost no time, and set to work with great energy to reform the institutions of Hungary, constitutionally, and to put into the form of law the ideas of liberty, equality, and fraternity. The salutary legislation met now with no opposition, either from the Upper House or from the court at Vienna, and in a short time the Diet passed the celebrated acts of 1848, which, having received the royal sanction, were proclaimed as laws on the 11th of April, at Presburg, amidst the wildest enthusiasm, in the presence of King Ferdinand V.

By these laws Hungary became a modern state, possessing a constitutional government. The government was vested in a ministry responsible to parliament, all the inhabitants of the country were declared equal before the law, the privileges of the nobility were abolished, the soil was declared free, and the right of free worship accorded to all. The institution of national guards was introduced, the utmost liberty of the press was secured, Transylvania became a part of the mother country—in a word, the national and political condition of the country was reorganized, in every particular, in harmony with the spirit, the demands, and aspirations of our age. At the same time the men placed at the head of the government were such as possessed the fullest confidence of the people. The first ministry was composed of the most distinguished patriots. Count Louis Batthyányi was the president, and acting in conjunction with him were Francis Deák, as minister of justice, Count Stephen Széchenyi, as minister of home affairs, and Louis Kossuth, as minister of finance.

The great mass of the people hailed with boundless enthusiasm the new government and the magnificent reforms. The transformation, however, had been so sudden and unexpected, and the old aristocratic world, with all its institutions and its ancient organization, had been swept away with such vehement, precipitation, that even under ordinary circumstances in the absence of all opposition, the new ideas and tendencies could have hardly entered into the political life of the nation without causing no little confusion and disorder. But, in addition to these natural drawbacks, the new order of things had to contend with certain national elements in the population, which, feeling themselves injured in their real or imaginary interests, were bent on mischief, hoping to be able to rob the nation, in the midst of the ensuing troubles, of the great political prize she had won. Certain circles of the court and classes of the people strove equally hard to surround with difficulties the practical introduction of the constitution of 1848. The court and the standing army, the party of the soldier class, feared that their commanding position would be impaired by the predominating influence of the people. The non-Hungarian portion of the inhabitants, choosing to ignore the fact that the new laws secured, without distinction of nationality, equal rights to every citizen of the state, were apprehensive lest the liberal constitution would chiefly benefit the Hungarian element of the nation. They, therefore, encouraged by the secret machinations of the government of Vienna, took up arms, in order to drag the country, which was preparing to take possession of her new liberties, into a civil war. The Croatians, under the lead of Ban Jellachich, and the Wallachs and Serbs, led by other imperial officers, and yielding to their persuasions, rose in rebellion against Hungary, and began to persecute, plunder, and murder the Hungarians living among them. Dreadful atrocities were committed in the southern and eastern portions of Hungary, hundreds and hundreds of families were massacred in cold blood, and entire villages and cities were deserted by their inhabitants, just as had previously happened at the approach of the Turks, and thousands were compelled to abandon their all to the rebels, in order to escape with their bare lives. In the course of a few weeks, the flames of rebellion had spread over a large part of the country, and the Hungarian element, instead of enjoying the liberties won for the whole nation after a bitter struggle of many decades, was under the sad necessity of resorting to armed force in order to reestablish the internal peace. The Hungarians now had to prove on the battle-field and in bloody engagements that they were worthy of liberty and capable of defending it.

The government, which, by virtue of the new laws, had meanwhile transferred its seat to Buda-Pesth, displayed extraordinary energy in the face of the sad difficulties besetting it. As it was impossible to rely upon the Austrian soldiers who were still in the country, it exerted itself to create and to organize a national army. A portion of the national guard entered the national army under the name of honvéds (defenders of the country), a name which became before long famous throughout the civilized world for the glorious military achievements coupled with it. The Hungarian soldiers, garrisoning the Austrian principalities, hastened home, braving the greatest dangers, partly accompanied by their officers and partly without them. The famous Hungarian hussars, especially, returned in great number to offer their services to their imperilled country. But all this proved insufficient, and as soon as the National Assembly, elected under the new constitution, met, Kossuth, who had been the life and soul of the government during this trying and critical period, called upon the nation to raise large armies for the defence of the country. The session of the 11th of July, during which Kossuth introduced in the House of Representatives his motions relating to the subject, presented a scene which beggars all description. Kossuth ascended the tribune pale and haggard with illness, but the never-ceasing applause which greeted him after the first few sentences soon gave him back his strength and his marvellous oratorical power. When he had concluded his speech and submitted to the House his request for 200,000 soldiers and the necessary money, a momentary pause of deep silence ensued. Suddenly Paul Nyáry, the leader of the opposition, arose, and lifting his right arm towards heaven, exclaimed: "We grant it!" The House was in a fever of patriotic excitement; all the deputies rose from their seats, shouting: "We grant it; we grant it!" Kossuth, with tears in his eyes, bowed to the representatives of the people and said: "You have risen like one man, and I bow down before the greatness of the nation."

These sacrifices on the part of the country had become a matter of urgent necessity. The Serb and Wallach insurrection assumed every day larger proportions, while the Croats, under the leadership of Jellachich, entered Hungarian territory with the fixed determination of depriving the nation of her constitutional liberties. But the Hungarian government was already able to send an army against the Croatians, who were marching on Buda-Pesth, plundering and laying waste every thing before them. They were surrounded by the Hungarian forces, and a portion of their army, nine thousand men strong, were compelled to lay down their arms, while Jellachich, with his remaining forces, precipitately fled from the country. The young Hungarian army had thus proved itself equal to the task of repulsing the attack of the Croats, but the recent events were nevertheless fraught with the gravest consequences. The news of the Croatian invasion filled the Hungarians with deep anxiety, and the extraordinary excitement caused by it cast a permanent cloud over the soul of that noble and great man, Count Széchenyi. The mind of the great patriot who had initiated the national movement gave way under the strain of the frightful rumors coming from the Croatian frontier. He had been ailing for some time back, and his nervousness constantly increased under the pressure of the great events following each other in rapid succession, so that when the news came that the enemy had invaded the country he thought that Hungary was lost. His despair darkened his mind and he sought death in the waves of the Danube. His family removed him to a private asylum near Vienna, where he recovered his mental faculties, and even wrote several books. But he was never entirely cured of his hallucination, and, exasperated by the vexations he was subjected to by the Viennese government, even in the asylum, the great patriot put an end to his own life on the 8th of April, 1860, by a shot from a pistol. Jellachich's incursion had other important political consequences. The attack on Hungary had been made by Jellachich in the name of the Viennese government, and the intimate connection between the domestic disorders and the court of Vienna became more and more apparent. This state of things rendered inevitable a struggle between Hungary and the unconstitutional action of the court. The Austrian forces were arming against Hungary on every side. Vienna, too, rose in rebellion against the court, and now the Hungarians hastened to assist the revolutionists in the Austrian capital. Unfortunately the young national army was not ripe yet for so great a military enterprise, and Prince Windischgrätz, having crushed the revolution in Vienna, invaded Hungary.

A last attempt was now made by the Hungarians to negotiate peace with the court, but it failed, Windischgrätz being so elated with his success that nothing short of unconditional submission on the part of the country would satisfy him. To accept such terms would have been both cowardly and suicidal, and the nation, therefore, driven to the sad alternative of war, determined rather to perish gloriously than to pusillanimously submit to be enslaved by the court. They followed the lead of Kossuth, who was now at the head of the government, whilst Görgei was the commander-in-chief of the Hungarian army. The two names of Kossuth and Görgei soon constituted the glory of the nation. Whilst these two acted in harmony they achieved brilliant triumphs, but their personal antagonism greatly contributed, at a subsequent period, to the calamities of the country.

Windischgrätz took possession of Buda in January, 1849, thus compelling Kossuth to transfer the seat of government to Debreczen, whilst Görgei withdrew with his army to the northern part of Hungary, but the national army fought victoriously against the Serbs and Wallachs, and the situation of the Hungarians had, in the course of the winter, become more favorable all over the country. The genius of Kossuth brought again and again, as if by magic, fresh armies into the field, and he was indefatigable in organizing the defence of the country. Distinguished generals like Görgei, Klapka, Damjanics, Bem, and others transformed the raw recruits, in a wonderfully short time, into properly disciplined troops, who were able to hold their own and bravely contend against the old and tried imperial forces whom they put to flight at every point.

The fortunes of war changed in favor of the Hungarians in the latter part of January, 1849. Klapka achieved the first triumph, which was followed by the brilliant victory won by one of Görgei's divisions commanded by Guyon in the battle of Branyiszkó, and very soon the Hungarian armies acted on the offensive at all points. In the course of a few weeks they achieved, chiefly under Görgei's leadership, great and complete victories over the enemy near Szolnok, Hatvan, Bicske, Vácz, Isaszegh, Nagy Sarló, and Komárom. Windischgrätz lost both the campaign and his position as commander-in-chief. Towards the close of the spring of 1849, after besieged Komárom had been relieved by the Hungarians, and Bem had driven from Transylvania not only the Austrians, but the Russians who had come to their assistance, the country was almost freed from her enemies, and only two cities, Buda and Temesvár, remained in the hands of the Austrians. The glorious efforts made by the nation were attended at last by splendid successes, and the civilized world spoke with sympathy and respect of the Hungarian people which had signally shown its ability to defend its liberties, constitution, and national existence.

It should have been the mission of diplomacy, at this conjuncture, to turn to advantage the recent military successes by negotiating an honorable peace with the humbled dynasty, as had been done before in the history of the country, after similar military achievements by the ancient national leaders, Bocskáy and Bethlen. Görgei, the head of the army was disposed to conclude peace. But the Hungarian Parliament sitting in Debreczen, led by Kossuth and under the influence of the recent victories, were determined to pursue a different course. The royal house of Hapsburg, whose dynasty had ruled over Hungary for three centuries, was declared to have forfeited its right to the throne by instigating and bringing upon the country the calamities of a great war.

This act had a bad effect, especially on the army, tending also to heighten the personal antagonism between Kossuth and Görgei. But its worst consequence was that it gave Russia a pretext for armed intervention. The emperor Francis Joseph entered into an alliance with the Czar of Russia, the purpose of which was to reconquer seceded Hungary and ultimately to crush her liberty.

One more brilliant victory was achieved by the Hungarian arms before the fatal blow was aimed at the country. The fortress of Buda was taken after a gallant assault, in the course of which the Austrian commandant bombarded the defenceless city of Pesth on the opposite bank of the Danube, and thus the capital, too, was restored to the country. Yet after this last glorious feat of war, good fortune deserted the national banners. The grand heroic epoch was hastening to its tragic end. Two hundred thousand Russians crossed the borders of Hungary, and were there reinforced by sixty thousand to seventy thousand Austrians, whom the Viennese government had succeeded in collecting for a last great effort. It was easy to foresee that the exhausted Hungarian army could not long resist the superior numbers opposed to them. For months they continued the gallant fight, and it was in one of these engagements that Petőfi, the great poet of the nation, lost his life, but in the month of August, the Russians had already succeeded in surrounding Görgei's army. Görgei, who was now invested with the supreme power, perceiving that all further effusion of blood was useless, surrendered, in the sight of the Russian army, the sword he had so gloriously worn in many a battle, near Világos, on the 13th of August, 1849. The remaining Hungarian armies followed his example, and either capitulated or disbanded. The brave army of the *honvéds* was no more, and the gallant struggle for liberty was put an end to by the superior numbers of the Russian forces. Kossuth and many other Hungarians sought refuge in Turkey.

Above Komárom, the largest fortress in the county, alone the Hungarian colors were still floating. General Klapka, its commandant, bravely defended it, and continued to hold it for six weeks after the sad catastrophe of Világos. The brave defenders, seeing at last that further resistance served no purpose, as the Hungarian army had ceased to exist, and the whole country had passed into the hands of the Austrians, capitulated upon most honorable terms. This was the concluding act of the heroic struggle of the Hungarian people, the brave attitude of the garrison and their commander adding another bright page to the already honorable record of the military achievements of 1848 and 1849.

As soon as the imperialists had obtained possession of Komárom, their commander-in-chief, Baron Haynau, began to persecute the patriots, and to commit the most cruel atrocities against them. Those who had taken part in the national war were brought before a court-martial and summarily executed. The bloody work of the executioner commenced on the 6th of October. Count Louis Batthyányi was shot at Pesth, and thirteen gallant generals, belonging to Görgei's army, met their deaths at Arád. Wholesale massacres were committed throughout the country, until at last the conscience of Europe rose up against these cruel butcheries, and the court itself removed the sanguinary baron from the scene of his inhuman exploits. The best men in the country were thrown into prison, and thousands of families had to mourn for dear ones who had fallen victims to the implacable vindictiveness of the Austrian government. Once more the gloom of oppression settled upon the unhappy country.

Many of the patriots had accompanied Kossuth to Turkey, or found a refuge in other foreign countries, and for ten years a great number of distinguished Hungarians were compelled to taste the bitterness of exile. Kossuth himself went subsequently to England, and visited also the United States. In the latter country he was enthusiastically received by the free and great American nation, who took delight in his lofty eloquence. During the Crimean war, and the war of 1859 in Italy, Kossuth and the Hungarian exiles were zealously laboring to free their country by foreign aid from the thraldom of oppression. At last, however, the Hungarian nation succeeded in reconquering, without any aid from abroad, by her own exertions, her national and political rights, and made her peace with the ruling dynasty. But the Hungarian exiles had their full share in the work of reconciliation, for it was owing to their exertions that the nations of Europe remembered that, in spite of Világos, Hungary still existed, and that again, at home, the people of Hungary were not permitted to lose their faith in a better and brighter future. Kossuth, the Nestor of the struggle for liberty, lives at present in retirement in Turin, and, although separated from his people by diverging political theories, his countrymen will forever cherish in him the great genius who gave liberty to millions of the oppressed peasantry, and who indelibly inscribed on the pages of the national legislation the immortal principles of liberty and equality of rights.

It is proper, however, to present in their regular order the chief events through which down-trodden Hungary of 1849 became from a subordinate province again an independent kingdom, taking part as an equal partner in the great realm of Austria-Hungary.

It was not until 1854 that the state of siege inaugurated in 1849 was abolished, and only in 1856 that an amnesty was proclaimed. In 1857 the emperor visited Hungary, and during his stay, he decreed the restoration of their confiscated estates to the late political offenders. From this time the emperor and the government of Vienna seemed anxious, by means of concessions to the national aims, to cause the Hungarians to forget the bitterness and strife of 1848 and 1849. In 1858 agricultural colonists were given special inducements to settle in specified districts, and were allowed certain exemptions from taxation.

In 1859 a most important concession was made by the imperial government to the spirit of nationality. By a ministerial order the language used in the higher schools was for the future to be regulated according to the circumstances of nationality, the predominance of German being thereby abolished. In the same year was issued what was known as the Protestant patent, which granted to the communes the free administration of their own educational and religious matters.

In 1860 the supreme court of judicature, known as the *curia regia*, and the county assemblies were reinstated, and the Magyar was recognized as the official language. Later in the year the district called the Banate of Temesvár was re-annexed to Hungary. In 1861 the old constitution was restored to Hungary, including Transylvania, Croatia, and Slavonia, and the Hungarian Diet reassembled in the old capital, Buda, afterwards removing across the river to Pesth. Within a few months, however, an address was presented at Vienna demanding the fullest autonomy for Hungary. To this the emperor declared himself unable to accede, and the Diet was dissolved. Stringent measures were again put into force by the imperial government, and military aid was invoked to enforce the collection of the taxes.

In 1865 the Diet was opened by the emperor in person, and the imperial assent was given to the principle of self-government for Hungary. The provisions of the Pragmatic Sanction (of 1722) were proposed as the basis for the settlement of the questions still at issue. The Diet also demanded, however, an acknowledgment of the continuity of the constitutional rights of 1848. Before an imperial decision had been reached on this point, the war of 1866 broke out between Austria and Prussia (allied with Italy), and the Diet was prorogued. The Hungarian troops formed an important contingent in the Austrian army which faced the Prussians in Bohemia, and the general in command, Marshal Benedek, was himself by birth a Hungarian. Hungarians also fought in the army of the south, which, under the leadership of the

Archduke Albrecht, made a brief but brilliant campaign against the Italians. In Bohemia the Austrians met with a decisive defeat at Sadowa (in July, 1866), and although in Italy Archduke Albrecht gained the important battle of Custozza, and Admiral Tegetthoff a naval victory near Lissa (in the Adriatic), the general results of the summer's campaign were adverse to Austria, and brought about material changes in its relations to Germany and in its own imperial organization.

By the peace of Prague (August, 1866) the German confederation was dissolved, and Austria's long preëminence among the states of Germany came to an end, the leadership in German affairs being transferred to Prussia. The centre of gravity of the Austrian empire (which was thus, as it were, pushed out of Germany) was thrown southward and eastward, and the most important result for Hungary was the constituting of the present dual monarchy of Austria-Hungary, finally sanctioned in February, 1867.

Under this arrangement the constitutional, legal, and administrative autonomy of 1848 was secured to Hungary, while the full control of the army rested with the emperor-king. The representative committee of the Diet, which conducted and completed the new constitutional arrangements, was headed by Deák, and the presidency of the first ministry was given to Count Andrássy.

In June, 1868, the emperor and empress were crowned at Buda-Pesth King and Queen of Hungary, and a complete pardon was proclaimed for all political offenders. It is worthy of note that twice in the checkered history of Hungary has Prussia been instrumental in securing for the kingdom from its Austrian rulers recognition and privileges which, had it not been for the pressure of the Prussian attacks, might long have been delayed.

In 1765, Maria Theresa, in grateful acknowledgment of the cordially loyal support given her by her "faithful Hungarians" in the bitter struggle against Frederic the Great, initiated various most important reforms, while just a century later, under the convincing influence of the second great struggle with Prussia, the Austrian ruler again falls back on his Hungarian subjects as the chief support of his reorganized realm, and in the new dual empire of Austria-Hungary the ancient kingdom of the Magyars, whose wonderfully elastic national vitality had withstood so many vicissitudes and disasters, again takes a commanding place among the nations of Europe.

THE END.